Sun Performance and Tuning

SPARC® *& Solaris*™

Adrian Cockcroft

sun
microsystems

≡

Editorial/production supervision and interior design: *Harriet Tellem*
Cover designer: *Tom Nery*
Cover photo: *Tim Wren — CAR Magazine, EMAP Publications Publications Ltd., London*
Buyer: *Alexis R. Heydt*
Acquisitions editors: *Gregory G. Doench/Phyllis Eve Bregman*

The publisher offers discounts on this book when ordered in bulk quantities. For more information, contact: Corporate Sales Department, Prentice Hall PTR, 113 Sylvan Avenue, Englewood Cliffs, NJ 07632
Phone: 201-592-2863, Fax 201-592-2249, e-mail: dan_rush@prenhall.com

10 9 8 7 6 5 4 3 2 1

ISBN: 013-149642-3

About the Cover: The cover shows a 1992 Porsche 911 Carrera 4. There is a special analogy between the development over the years of the Porsche 911 and the UNIX® operating system. Both were created in the 1960s, in a form which is recognizably the same as the current product. Both have been revised and developed continuously since they were created—they have grown larger, heavier, and much more powerful. The four-wheel drive Porsche 911 Carrera 4 had a major redesign of its under-the-surface components to carry it through the 1990s. Solaris™ 2 is similarly a major update and redesign of the UNIX kernel, now fully multithreaded. Both represent the latest and best technology applied to a product that has endured despite its quirks—both are exceptional high performance tools.

SunSoft Press
A Prentice Hall Title

Acknowledgments

Thanks to my wife, Linda, for keeping me rooted in the *real* world.

This book is dedicated to Sun's Systems Engineers worldwide; the people who have to deal with configuration, performance, and tuning issues on a daily basis.

Special thanks to Brian Wong, Phil Parkman, Mike Briggs, Keith Bierman, Hal Stern, Gordon Irlam, Morgan Herrington, Rob Gingell, and Dave Rosenthal for their technical input and support over the years, and Stephen Walter, Peter VanDerLinden, Gordon Becker, Karin Ellison, and Phyllis Bregman for their help in reviewing and producing this book.

All the engineers in SMCC and SunSoft who work on tuning Solaris deserve a special mention for their advice and all the performance improvements they devise for each successive release. In particular Dwight Wilcox, Chaitanya Tikku, and Anup Pal in SMCC; and Jeff Bonwick, Joe Eyckholt, Tim Marsland, Michael Sebrée, Dave Singleton, Bart Smaalders, and Jim Voll in SunSoft.

Thanks also to all those system administrators and software developers who have given me the opportunity to investigate their systems over the past six years. Problems and solutions that are hard to see in isolation have become familiar to me after repeated exposure.

My father Nick Cockcroft, and the University of Hertfordshire in the UK, gave me my first contacts with computers while I was a school kid in the early 1970s. I first used UNIX in the Physics Department Lab at the City University, London (version 6 on a PDP-11). While working for Cambridge Consultants Ltd., I became the UNIX systems administrator at one of the first Sun user sites in the UK. I would like to thank all of them for their part in getting me where I am today.

— Adrian Cockcroft

Contents

≡

Contents

≣ Contents

☰ Contents

☰ *Contents*

Contents ≣

Figures

Figures

≡ Figures

Tables

≡ Tables

Preface

This book, *Sun Performance And Tuning,* has its origins in a white paper that outgrew the white paper format. The paper was originally written for a Sun® UK User Group conference in September 1991, it was extensively updated for a second Sun UK User Group conference in January 1993, and was revised and presented to the Sun User Group in the USA in December 1993. While some of the material covered will be familiar to those who have read the white paper, the book expands the explanations and covers many key new areas. It has also been updated to take into account subsequent hardware releases and many significant performance related changes in Solaris™ 2.4.

This book consists of everything I have learned over the years about performance and tuning. It includes a structured approach, opinions, heuristics, and every reference I can find to the subject. It contains the kind of hard recommendation and opinions that are often needed, but that are not normally found in the manual set. The book is exclusively concerned with SPARC® hardware and Solaris. All of Sun's operating system releases from SunOS™ 4.1 through to Solaris 2.4 are covered and compared.

Many other books, manual sections and white papers are referenced, criticized and recommended, so that this book can be used as a central point of reference. Some parts of the subject are covered well in other publications, so this book highlights the important points and brings things up to date with Sun-specific information (e.g. using optimizing compilers). Some other aspects of performance tuning are not discussed anywhere else, so are covered here in great detail (e.g.,virtual memory paging algorithms). One entire subject is ignored. Some references are provided that address the performance of window systems, graphics libraries, and graphics accelerators, but the author has conveniently managed to remain ignorant in this area.

With competitive pressures and the importance of "time to market," functionality and bugfixes get priority over designed-in performance in many cases. This book is aimed both at developers who want to design for performance and need a central reference to better understand Sun machines, and also at system administrators who have a Sun machine running applications and want to understand and improve overall performance.

This book covers an incredibly complex and fast changing topic. I have tried to organize it in a useful manner with the most important information up front in each chapter and many cross references. A book like this can never truly be complete and finished, but it has to be frozen at some point so it can be published!

How This Book Is Organized

This book is intended to be read sequentially, as it tries to cover the most significant and most common performance problems first. It can be used as a reference work by following the many cross references that link related topics.

Chapter 1, "Quick Tips and Recipes," is for those of you who need results *now,* and don't have time to read the whole book first.

Chapter 2, "Performance Measurement," tells you what kind of things to measure and how to decide whether your efforts at tuning have made any difference to the system performance.

Chapter 3, "Source Code," is aimed primarily at developers and end-users who have access to the source code of the application being tuned.

Chapter 4, "Applications," assumes you have an off-the-shelf application and tells you how to find out what it is doing. Changes in the execution environment are discussed.

Chapter 5, "Disks," investigates the performance characteristics of disk subsystems, how to monitor and tune them.

Chapter 6, "Networks," contains Sun-specific information on network hardware and performance issues.

Chapter 7, "Processors," looks at how to decide whether you have enough CPU power for your workload. The interactions between multiprocessor machines and UNIX is described at a high level.

Chapter 8, "System Architectures," takes a simplified look at the way uniprocessor and multiprocessor SPARC systems are put together.

Chapter 9, "Memory," looks at the memory system components. The implications of modern caches and memory management unit designs are covered.

Chapter 10, "SPARC Implementations," gets down to the implementation-specific performance differences of all the SPARC chips from 1987 to 1994 and beyond.

Chapter 11, "Kernel Algorithms and Tuning", provides a unique insight into the algorithms and tunable parameters of the SunOS 4 and Solaris 2 kernel. It also tells you how to decide if you have enough memory by monitoring the paging algorithm.

Appendix A, "Rules and Tunables Quick Reference Tables," summarizes the advice given elsewhere into performance monitoring rules. The tunable values are also summarized into table form.

Appendix B, "References," contains a long list of sources of further information, with a description of what is of interest in each document.

Related Books

There are a very large number of manual sections, books, and papers listed in Appendix B, "References." A few highlights are mentioned here.

My colleague Brian Wong explains how to analyze a workload and configure a server with the right capacity for the job in his book. The SPARC hardware information in this book is covered in much more detail by Ben Catanzaro. Hal Stern's early white papers on performance related topics provided me with some inspiration to do my own tuning paper; his definitive book on NFS and NIS is the main reason why my own network chapter is relatively short. I provided some input to the Solaris 2.4 NFS Server manual and it is up to date and a very useful guide.

- *"Configuration and Capacity Planning for Solaris,"* Brian Wong, SunSoft Press
- *"Multiprocessor System Architectures,"* Ben Catanzaro, SunSoft Press
- *"Managing NFS and NIS,"* Hal Stern, O'Reilly
- *"SMCC NFS Server Performance and Tuning Guide,"* Solaris 2.4 SMCC Manual

Typographic Changes and Symbols

The following table describes the type changes and symbols used in this book.

Table PR-1 Typographic Conventions

Typeface or Symbol	Description	Example
AaBbCc123	The names of commands, files, and directories; on-screen computer output	Edit your `.login` file. Use `ls -a` to list all files. system% You have mail.
AaBbCc123	What you type, contrasted with on-screen computer output	system% **su** password:
AaBbCc123	Command-line placeholder: replace with a real name or value	To delete a file, type `rm` *filename*.
AaBbCc123	Book titles, new words or terms, or words to be emphasized	Read Chapter 6 in *User's Guide*. These are called *class* options. You *must* be root to do this.

Code samples are included in boxes and may display the following:

| % | UNIX C-shell prompt | system% |
| # | Superuser prompt, either shell | system# |

Quick Tips and Recipes 1

There is too much detail in this book to be quickly absorbed by the reader. Based upon my own experience, there are a few recurring situations and frequently asked questions that I will list here, with references in the rest of the book for in-depth detail. This is followed by some performance-oriented configuration recipes for common system types.

Quick Reference for Common Tuning Tips

This list focuses primarily, but not exclusively, on servers running Solaris 2. It should help you decide whether you have overloaded the disks, network, available RAM, or CPUs.

1. **The system will usually have a disk bottleneck.**
   In nearly every case the most serious bottleneck is an overloaded or slow disk. Use `iostat -x 30`[1] to look for disks that are more than 30 percent busy and have service times of more than 50 ms. The service time is key; this is the time between a user process issuing a read and the read completing (for example), so it is often in the critical path for response time. If many other processes are also accessing that disk, a queue can form, and service times of over 1000 ms (not a misprint, over one second!) can easily occur as you wait to get to the front of the queue. See "Load Monitoring And Balancing" on page 75 for more details. Increasing the inode cache size can help reduce the number of disk I/Os required to manage filesystems, see "The Inode Cache and File Data Caching" on page 191.

2. **You will often be told that the system is not I/O bound.**
   If you are unfamiliar with the system and are being briefed by its system administrator, you are very likely to be told that the system is *not* disk bound. Ignore this advice and insist on seeing `iostat -x 30` output for the period when the system is running sluggishly. See Step 1. This situation occurs with depressing regularity!

3. **After first pass tuning, the system will *still* have a disk bottleneck!**
   Keep checking `iostat -x 30` as tuning progresses. When a bottleneck is removed, the system may start to run faster, and as more work is done, some other disk will overload. At some point you may need to stripe filesystems and tablespaces over multiple disks. See Step 1 again. (Hopefully, you are getting the message now).

---

1. The -x option is Solaris 2 specific. A 30 second interval tends to average out the peaks and show the sustained load.

4. Poor NFS response times may be hard to see.

Waiting for a network-mounted filesystem to respond is not counted in the same way as waiting for a local disk. The system will appear to be idle when it is really in a network I/O wait state. Use nfsstat -m to find out which NFS® server is likely to be the problem, go to it, and start at Step 1 again. You should look at the NFS operation mix with nfsstat on both the client and server and if writes are common or the server's disk is too busy, configure a prestoserve or NVSIMM in the server. See that the Ethernet is not overloaded by checking that the collision rate is around one or two percent. If collisions are above five percent, insist that the network is split up or replaced with something faster. See *SMCC NFS Server Performance and Tuning Guide* on the Solaris 2.4 SMCC Hardware AnswerBook® CD.

5. Avoid the common memory usage misconceptions

When you look at vmstat *please* don't waste time worrying about where all the RAM has gone. After a while the free list will stabilize around one sixteenth of the total memory configured[2]. The system stops bothering to reclaim memory above this level, even when you aren't running anything. See "Understanding vmstat and sar Output" on page 194.

6. Don't panic when you see page-ins and page-outs in vmstat.

These are normal since all filesystem I/O is done using the paging process. Hundreds or thousands of Kbytes paged in and paged out are not a cause for concern, just a sign that the system is working hard.

7. Use page scanner activity as your RAM shortage indicator.

When you really are short of memory the scanner will be running continuously at a high rate (over 200 pages/second averaged over 30 seconds). If it runs in separated high-level bursts, you should try patching *slowscan* to 100 so that the bursts are made longer and slower. See "The Paging Algorithm in Solaris 2" on page 207.

8. Look for a long run queue (vmstat procs r).

If the run queue or load average is more than four times the number of CPUs, then processes end up waiting too long for a slice of CPU time. This waiting can increase the interactive response time seen by users. Add more CPU power to the system and see "Understanding vmstat on a Multiprocessor" on page 95.

9. Look for processes blocked waiting for I/O (vmstat procs b).

This is a sign of a disk bottleneck. If the number of processes blocked approaches or exceeds the number in the run queue, see Step 1 again. If you are running database batch jobs, it is OK to have some blocked processes, but batch throughput can be increased by removing disk bottlenecks.

---

2. The actual level depends on the version of the operating system you are running, it may be fixed at a Mbyte or less.

10.Check for CPU system time dominating user time.

If there is more system time than user time and the machine is not an NFS server[3], you may have a problem. To find out the source of system calls, see "Tracing in Solaris 2" on page 52. To look for high interrupt rates and excessive mutex contention, see "Using mpstat to Monitor Interrupts and Mutexes" on page 98. To find out which kernel functions are busy see "Kernel Profiling with kgmon in Solaris 2" on page 219. If you have a large time-shared system see "Using Solaris 2 with Large Numbers of Active Users" on page 183.

11.Watch out for processes that hog the CPU.

Processes sometimes fail in a way that consumes an entire CPU. This can make the machine feel sluggish. Watch for processes that are accumulating CPU time rapidly when you don't think they should be. See "Monitoring the System with Proctool" on page 221. If you find that the system process fsflush is using a lot of CPU power, see the description of the kernel variables "autoup and tune_t_fsflushr" on page 210.

---

3. NFS service is entirely inside the kernel so system time will normally dominate on an NFS server.

Instant Configuration and Tuning Recipes

The rest of this book gives you the information you need to understand a lot about how SPARC systems running Solaris work and the basic principles involved in performance and tuning. Probably all you really want right now is to be told what to do or what to buy and how to set it up. This section just tells you *what* to do, with references to the rest of the book if you want to find out *why.* If you decide that you want to vary the recipes and do something a bit different, you should really read the rest of the book first! For (much) more information on configuration issues you should get a copy of the book *Configuration and Capacity Planning for Solaris,* by Brian Wong *(SunSoft Press).*

The intention is for these recipes to fit together to make up networks of machines that are all running within their capacity and providing good performance. I have allowed for some headroom but have tried to avoid grossly overconfigured recipes.

Single -user Desktop Workstation Recipe

Local Disks and NFS Mounts

My recommended configuration is to NFS-mount home, mail, and applications programs directories from one or more dedicated NFS servers. Configure a single local disk to have two partitions, one for the operating system and one for swap space. It is very easy to overload a single swap disk, so if you have more than one local disk, split any swap partitions or files evenly across all the disks (keep one clear for cachefs if necessary, see below).

Swap Space

Most application vendors can tell you how much swap space their application needs. If you have no idea how much swap space you will need, configure at least 64 Mbytes of virtual memory to start with. It's easy to add more later so don't go overboard. With SunOS 4, your swap space should be bigger than your RAM, but at least a 64-Mbyte swap partition will be needed. With Solaris 2 the swap partition size should be the difference between 64 Mbytes and the RAM size; that is 48-Mbyte swap with 16 Mbytes RAM, 32-Mbyte swap with 32-Mbyte RAM, no swap partition at all with 64 Mbytes or more RAM. If your application vendor says a Solaris 2 application needs 64 Mbytes of RAM and 128 Mbytes of swap, this adds up to 192 Mbytes of virtual memory. You could configure 96 Mbytes of RAM and 96 Mbytes of swap instead. If you run out of swap space, make a swap file (I put them in /swap) or add more RAM.

Filesystems and Upgrades

Try to make the rest of the disk into one big root partition that includes /usr, /opt, /var and /swap. The main reason for doing this is to pool all the free space, so that upgrade or install can easily be used to move up to the next OS release without running out of space in one of the partitions. It also prevents /var from overflowing and makes it easy to have a /swap directory to hold extra swap files if they are needed. In Solaris 2, /tmp uses the RAM-based tmpfs by default; the mount /tmp command should be uncommented in /etc/rc.local to enable it for SunOS 4.X.

Solaris 2 systems should be automatically installed from a JumpStart™ install server that includes a postinstall script to set up all the local customizations. Since the disk can be restored by using JumpStart™ and contains no local users files, it is never necessary to back it up over the network. A JumpStart™ install is much less frequent than a network backup, so this aids good performance of the network. A useful tip to free up disk space for upgrades is to remove any swap files before you run the upgrade, then re-create the swap file afterwards.

```
# swap -d /swap/swap20
# rm /swap/swap20
comment out the swap in /etc/vfstab
shutdown and run the upgrade
# mkfile 20M /swap/swap20
# swap -a /swap/swap20
```

Applications and cachefs

If possible NFS-mount the applications read-only, to avoid the write-back of file access times, which is unwanted overhead. If you are running Solaris 2.3 or later configure the cache filesystem for all application code mount points. First make /cache, then mount all the application directories using the same cache. If you use large applications check the application file sizes; if anything you access a lot is over 3 Mbytes increase the *maxfilesize* parameter for the cache with cfsadmin.

Do not use cachefs for mail directories. It might be useful for home directories if most files are read rather than written — try it with and without to see. Cache loads when a large file is read for the first time can overload the disk. If there is more than one disk on the system, then don't put any cache on the same disk as any swap space. Swap and cache are often both very busy at the same time when starting a new application. The cache works best for files that don't change often and are read many times by the NFS client.

If your application is very data-intensive, reading and writing large files, you are likely to need an FDDI or 100 Mbit fast Ethernet interface. This often occurs with EDA, MCAD, and Earth Resources applications. If large files are written out a lot, you should avoid cachefs for that filesystem. Figure 1-1 shows how to set up and use cachefs.

Figure 1-1   Setting Up Cachefs and Checking for Large Files

```
# cfsadmin -c /cache
# find /net/apphost/export/appdir -size +3000k -ls
105849 3408 -rwxr-xr-x  1 root       bin         3474324 Mar   1 13:16
/net/apphost/export/appdir/SUNWwabi/bin/wabiprog
# cfsadmin -u -o maxfilesize=4 /cache
cfsadmin: list cache FS information
   maxblocks       90%
   minblocks        0%
   threshblocks    85%
   maxfiles        90%
   minfiles         0%
   threshfiles     85%
   maxfilesize     4MB
# mount -F cachefs -o backfstype=nfs,cachedir=/cache apphost:/export/appdir
/usr/local
```

Example Filesystem Table

The filesystem mount table shown in Figure 1-2 is for a system with a single local disk. Application program code is mounted read-only from *appshost* using cachefs. Mail is mounted from *mailhost*. Home directories are automounted, so do not appear in this table. This system has a swap partition, and an additional 20-Mbyte swap file has been added. Direct automount mappings can be used to mount applications (including the cachefs options) and mail.

Figure 1-2   Sample /etc/vfstab *for Workstation Recipe*

#device #to mount	device to fsck	mount point	FS type	fsck pass	mount at boot	mount options
/proc	-	/proc	proc	-	no	-
fd	-	/dev/fd	fd	-	no	-
swap	-	/tmp	tmpfs	-	yes	-
/dev/dsk/c0t3d0s0	/dev/rdsk/c0t3d0s0	/	ufs	1	no	-
/dev/dsk/c0t3d0s1		-	swap	-	no	-
/swap/swap20	-	-	swap	-	no	-
appshost:/usr/dist	/cache	/usr/dist	cachefs	3	yes	
ro,backfstype=nfs,cachedir=/cache						
mailhost:/var/mail	-	/var/mail	nfs	-	yes	rw,bg

Kernel Tuning

Since this setup is the most common, Solaris is already reasonably well tuned for it. Solaris 2 systems predating Solaris 2.4 can free up some RAM by setting the pager thresholds lower as show in Figure 1-3. These are the 2.4 defaults for small machines only[4], and you don't need to set anything in Solaris 2.4. See "The Paging Algorithm and Memory Usage" on page 194 for more information.

Figure 1-3   Sample `/etc/system` *Kernel Tuning Parameters for Workstation Recipe*

```
set slowscan=100
set minfree=25
set desfree=50
set lotsfree=128
```

Dedicated NFS, Mail and Print Server Recipe

Workload Mixture

For good performance an NFS® server should be dedicated to its task. NFS requests will always run in the kernel at a higher priority than user level programs, so a busy NFS server is unlikely to provide high performance for interactive use. For example, if a machine is configured as a combined database and NFS server, NFS will win, and the database will slow down whenever a lot of NFS requests need to be processed. A useful way to soak up the spare CPU cycles on an NFS server is to use it as a mail server. The process of delivering mail and expanding aliases is a background batch job, and users won't notice it being slowed down at any time to provide NFS service. Users' mail files are exported to workstations via NFS. Another common batch workload comes from printing. The NeWSprint™ code is CPU-intensive, but NFS will always be higher priority, so it shouldn't impact NFS service much.

RAM Requirements

Dedicated NFS and mail servers do not need much RAM. The kernel will be configured to be a little larger than normal, but the main, active user program will be `sendmail`. The rest of RAM is a cache for the filesystems. UNIX based NFS clients do a great deal of caching, so don't usually ask for the same data more than once. Home directories and mail files are specific to a single user, so there will not be multiple reads of the same data from different machines very often. Anything that is constantly reread from the server by multiple workstations is a prime candidate for setting up with cachefs on the clients.

---

4. That is, everything except the SPARCserver™ 1000 and SPARCcenter™ 2000.

NFS clients that are PCs running MS-DOS™, MS-Windows™, or MacOS™ put much less load on an NFS server than a UNIX client does, but require fast response times for short bursts of activity and do very little caching themselves. It may be worth having extra memory on the server to try and cache requests to common files.

Allow 16 Mbytes of RAM for the kernel, `sendmail`, printing and other Solaris daemons, then another 16 Mbytes for each 10-Mbit Ethernet or 16-Mbit token ring being served, and 64 Mbytes for each FDDI or 100-Mbit Ethernet being served. To run NeWSprint, allow another 16 Mbytes so that the NFS service is not competing with the printer for RAM.

Prestoserve

Dedicated NFS servers should always be configured with the Prestoserve™ option, using NVSIMM memory options if possible, and an SBus Prestoserve otherwise. A limitation of the Prestoserve is that it cannot be used to accelerate accesses to the root filesystem.

The recommended disk configuration is to have a single large root partition like the workstation recipe with the exception of the `/var` directories. `/var/mail` needs to be on a separate disk partition because it needs to be accelerated by the Prestoserve. Mail programs on the NFS clients rewrite the entire mail file when the user saves changes; the time this takes is very noticeable and a prestoserve speeds it up a great deal. The `/var` filesystem should be big enough to hold a lot of mail (several Mbytes per user account) and printer jobs (at least 10 or 20 Mbytes, sometimes much more).

Network Loading

For optimal performance, the NFS server should be configured with enough networks to allow a maximum of only 10 active NFS clients per 10-Mbit Ethernet. Concurrent, continuously active NFS clients tend to occur in student classrooms when the students all log in and start their applications at the beginning of the class. In most other situations only half the workstations are likely to be concurrently active, so configure a maximum of 20 to 25 per Ethernet. The most efficient Ethernet controller is the Sbus Quadruple Ethernet Controller (SQEC/S), which provides four independent Ethernets in a single SBus slot and consumes much less CPU to drive it than the common Ethernet interfaces, especially on the SPARCserver™ 1000 and SPARCcenter™ 2000 machines.

If you need to support a large number of client machines, the SPARCcluster™ 1 provides an excellent way to support a large number of Ethernets from a single system without requiring subnetted IP addresses.

Since 100-Mbit networks are only justified in data-intensive environments the client machines are usually much more demanding, and fewer than 10 fully active NFS clients should be configured. With typical applications, a maximum of 25 to 40 clients can be supported per network.

CPU Loading for NFS Servers

A SPARCstation™ 2 or SPARCclassic™ is plenty for one or two Ethernets. A SuperSPARC™ can handle four or five Ethernets. Each fully loaded 100-Mbit Ethernet or FDDI should have two SuperSPARC processors to handle the network, NFS protocol, and disk I/O load.

Always Use Solaris 2.3 or Later

The NFS server code in Solaris 2.3 and 2.4 is more efficient than SunOS 4.1.3 or Solaris 2.2 and takes full advantage of multiple processors (unlike SunOS 4.1.3). A *dedicated* NFS server should be one of the first systems to be upgraded when moving from SunOS 4.1.3 to Solaris 2 (if it is dedicated, there should be no application support issues). It can then also act as a JumpStart install server for the desktop machines as they migrate over time.

Disk Configurations

Since an NFS lookup or read can involve two trips over the network from the client as well as a disk I/O, getting good perceived performance from the server requires a low latency disk subsystem that averages better than 40 ms service time. Use Online: DiskSuite™ or SPARCstorage™ Manager to stripe filesystems so that the load is evenly balanced across as many independent disks as possible. You will get two to three times better performance from a stripe of three 1.05-Gbyte disks than you will from one 2.9-Gbyte disk. For good performance, configure four disks in the stripe for each loaded Ethernet you serve and eight disks for each loaded 100-Mbit network. The data-intensive clients that need faster networks tend to do more sequential accesses, and so get more throughput from the disks than the typical random access load from Ethernet clients. The logging filesystem supported by Online: DiskSuite 3.0 on Solaris 2.4 is especially useful with multigigabyte filesystems, since it never needs a time-consuming full filesystem check. It also helps performance a lot in write-intensive situations.

Setting the Number of NFS Daemons

In SunOS 4.X, each NFS daemon appears as a separate process, although they do all their work in the kernel. In Solaris 2, a single NFS daemon process and a number of kernel threads do basically the same job. Configure two threads per active client machine, or 32 per Ethernet. The default of 16 is suitable only for casual NFS use, and there is little overhead from having several hundred of them, even on a low-end SPARCclassic server. Since kernel threads all use the same context, there is very little thread switch overhead in either SunOS 4 or Solaris 2.

For example, a server with two Ethernets running SunOS 4 would need `nfsd  64` set in `/etc/rc.local` and, when running Solaris 2, would need `/usr/lib/nfs/nfsd -a 64` to be set in the file `/etc/init.d/nfs.server` (which is hardlinked to `/etc/rc3.d/S15nfs.server`).

Kernel Tuning

NFS servers don't often need a lot of RAM but do need large, name lookup caches, which are sized automatically, based on the RAM size in Solaris 2. The two main changes recommended are to make the directory name lookup cache have at least 5000 entries and to make the inode cache twice as big as the DNLC in releases prior to Solaris 2.4. See "Vnodes, Inodes and Rnodes" on page 189 for more details.

The default size of both caches in Solaris 2.3 and 2.4 will be (RAM-2)*17+90. For a 64-Mbyte system this works out at 1144. If you have more than 256 Mbytes of RAM, the cache is big enough, so you just need to double the inode cache size.

Figure 1-4   Sample `/etc/system` *Kernel Tuning Parameters for a 64- Mbyte Solaris 2.3 NFS Server*

```
set slowscan=100          not needed on Solaris 2.4
set ncsize=5000           for NFS servers with under 256MB RAM
set ufs_ninode=10000      for NFS servers running 2.3 & under 256MB
```

Database Backend Server Recipe

Workload Mixture

For good performance, a database server should be dedicated to its task. If a machine is configured as a combined database and NFS server, NFS will win, and the database will slow down whenever a lot of NFS requests need to be processed. It is also more efficient to run large database configurations as a single backend server, with no user logins, and one or more database clients to handle user logins. Communication between the database clients and the server is typically done by using SQL over a TCP/IP connection. A single time-shared machine with everything on it also works well, but keep the number of active users below 200 unless you are running Solaris 2.4. See "Using Solaris 2 with Large Numbers of Active Users" on page 183 for more details.

RAM Requirements

Database servers need a lot of RAM. Each database and application vendor should provide detailed guidelines on how to configure the system. If you have no other guidance, I will suggest a starting point that has been used with Oracle®. For the database back end, allow 64 Mbytes of RAM for the kernel, Solaris daemons, database backend processes, and shared memory area. Then allow another 2 Mbytes for each user if time-shared, or 512 Kbytes per user on a pure back end. For each client machine allow 16 Mbytes of RAM for the kernel and Solaris daemons, then 1.5 Mbytes per user for each database forms-based client.

Prestoserve and Log -based Filesystems

Database back-end servers that use filesystems to hold database tables rather than raw disks should be configured with the prestoserve option, using NVSIMM memory options if possible, and an SBus Prestoserve otherwise. A limitation of the Prestoserve is that it cannot be used to accelerate accesses to the root filesystem. The log-based UFS filesystem supported by the combination of Solaris 2.4 and Online: DiskSuite is a good alternative to a Prestoserve. In high availability configurations, the log-based filesystem has faster fsck recovery and can also be switched between two machines for fail-over.

Network Loading for Database Servers

There are three components to network loading from database workloads: NFS, telnet, and SQL. If possible, avoid heavy NFS activity on a database server. Tests indicate that 200 *active* telnet connections on an otherwise idle Ethernet give good performance, and that 400 or more worked well but the network was rather busy. Telnet and Rlogin cause a large number of very small packets. If possible this traffic should be run on a dedicated network separated from NFS or SQL activity in large configurations.

The network activity caused by SQL is so application-dependent that it is hard to give general guidelines. Some work with the snoop command or a network analyzer on a live system or a similar application is likely to be needed to work out the load. Some applications may work well over a 56-Kbit leased line, whereas others will need 100-Mbit FDDI or may only work well when the client and server are on the same machine.

CPU Loading

CPU loading is hard to estimate; any guidelines provided in this book would lead to a mixture of very overconfigured and very underconfigured systems. Database sizing involves too many variables and is outside the scope of this book. Sizing data for common application and database combinations is being generated within Sun for use by systems engineers and resellers. Database vendors often place restrictions on the publication of performance-related information about their products.

Disk Configurations

Getting good, perceived performance from the server requires a low latency disk subsystem that averages better than 50-ms service time on all disks. Use Online: DiskSuite or SPARCstorage Manager to stripe filesystems so that the load is evenly balanced across as many independent disks as possible. You will get two to three times better performance from a stripe of three 1.05-Gbyte disks than you will from one 2.9-Gbyte disk. Stripes created with Online: DiskSuite or SPARCstorage Manager can be used to provide very large and fast raw tablespaces. If tablespaces are to be placed in filesystems, the logging filesystem supported by Online: DiskSuite 3.0 on Solaris 2.4 should be used. It never needs a time-consuming full filesystem check and it also helps performance a lot in write-intensive situations.

Setting the Shared Memory Size

Shared memory size is often set too small. On a database using raw disks, it needs to be set higher than on a system with UFS. The effect of UFS is to provide additional data buffering and a duplicate copy of the data in shared memory. This improves read performance and can help sequential table scan rates when UFS prefetching is more aggressive than the database's own prefetching. The drawback is that more RAM and CPU time is used. When running raw, you can choose to run with less caching and use less RAM, or you can go for higher performance by using a much bigger shared memory area and similar total RAM usage.

Kernel Tuning

Databases tend to use lots of shared memory and semaphore settings. These do not affect performance; as long as they are big enough, the programs will run. Each database vendor supplies its own guidelines. See "autoup and tune_t_fsflushr" on page 210 for advice on tuning the `fsflush` daemon.

Figure 1-5   Example `/etc/system` *Entries for a Database Server*

```
* example shared memory settings needed for database
set shmsys:shminfo_shmmax=268435456
set shmsys:shminfo_shmmni=512
set shmsys:shminfo_shmseg=150
set semsys:seminfo_semmap=350
set semsys:seminfo_semmni=350
set semsys:seminfo_semmns=1000
set semsys:seminfo_semmnu=700
set semsys:seminfo_semume=100
* slow down the pager for large memory systems not needed on Solaris 2.4
set slowscan=100
set fastscan=16000
* keep fsflush from hogging a CPU
set autoup=240
```

Multiuser, Time-shared Server with ASCII or X Terminals Recipe

Terminal Types

There is little difference in kind between dumb ASCII terminals, proprietary graphics terminals connected over serial ports, IBM 3270 terminals connected over SNA, and X terminals. The terminal understands a fixed, low-level display protocol and has varying amounts of built-in functionality, but all application processing is done on time-shared multiuser servers.

Sun's own X terminal product, the SPARCclassic X, is a stripped down, low-end SPARCclassic workstation that is booted with dedicated X terminal software. It is faster than most X terminals, is one of the easiest to install, and is supplied with networked administration tools. It can be upgraded to a full SPARCclassic workstation if required at a later date by basically adding more RAM and a Solaris license.

What's the Difference between Client-Server and Time-shared Configurations?

The term *client-server* is sometimes used to describe a time-shared system with X terminals. Personally, I don't like this use of the term as I think it is misleading. The primary extra capability of an X terminal over other types of terminals is that it can make direct connections to many servers at the same time. As an example consider upgrading a time-shared server by replacing ASCII terminals with X terminals running the same application in a terminal emulator window. There is still no separate client processing going on. An upgrade to client-server would be to have users running part or all of the application on a SPARCstation or PC on their desk, with an application-specific protocol linking them to a database or an NFS server back-end.

Performance Is Usually a Problem on Time-shared Systems

From a performance point of view, time-shared systems are usually a source of problems. Part of the problem is that UNIX assumes that its users will be well behaved, and has few ways to deal with users or programs that intentionally or accidentally take an unfair share of the system. It is sometimes known as a *Denial-of-Service Attack* when a user tries to consume all the CPU, RAM, disk space[5], swap space, or overflow kernel tables. Even unintentional overload can cause serious problems. Instead, if you can configure a client-server system where users get their own SPARCstation or PC to use and abuse, then it is much harder for one user to affect the performance for the rest of the user community.

---

5. If this is a problem, then you can use the standard BSD UNIX disk quotas system in Solaris.

Another problem occurs when applications that were developed for use on high-end SPARCstations are installed on a server and used via X terminals. If the application runs well on a low-powered machine like a SPARCstation 1, then sharing a more powerful machine makes sense. If it's normally used on a SPARCstation 10, then don't expect many copies to run simultaneously on an X-terminal server.

X terminals work very well in a general office environment where most users spend a small proportion of their time actually working at the X terminal. They don't work well if all the users are active all the time. Try to avoid configuring data entry or telephone sales sweatshops, or student classrooms full of X terminals; the back-end system needed to support them will often be very large and expensive or seriously underpowered. Some software licensing practices can make a single large system with X terminals cheaper than lots of smaller systems. Hopefully, more software vendors will convert to floating per-user licenses for software.

NIS, NIS+, License, and Internet Server Recipe

This general class of network information servers differs from NFS servers in that the service is performed by a user-level daemon process. To provide the service, the process forks to create a new process to handle the request. This puts a very different load on the server from the kernel-based NFS service.

Swap Space Requirements

When the server process is large, the forked child processes can lead to a large requirement for swap space. NIS+ servers for large and complex NIS+ domains often need several hundred Mbytes of swap space to service a large number of client requests. This space is reserved for use but isn't often used heavily, since the forked process has a short and active lifetime and is unlikely to be paged or swapped out.

Monitoring Activity

The only way to track what is happening on these systems is to turn on accounting. For example, an Internet World Wide Web server with Mosaic clients services many requests by forking an httpd process that typically lasts for less than one second. You never see this load if you run ps because the processes are so short-lived. See "Using Accounting to Monitor the Workload" on page 25.

Understanding Information Server Architectures

There are three ways to implement an information server.

The most common way is to start a UNIX daemon to service each request. This is done either by having a master daemon running all the time that forks children to service each request, or by using `inetd` to start the appropriate daemon for the request. Either way, each request involves the relatively high overhead of process creation. The benefit is that many simultaneous requests can be serviced at once. This solution is relatively slow but scales well as the number of requests increases. It also takes advantage of multiple processors when they are configured. A multiprocessor SPARCserver system can be used to support a large number of Mosaic clients. The default options for the Solaris 2.3 NIS+ `rpc.nisd` daemon allow it to fork up to 128 child processes. Relatively few NIS+ master and replica servers will be needed even in large networks, but it may be worth configuring dedicated NIS+ server machines in large complex networks[6].

The second way of implementing an information server is to handle requests one at a time in a single-threaded daemon that is always running. This is the way that NIS works with the `ypbind` and `ypserv` processes. The `portmapper` process is involved in directing incoming RPC calls to the daemon. Each request is handled quickly with little overhead, but when many simultaneous requests occur, a queue forms and the response time increases. The implication for NIS is that `ypserv` is quite quick and efficient, but many slave server machines may be needed in large networks.

The third way to implement an information server is to take advantage of the Solaris 2 user-level threads libraries and implement a single, multithreaded server daemon. New threads can be created to service each request more efficiently than by forking the entire process, so this provides the best of both worlds and is both fast and scalable. There are few examples of multithreaded daemons at present, but Solaris 2.4 contains options to the `rpcgen` program to automatically generate the code for a multithreaded RPC server, so it is getting easier to build one[7].

Ultimately for high performance and scalability, services can be implemented in the kernel. This is the way NFS works, and a number of kernel threads are used which increases and reduces dynamically, depending upon the workload. This reduces thread creation overhead, the same trick could be used in a daemon.

---

6. The 32-Mbyte SPARCserver5 is a good starting point for a dedicated NIS+ server configuration.

7. The `vold` volume daemon process is the only multithreaded daemon shipped in Solaris 2.3.

☰ *1*

Sun Performance and Tuning

Performance Measurement 2 ≣

In some cases, it is obvious that there is a performance problem; when it is fixed, there may be a noticeable improvement and your job is finished. It is much more common for performance tuning to consist of many small cumulative steps. Some of the steps may reduce performance overall or make one part of the system faster at the expense of another part of the system

Problems can arise when it is necessary to quantify the changes or to measure minor performance changes in complex systems. If the aim of the work is to improve the performance in a well-defined benchmark, such as one of the SPEC or TPC measures, then the measurement can be well defined. In real life, it may be necessary to design a controlled set of experiments to measure performance on the system being worked on.

The analysis of test results can be used to produce sizing or performance models. A method for producing a configuration and sizing model for multiuser systems is described at the end of this chapter.

A Conceptual Model of Performance

The normal situation illustrated in Figure 2-1 is that you have a computer system with a particular configuration and an application workload running on that system. You then measure the performance, analyze the results, and make changes to the configuration.

Figure 2-1   A Conceptual Model of Performance

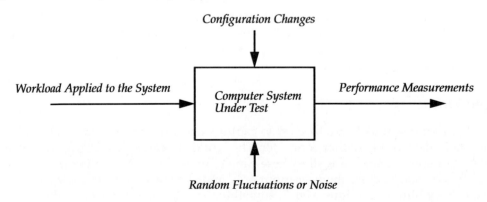

The Workload

The workload is actually one of the hardest things to deal with. In some cases, you can have total control, for example, when running a single CPU-bound application with fixed input data. In other cases, the workload is totally beyond your control, for example, on a times-sharing server with many users running different applications.

The workload selection is also your weakest point if someone wants to challenge the results you are claiming credit for. If you didn't spend a lot of time researching your workload, then you have no comeback to a critic who says, "That's all very well, but in real life the applications aren't used like that, and you have measured and tuned the wrong things." It is much harder for someone to dismiss a detailed, written justification of the workload you have used. For this reason it is worth writing up the workload and circulating the workload justification to interested parties before you start to collect data. You are likely to get valuable review feedback that will help you target your efforts more precisely.

Fixed Workloads

The biggest problem with a fixed workload is that because you have total control, you have to make decisions yourself that can affect the results you get. In real situations, the same program is usually run with different input data each time it is used. You must make sure that the input data you use is somehow representative of the kinds of data for which you want to optimize the system performance. It is worth spending a lot of time investigating the typical usage of an application by your user base. If you don't, then your carefully tuned optimizations may not have the desired effect.

Random Workloads

Random workloads are in some ways easier to deal with. If you can't control the workload, you don't have to spend so much time investigating it. Instead, you have to spend more time analyzing the measured results to separate out the random fluctuations from the effect of your tuning. Some fluctuations will occur, depending on the time of day, or whether a departmental staff meeting is in progress, or if a particular project team is trying to meet a delivery deadline.

Managed Workloads

An increasing number of tools can be used to capture, encapsulate, and drive a workload into your test system from another computer. The workload can either be captured from a live session or constructed manually. These can be divided into two categories. *Journalling*-based tools capture the user input only and simply attempt to replay it at a fixed speed. They blindly continue even if something unexpected happens or the system responds more slowly than during capture, and they cannot be programmed to react appropriately to variable responses from the system being tested. *Emulator*-based systems pattern-match the received responses to ensure that the system is still on track, measure response times, and decide when the next input is due. These are sophisticated and expensive tools, so are not for the casual user. They allow complex and sophisticated workloads to be run reliably and repeatedly and are normally used to produce system sizing information or capacity planning guides. Traditionally, these tools have worked with ASCII text applications on directly connected lines or telnet over Ethernet, but recently they have been extended to work with the much more complex X11 window system protocol. The main vendors are Performix Inc., with Empower™ and Empower/X™; Performance Awareness Corp, with PreVue™ and PreVue/X™; and Mercury, with LoadRunner™ and X Runner™. These tools are often known as RTE systems, for Remote Terminal Emulator.

Workload Characterization

If your workload consists of multiple users or individual components all running together, then it can be very useful to run each component separately (if possible) and measure the utilization profile over time. A plot of the CPU, disk, and network activity will show you when the peak load occurs and whether the load is even or peaks with idle time in between. Capacity planning tools, like the Best/1™ product from BGS Inc., sample the resource usage of each process on the system to measure the profile over time. This information is fed into a queuing model that can be used to predict the behavior of the system under various conditions. The most common uses are to see what would happen to response times if more users were added to the system and to predict the effect of hardware upgrades.

Configuration Changes

There is a tendency to make a bunch of small changes at one time, in the hope that they will have a big effect on the system. What is needed instead is a systematic approach that gives you the results you need to decide which changes are making a significant difference and which changes can be ignored.

2

Configuration Factors and Levels

There are always too many possibilities. To illustrate, I will pick some possible configuration factors from the subsequent chapters of this book. The important thing is to clearly identify the factors you wish to vary and then to pick a small number of levels that span the usable range for the factor.

Table 2-1   Example Configuration Factors and Levels

Factor	Example Levels for the Factor
Algorithm design	Bubblesort, shellsort, quicksort
Compiler flags	Debug, base optimization (`-O`), high optimization (`-fast`)
I/O library	`stdio.h`, direct unbuffered read/write, mmap, asynchronous I/O
Filesystem type	Some subset of: NFS, ufs, tmpfs, raw disk, cachefs, logfs
Application version	Compare new and old releases of the application
User count	Vary the number of simultaneously active users of the machine
Database shared mem	Minimum default, 10MB, 50MB
Database parameters	Defaults, simple DB tuning guide changes, database guru fixes
OS version	Compare several releases of the operating system
Kernel buffer sizes	Defaults, minimum sizes, extra large sizes
Paging parameters	Defaults, reduced values
Cache configuration	On-chip, on-chip + external 1 MB, on-chip + external 2 MB
Memory size	Subset of 16 MB, 32 MB, 64 MB, 128 MB, 256 MB, 512 MB, 1 GB, 2 GB
Disk type	535 MB, 1.05 GB, 2.1 GB, 2.9 GB, SPARCstorage™ Array
Disk configuration	4 striped, 8 individual, 6 mirrored, RAID5, etc.
CPU type	microSPARC™, microSPARC II, SuperSPARC, UltraSPARC™
CPU clock rate	Subset of 40 MHz, 50 MHz, 60 MHz, 70 MHz, 85 MHz, 100 MHz, etc.
CPU count	Subset of 1, 2, 4, 6, 8, 10, 12, 16, 20, 32, 48, 64
Backplane type	MBus, Single XDBus, Dual XDBus, Quad XDBus
Network type	Ethernet, Token Ring, FDDI, Fast Ethernet, ATM155, ATM622
NetWork protocol	TCP/IP, UDP/IP, PPP, NFS, etc.
Network count	1, 2, 3, 4, etc.

The best way to approach a large-scale set of tests is to perform an initial small set of tests with just two levels for each factor. In *The Art of Computer Systems Performance Analysis* by Raj Jain, a sophisticated statistical technique is described that drastically reduces the number of tests required to work out the factors that make a significant difference and those that can be ignored. To fully measure every combination of six different factors with four levels for each factor would take $4^6 = 4096$ separate measurements. Reducing to two levels for each factor brings this number down to $2^6 = 64$ separate measurements. Using the statistical methods to analyze the results, you carefully pick certain combinations of levels to measure and do the analysis on only seven measurements to find out which factors can be ignored for a more complete set of tests.

One extra benefit of doing a small preliminary test is that you start analyzing the results sooner than you would if you did all the measurements in one session. Since you will often find some bug in your measurement methods, you have a chance to fix it before you spend a lot longer taking bad measurements. It is common for a large proportion of the measured data to be useless for some reason, even in the best designed experiments.

Measurement Techniques

The Fundamentals —Throughput, Response Time, Utilization

Nearly all the measurements you can make fit into one of these three categories. You can perform a simple mental check whenever you are collecting a set of measurements to make sure that you are collecting at least one of each type. You do not have the complete picture and can easily be misled, if you don't have all three types of measurement available to you.

Example Throughput Measures

Throughput is generically the amount of work that is completed in a given amount of time. The Transactions Per Second (TPS) measures quoted for databases are one example. The SPECrate92 measures are another. Do not confuse *throughput* with *bandwidth*. Bandwidth is typically the peak, possible speed ignoring any overheads. Throughput is how much work you can actually get done at 100 per cent utilization.

- A Fast SCSI bus rated at 10.0 Mbytes/s bandwidth has a maximum throughput of about 7.5Mbytes/s when you take the SCSI protocol overhead into account. A Fast Wide SCSI bus rated at 20.0 Mbytes/s has a throughput of about 16 Mbytes/s.

- The MBus used on the SPARCstation™ 10 and the XDBus™ used on the SPARCserver 1000 both have the same bandwidth of 320 Mbytes/s. Assuming a typical mix of transaction types, the throughput of the MBus is about 100 Mbytes/s and the throughput of the XDBus is about 250 Mbytes/s. The large variation is due to a totally different protocol on each bus. The MBus is not good for throughput, but it does have substantially less latency than the XDBus.

Response Time or Latency

Response time is a measure of the time that the user has to wait for some work to complete. When measured by an RTE system this can be as fine as the time taken to echo characters being typed, or it can be the time taken for a database transaction to complete for that particular user. If you run a single job and measure the elapsed time it took to complete, then you have a measure of response time for a throughput of 1. Latency is the same thing, but this term is more often used when a protocol is being discussed.

Utilization

Utilization is a measure of how much of the computer's resources were used to do the work. The measures reported by sar and iostat are typical utilization measures. If you run a single job and measure how much CPU time it uses, then you are concentrating on the utilization level of the job.

Typical Interactions for a Multiuser System

If a particular configuration of a multiuser system is tested by using an RTE, then the test can be repeated under controlled conditions with different load levels or user counts. The throughput, response time, and utilization can be measured at each load level and plotted. The resulting set of plots normally takes the form shown in Figure 2-2.

If a single job contains some thinktime or does I/O, then it is unlikely to fully utilize a system[1]. It will have a response time, which is the time taken to complete the job, and a throughput, which is the simple inverse of the response time.

If several users run the job at once, then the utilization level will be higher, the response time will be similar, and the throughput will have increased. At some point as users are added the utilization reaches 100 percent and the user jobs must wait in a queue before they can be run. Utilization is a generic term. In practice the CPU usage level is the most common utilization measure, although it is also common for the initial bottleneck in the system to be an overloaded disk drive at 100 percent utilization.

As shown in Figure 2-2, once we reach 100 percent utilization, throughput stops increasing and the response time starts to climb. This is the saturation point of the system. If still more users are added, the overhead of managing long queues and switching between users takes an increasingly large proportion of the CPU, the system CPU time climbs, the user CPU time drops, and the throughput drops with it.

---

1. This is particularly true on large multiprocessor servers and for window system tools.

The ideal situation is to always run at the 90 percent utilization level, with a very stable workload. In practice, most machines have a widely fluctuating workload and spend most of the time at a low utilization level. When a peak occurs, it may exceed the saturation point; what happens after saturation can make a big difference to the perceived performance of the system.

After saturation, the response time increases. The goal should be to have a steady increase over a wide load range; that way, users find that the system gradually seems to slow down, and they tend to reduce their demand on the system. If the response time increases sharply over a short load range, users find that the system suddenly stops responding with little advance warning, and they will complain about poor performance.

Real systems are more complex than this, but one way to deal with this problem is to assume that each type of user has its own collective saturation point, and to think in terms of the number of each distinct user category, rather than an overall, homogeneous, user load. One example is the distinction between database users who process mainly inquiries against existing data and users who do mainly data entry. The data entry users can encounter an I/O bottleneck with a relatively small number of users as they process updates against the database. The inquiry users often run from cached data in memory and will encounter a CPU bottleneck on the same machine at a much higher number of users.

When you are installing a new system or tuning an existing one, you should deliberately drive it into a saturated state if you can. If you then carefully tune the performance under excessive load, you may be able to get a gradual response degradation curve. This may mean that the system begins to slow down a little earlier than before, which acts as a warning to the users. Be aware that if a system is tuned so that every resource hits 100 percent utilization at the same time, you will have a very fast degradation at the saturation point.

Figure 2-2 *Saturation Points and the Relationship Between Performance Measures*

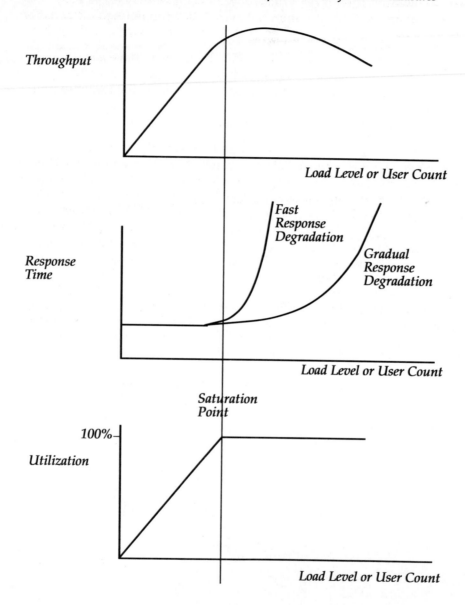

Heisenberg's Principle

It is a basic rule of physics that you cannot measure something without also affecting it in some way. When you measure the performance of a system, be aware of the effect that your measurement tools may have. Fortunately most of the data collection utilities have a negligible impact on the system. A sar, vmstat, or iostat collecting data at 5-second intervals is not going to make a noticeable difference. Collecting a system call trace of an active process is an example of the kind of high-speed data collection that should be avoided while taking performance measurements.

Using Accounting to Monitor the Workload

If you have access to a group of real end-users over a long period of time, then enable the UNIX system accounting logs. This can be useful on a network of workstations as well as on a single time-shared server. From this you can identify how often programs run, how much CPU time, disk I/O, and memory each program uses, and what work patterns throughout the week look like. To enable accounting to start immediately, enter the three commands shown at the start of Figure 2-3. Check out the section "Administering Security, Performance, and Accounting in Solaris 2" in the *Solaris System Administration Answerbook* and see the acctcom command. Some crontab entries must also be added to summarize and checkpoint the accounting logs. Collecting and checkpointing the accounting data itself puts a negligible additional load onto the system, but the summary scripts that run once a day or once a week can have a noticeable effect, so they should be scheduled to run out of hours.

Figure 2-3   How to Start Up System Accounting in Solaris 2

```
# ln /etc/init.d/acct /etc/rc0.d/K22acct
# ln /etc/init.d/acct /etc/rc2.d/S22acct
# /etc/init.d/acct start
Starting process accounting
# crontab -l adm
#ident   "@(#)adm      1.5      92/07/14 SMI"    /* SVr4.0 1.2    */
#min    hour    day    month    weekday
0       *       *      *        *        /usr/lib/acct/ckpacct
30      2       *      *        *        /usr/lib/acct/runacct 2> \
  /var/adm/acct/nite/fd2log
30      9       *      *        5        /usr/lib/acct/monacct
```

Collecting Long-term System Utilization Data

Collect overall system utilization data on all the machines you deal with as a matter of course. For Solaris 2, this is already set up and just needs to be uncommented from the crontab file for the sys user. For SunOS 4.X, you need to invent your own scheme along the same lines by logging iostat and vmstat output to a file. An example to get you started is listed in Figure 2-4. This script should run on either release.

Figure 2-4   perflog - Long-term Performance Collection Script for SunOS 4 and Solaris 2

```
#!/sbin/sh
# perflog - long term performance collection script
#
# run from crontab, pass the number of seconds between samples as
# the first argument and make the crontab period the same
# make the log filename the second argument
#
# run iostat -D, vmstat and netstat into temporary files then
# concatenate them onto the log with a datestamp
# iostat and vmstat need to throw away the first data since it is
# the average since boot time.
#
# first check to see if file exists
if [ ! -w $2 ]; then
        echo "Performance Log File Collected By perflog" > $2
        echo >> $2
fi
( iostat -tDc -l 32 $1 2 > /tmp/iolog$$ &
vmstat $1 2 >/tmp/vmlog$$
# its now the end of the period, while cron is starting another copy
# save away this one to the log.
echo >> $2
echo "Performance for" $1 "seconds ending at " 'date'>> $2
# put absolute network counts for all interfaces into the log
netstat -i >> $2
# wait to make sure iostat has finished
wait
head -2 /tmp/vmlog$$ >> $2
tail -1 /tmp/vmlog$$ >> $2
rm /tmp/vmlog$$
head -2 /tmp/iolog$$ >> $2
tail -1 /tmp/iolog$$ >> $2
rm /tmp/iolog$$ ) &
```

This script could easily be extended to collect other information such as NFS activity counts.

The Solaris 2 utilization log consists of a `sar` binary log file taken at 20-minute intervals throughout the day and saved in `/var/adm/sa/saXX`, where XX is the day of the month. This collects a utilization profile for an entire month. See "Using sar Effectively in Solaris 2" on page 216. The monthly records should be saved for future comparison.

When a performance-related problem occurs, it is far easier to identify the source of the problem if you have measurements from a time when the problem was not present. Remember that the real-life, user workload is likely to increase over time. If you are trying to justify the purchase of an upgrade to a manager, it is hard to dismiss a plot showing a long-term utilization trend.

The example `crontab` file shown in Figure 2-5 has an extra entry that runs the perflog script every 20 minutes as well so that network traffic counts are collected. `sar` does not collect network-related information.

Figure 2-5   Extended `crontab` *Entry for Long-term* `sar` *Data Collection*

```
# crontab -l sys
#ident"@(#)sys1.592/07/14 SMI"/* SVr4.0 1.2*/
#
# The sys crontab should be used to do performance collection. See cron
# and performance manual pages for details on startup.
#
0 * * * 0-6 /usr/lib/sa/sa1
20,40 8-17 * * 1-5 /usr/lib/sa/sa1
5 18 * * 1-5 /usr/lib/sa/sa2 -s 8:00 -e 18:01 -i 1200 -A
0,20,40 * * * * /usr/lib/sa/perflog 1200 /var/adm/sa/perf.log
```

Processing and Analyzing the Measurements

Processing and analyzing the measured results of a set of experiments is an open-ended activity. Collected data is often simply processed into averages and tabulated or plotted. I'm sure that even with the best of intentions, the post-processing and analysis of results could often be described as cursory. Part of the problem is a lack of tools and techniques, so I will explore some simple methods and give examples of the kind of advanced results that can be obtained by using a good statistics package like SAS/CPE™ or S-PLUS™.

Generating Averages with Sar

If you have the automatic utilization log enabled, then the default for a `sar` command is to print out the log for the day with an average at the end. Figure 2-6 shows the `sar` summary for an evening's work writing this book with FrameMaker® software. Whenever `sar` is used to read a `sar` log file, start and end times can be specified, and an average will be produced.

Figure 2-6   Looking at Today's Utilization Log

```
% sar

SunOS hostname 5.3 Generic sun4c    03/04/94

19:34:10    %usr    %sys    %wio    %idle
19:34:10unix restarts
20:00:03      4       4       4       88
21:00:00      3       1       0       95
22:00:01      8       2       0       89
23:00:01      9       2       0       89

Average       6       2       1       91
```

See "Understanding vmstat and sar Output" on page 194 and "Using sar Effectively in Solaris 2" on page 216 for more details. `sar` records all the information that the more familiar `iostat` and `vmstat` commands report, as well as many other useful measurements. Its major flaw is that it does not store any network-related information, so a supplemental `netstat` output log may be needed.

An `awk` script[2] can be used to pick out the information of interest from `sar`, and data from several measurements can be combined into a table like the one shown in Figure 2-7. This table shows how the CPU and disk utilization varies as the number of users is increased on a complex RTE-driven, database workload that has a large batch processing component.

Figure 2-7   Example Data from `Sar` *Averages Tabulated with* `Awk`

users	cpu.usr	cpu.sys	cpu.wio	cpu.idl	disk.sd32	disk.sd33
16	58	19	22	1	9	62
32	73	24	3	0	14	37
48	72	26	2	0	15	34
64	74	26	0	0	15	12
96	70	28	1	0	11	50
128	70	30	0	0	10	17
160	58	42	0	0	7	9

Using the Results Generated by an Emulator System

Emulator systems run a program to emulate each user. This program uses a script of commands and responses and includes defined operation sequences (sometimes known as user functions). Each user program writes a log of every command and response that has the function start and end points with accurate time stamps embedded in it. After a mixture of these programs has been run as a workload, special postprocessing commands extract the named functions and time stamps. Reports can then be generated for a particular start and end time during the test (which should match the start and end time used for the `sar` utilization averages). The report lists the number of times each named function completed in the specified time interval and the maximum, minimum, mean, and standard deviation of the time taken.

The number of functions completed in the time interval is a throughput measure, and the average time taken is a latency measure. Together with the `sar`-based utilization information, we have a good basis for further analysis.

If a set of results is taken with varying numbers of users, then the measurements will often have the form shown in Figure 2-2 on page 24.

---

2. Details of this script are left as an exercise for the reader, but the Solaris head, tail, cut, and paste commands may also be useful.

Obtaining Results on a Live System

If you are monitoring a live system with real users, then you will need to find a way of quantifying the throughput. Response times are very hard to obtain on a live system but can be inferred from the throughput and utilization measures in many cases. To find a throughput measure, look at the system accounting reports to see if there is a key application program associated with the users that uses a significant amount of CPU or I/O. You can also look at the typical execution times for the program, and it may be possible to derive a throughput measure from either the number of times the program executed or from the total amount of CPU time or I/O consumed by that program in a given time period. Database applications are somewhat easier, as it is usually possible to identify how many transactions of a given type have occurred in a given time period and to use this as the throughput measure.

Whereas a managed workload using an RTE may process data over a time period measured in minutes, a real-life workload will often need measurement periods measured in hours or days. If users log in only once each day and use a single instance of an application throughout the day, then the daily CPU usage for that application could be extracted as a throughput measure from the accounting logs with awk each night.

Analyzing the Results

The analysis required depends on the situation. If you are conducting a sizing or capacity planning study, then many results for different configurations of the system can be combined into a sizing model. If you are monitoring a live system and trying to identify where the next bottleneck will occur, then you need to build a model of changes in the system over time.

How to Produce a Sizing Model

I will briefly describe a method that has worked well for sizing multiuser workloads using the Performix Empower RTE and the StatSci S-PLUS statistical modelling package.

The tabular data on utilization, throughput, and response time at varying user counts was produced for each system configuration that was tested. A system was set up with a particular disk, memory, and CPU configuration and then a series of measurements were made with increasing numbers of users. At the high user counts the system was pushed well into an overloaded state for some configurations. Configuration changes were made by varying the number of CPUs[3], changing the disk setup, and changing the amount of thinktime in the workload scripts.

---

3. This can be done programmatically; see "CPU Control Commands — psrinfo and psradm" on page 97.

The first thing to do is produce plots of the data, to make sure that it looks "clean." The next task is to estimate the saturation point for each configuration in terms of users. The technique used was to take the throughput data and to fit a straight line from the origin through the first few points. This represents the region where the system is underutilized; the only constraint on throughput is the thinktime of the users (the rate at which they ask the system to do work for them). Another straight horizontal line is taken from the point of peak throughput; the intersection of the two lines was defined as the saturation point; projected down to produce a user count. This measure was found to be very stable and didn't fluctuate much when repeated measurements were made on the same configuration whereas the position of the peak throughput varied much more. It has the additional benefit of not requiring measurements of response time, so it can be used in situations where the response time measurement cannot be obtained.

Figure 2-8   Finding the Saturation Point

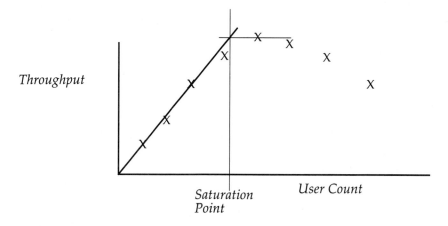

Each test can now be characterized by its saturation point measured in users, the peak throughput level, the utilization levels of the various parts of the system at the measured saturation point, and the configuration factors used for the test. The response time at this point should always be good, so it does not need to be included.

The test results are stored in S-plus as a *data frame* for modeling. A model can be calculated that produces a set of coefficients relating the configuration factors to the saturation point. Each coefficient is used for one level of the factor, for example, in an ideal world the CPU coefficients might be 0.5 for two CPUs, 1.0 for four CPUs and 2.0 for eight CPUs. When the model was used to predict results, the values predicted by this model were within a few user values of the measured results across the entire range. The residual errors were small, and a good fit for the model was obtained. A similar formula for predicting the peak throughput can also be obtained.

Figure 2-9   Model Formula and Coefficients Produced for System Sizing

$$Users \ = \ Intercept \times \begin{bmatrix} Timeshare \\ ClientServer \end{bmatrix} \times \begin{bmatrix} 2CPU \\ 4CPU \\ 6CPU \\ 8CPU \end{bmatrix} \times \begin{bmatrix} ShortThink \\ MediumThink \\ LongThink \end{bmatrix}$$

In the formula shown above, a coefficient is produced for each value shown. To get the saturation point value in users for a particular combination, the coefficients for that combination are multiplied, for example, Intercept × Timeshare × 6CPU × MediumThink.

A useful aspect of this method is that the statistics package maintains information on the variance of each coefficient, and when the formula is used to predict the value of a saturation point, the standard deviation of that prediction is also calculated. The tests used to calculate the model represent a sparse subset of the complete configuration space (i.e. not every possible combination of configuration options was tested, which saved time), so if a group of related predictions are calculated to have a large standard deviation, then more tests can be performed in the region of that group, and the model can be regenerated with reduced variance.

The statisticians among you may be curious about the method used to produce a multiplicative model equation, when the standard techniques work with additive models. There are two ways to handle this in S-Plus. One way is to take logarithms of the data before calculating the additive model, then use exponents to regenerate the coefficients. A more sophisticated method is to use the generalized linear model with a Poisson link function, which sounds complicated but is actually easier to use. (It took me a while to work out that this was the right thing to do, since S-Plus has hundreds of possible modeling options!). This, has the property that the variance of the result is proportional to its value, so the error in a 10-user prediction might be 1 user, while for a 200-user prediction, the error might be 20 users.

Looking for Trends

Take many short samples of utilization data (like the hourly sar measures) and plot them to produce a distribution curve or histogram over a longer period (perhaps weekly). This way, you count the number of hours per week that utilization was in a certain range and, as time goes on you can compare the weekly distribution plots to see if there is an increase in the number of hours per week at high utilization levels. Do this for CPU run queue size, for each disks service time, and for the page scan rate[4].

Further Reading

A recent book on this subject is highly recommended. *The Art of Computer Systems Performance Analysis*, by Raj Jain, provides comprehensive coverage of techniques for experimental design, measurement, simulation, and performance modeling. If you are embarking on a large project that involves a lot of measurement and analysis, you can save a great deal of effort and get much better results by using the right techniques.

Statistical Models In S, by John M. Chambers and Trevor J. Hastie, is quite specific to the S-Plus statistics package, but it gives an excellent insight into the range of techniques available in modern statistics and how the combination of statistics and numerical modelling can be used to make sense of data.

---

4. A high scan rate indicates a memory shortage, see "The Paging Algorithm in Solaris 2" on page 207.

Source Code 3≡

This chapter is concerned with the aspects of a system that programmers specifying and writing the software can control to affect system performance.

Algorithms

Many algorithms are invented on the fly while writing a program and are as simple to code as possible. More efficient algorithms are often much more complex to implement and may need to be retrofitted to an application that is being tuned. A good book of algorithms and a feel for which parts of the program are likely to be hot spots can make more difference to performance in some cases than all other tuning tweaks put together.

Algorithmic Classification

Some general behavioral classes of algorithms are shown in Figure 3-1. There is an initial overhead or setup time; then, as the amount of data increases, the time taken increases in various ways. This is a very generalized discussion, but some examples are included to illustrate the point.

Figure 3-1   Time Taken to Run vs. Dataset Size for Different Classes of Algorithms

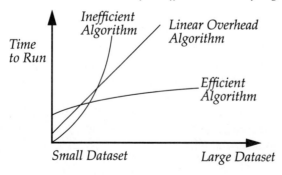

Inefficient Algorithms

For example, the time taken to sort some data with a bubblesort algorithm more than doubles when there is twice as much data to be sorted, so it is an inefficient algorithm. These algorithms are relatively simple to implement and can have a smaller setup time than more complex algorithms. For very small data sets, the setup time can dominate, so inefficient algorithms can be useful in some restricted areas. An application using inefficient algorithms in critical areas can suffer from a brick wall effect, where it rapidly becomes unusable when given data sets that are not much larger than usual.

Linear Algorithms

There may be a slightly larger setup overhead for linear algorithms than for an inefficient algorithm, but the application will degrade gracefully when it is given an oversized data set to work on if all the algorithms are linear or better. It simply means that the time taken is directly proportional to the amount of data. Simple linear searches are an example.

Efficient Algorithms

The time taken to locate a database record from an indexed table is mostly independent of the actual size of the table, so it is a very efficient search algorithm. The setup time is often considerable, as an index must be built and maintained in advance, and there is often a complex hashing function to execute for each lookup.

As long as a program is being used with a small data set, the difference between each class of algorithms is minor. This is often the case during testing or in the early lifetime of a product, but problems often occur when the data-set size increases.

An Example Problem

One real-life example was a CAD system that kept each object in a drawing on a linked list and performed a linear search through the list whenever it needed to find an object. This worked all right for small drawings, since the time taken to perform other operations dominated the execution time. When the CAD system was ported from a Sun-3™ /60[1] to a SPARCstation 2, many parts of the code speeded up by a factor of up to 10 times. The users now expected to run drawings with many times the complexity at the same speed as they used to run them on a Sun-3/60.

---

1. This example is based upon a situation that occurred in 1991. The Sun3/60 is a 3-MIP machine and the SPARCstation 2 is a 28-MIP machine. Both are now obsolete, but this kind of situation recurs every year as performance increases.

Unfortunately for some operations, the time taken to search through the linked list dominated due to the larger data-set size, and the linked list code didn't see a 10-times speedup due to caching effects. (The Sun-3/60 has no data cache, see "A Problem with Linked Lists" on page 186.) This was identified as the performance problem, and the algorithm was improved. The solution in this case was to move from a linear search to a more complex search based on hash tables or tree structures.

Another approach that could be used in similar situations is to incrementally sort the linked list. You can do this by taking the entry that you have just located on the list and moving it to the front of the list. Eventually, all the uninteresting entries end up at the end of the list, the entries that are in most demand congregate at the front of the list where they are searched first, and the first few entries of the list may stay in the cache.

Space versus Time

Another issue to consider is space versus time optimization. There's no sense in making an algorithm that's inefficient run more quickly if doing so requires a large increase in the memory space required. The increase in storage may make the application miss the cache more often or page, and the cache or disk accesses can outweigh any improvement in CPU runtime. It is possible to make an algorithm efficient, only to use so much space that it doesn't run at full speed.

Optimize for the Common Code Path

When you write code there are often many places where optional cases or error conditions are tested for. Wherever possible, try to make the common case the straight-through path, as this causes fewer branches to be taken. Straight-line code has a better cache hit rate and also helps processors prefetch and execute more useful instructions in a given number of clock cycles. The disadvantage is that the code can sometimes be a little harder to read, because the test and the action for each exception will be separated. A trivial example is shown in Figures 3-2 and 3-3; most benefit comes when multiple options and error conditions are being handled.

Figure 3-2   Example Pseudocode for Branching in the Usual Case

```
do some work
if (option)
        deal with option
else
        do the usual case
return
```

Figure 3-3   Example Pseudocode for Straight Line Code in the Usual Case

```
do some work
if (option not set)
        do the usual case
        return
else
        deal with option
return
```

Layering and Fast Paths

It is good software engineering practice to have a well-defined interface at each level in the system. This tends to increase the code path, as high-level operations descend through the hierarchy of layers. The solution is to profile the code, looking for the most common operations, then to implement well-documented and commented fast paths through the code for the most common operations. The danger is that you end up with two ways of performing the same operation, the slow path and the fast path. When functional changes are made, they can cause problems with trying to keep both in sync. The best approach is to make the fast path a conditional compilation option where possible and to delay implementing the fast path until the whole system is tested and functionally stable. The temptation to implement the fast path at the design stage must be resisted, as the measured hot spots on a finished application are often subtly different cases from those that the designer anticipated. Figures 3-4 and 3-5 illustrate examples.

Figure 3-4   .Layered Code Example Calling Sequence

```
save_everything()
  write_special_header()
    fwrite()
      write()
  get_thinglist()
  for (everything there is)
    get_next()
    save_thing()
      my_save()
        save_thing_header()
          fwrite()
            write()
        save_thing_body()
          fwrite()
            write()
```

Figure 3-5   Fast-path Code Example Calling Sequence

```
save_everything()
  /* patch up a pre-built header */
  /* build a linked list of all the stuff to be written */
  /* by chasing pointers through data structures directly */
  writev()  /* let the kernel handle the whole list in one go */
```

Programming Model

There is often a conceptual framework underlying an application which can be thought of in terms of a programming model. Some example models are:

- Hierarchical, structured programming via Jackson diagrams

- Object-oriented

- Data flow, the Yourdon/DeMarco methods

- Numerical algorithms

- AI-based, rules- or knowledge-based design

- Forms and records

Examples to illustrate some of these models are shown in Figures 3-6, 3-7, and 3-8. I've tried to illustrate the flavor of each programming model on a similar task.

Figure 3-6   Hierarchical, Structured Programming via Jackson Diagrams

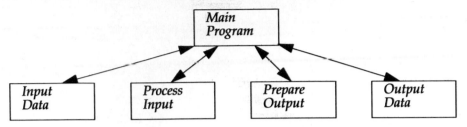

Figure 3-7   Object-oriented Programming

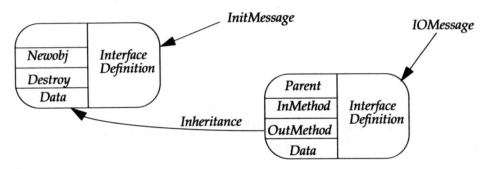

Figure 3-8   Dataflow, the Yourdon/DeMarco Method

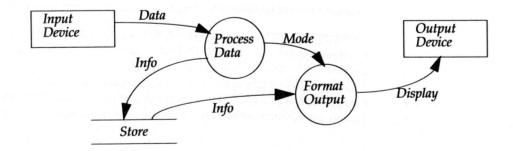

Figure 3-9   Numerical Algorithms

$$output = \alpha \times \prod_{1}^{n} \left(input[n-1] \times \begin{bmatrix} 1 & \beta & \zeta \\ 0 & 1 & \beta \\ 0 & 0 & 1 \end{bmatrix} \right)$$

Sometimes, the model that a programmer or system designer prefers is chosen regardless of the type of system being written. An inappropriate match between the programming model and the problem to be solved is a remarkably common cause of performance problems.

Choice of Language to Express the Algorithm or Model

The programmer may decide to choose a language that is familiar to him or may have a language imposed on him. Often the language ends up dictating the programming model, irrespective of the needs of the application, but sometimes languages are forced to implement programming models that are inappropriate. Real examples that I have encountered include a database system written in APL, a real-time control system written in Prolog, and a very large message-passing, object-oriented system written in C.

If there is a good match of problem to programming model to language, then there is a good chance that the system overall will respond well to tuning. Poorly matched systems sometimes contain so much unnecessary complexity that they are impossible to profile and tune. Brute-force increases in CPU and I/O throughput are the only thing that have a significant effect on performance.

The moral is that if you come across an application like this and first attempts at tuning have little effect, you may as well put your money into buying a faster SPARCstation and your time and effort into redesigning the system from scratch.

It comes down to using the right tool for the job. Most people know what languages to use for particular jobs, but some non-obvious points are listed below[2].

FORTRAN

FORTRAN is usually the fastest language for anything that is numerically intensive. For an equivalent level of compiler technology, it will always be faster than C. This is because it has a simple structure that compilers can handle more easily than C and it doesn't have pointers so there is less chance of side effects during expression evaluation. The key to

---

2. *High Performance Computing*, by Keith Dowd covers these issues very well.

optimization is *code motion,* and this can be performed more safely in FORTRAN than in C. A second reason is that FORTRAN defaults to passing floating-point variables to subroutines by reference (i.e., passing an address rather than the number itself). This is more efficient, especially on RISC processors such as SPARC that have separate integer and floating-point registers and where the calling convention is to pass variables in integer registers.

Assembler

In theory, assembler is the fastest language possible. In practice, programmers get so bogged down in the huge volume of code and the difficulty in debugging it that they tend to implement simple, inefficient algorithms in poorly structured code. It is hard to find out where the hot spots in the system are, so the wrong parts of the system get optimized. When you discover a small routine that dominates the execution time, look at the assembler generated by the compiler and tweak the source code. As a last resort, consider rewriting it in assembler.

It is often very helpful to understand what sort of code is generated by your compiler. I have found that writing clean, simple, high-level language code can help the compiler to understand the code better and that this can improve the optimization of the generated assembler. Just think of assembler as read-only code. Read it and understand it if you can, but don't try to write it.

C and C++

It seems that just about everything is written in C nowadays. Its biggest weakness is that hardly anyone seems to use `lint` to check code as a standard part of their compilation makefiles. Wading through the heaps of complaints that `lint` produces for most systems written in C gives a pretty good insight into the sloppy nature of much C coding. Many problems with optimizers breaking C code can be avoided by getting the code to lint cleanly first! ANSI C is an improvement but not a substitute for `lint`.

C++ should be used whenever an object-oriented design is called for. In most cases C could be used, but sloppy coding and programmers who take shortcuts make the resulting systems very hard to debug, and give optimizers a hard time. Writing C++-like code in C makes the code very hard to understand; it is much easier to use a C++ preprocessor with a debugger and performance analyser that understand the language.

A common problem with C++ is that too many trivial objects or complex hierarchies are created. Objects should not be used when a function call would do the job just as well. Objects work best when they are used to represent something concrete. The more abstract an object is, the less useful it is.

Debug and Test Tools

lint has just been mentioned; build it into your default makefiles and use it regularly. A little known utility called tcov[3] performs test coverage analysis and produces an annotated listing showing how many times each block of code has been executed and a percentage coverage figure. This utility is bundled with SunOS 4 and is bundled with the SunPro™ compilers for Solaris 2.

The execution profile of a program can be obtained by means of the prof or gprof tools provided with the system. One problem with these tools is that they measure the total execution from start to finish, which is less useful for window system tools that have a long start-up time. The SunPro SPARCworks™ collector and analyzer can be used on Solaris 2 to obtain this type of profile information for specific parts of a program.

The SunPro SPARCworks 3.0 debugger includes a sophisticated runtime checking option. There are also similar products from Purify, Inc. and Sentinel, Inc. These can be used to debug subtle errors in C and C++ programs, such as used-before-set data, memory allocation errors, and array bounds violations. Purify works by modifying object files to instrument memory references, and it can even find errors in library routines.

Compiler and Optimizations

Having chosen a language, there is a choice of compilers for the language. There are typically several compilers for each major language on SPARC. The SPARCompilers™ from SunPro tend to have the largest user base and the best robustness on large programs. The Apogee C and FORTRAN compilers seem to have a performance advantage of 10 - 20 percent over the commonly used SunPro SPARCompilers™ for benchmarks and programs that run reliably with maximum optimization. Results for the SPARCompilers™ 3.0 and Apogee 2.3 releases show substantial performance improvements over previous releases for both vendors. Competition between SunPro, Apogee, and others will lead to better compilers. Using compilers effectively to tune code is not covered in this book since it has been addressed in great depth in previous publications[4]. To summarize in a sentence: Clean C code with lint, turn up the optimizer most of the way (-O3), profile to find hot spots, and turn up the optimizer to maximum for those parts only (-O4). Look at the assembly language code produced for the hot spots to see if it is efficient. If the code doesn't look good, tweaking the source

---

3. See the tcov manual page.

4. Some of the publications are: (1) *Performance Tuning an Application,* supplied with Sun® C™, and Sun®FORTRAN; *(2) You and Your Compiler,* by Keith Bierman; *(3) SPARC Compiler Optimization Technology Technical White Paper; (4) High Performance Computing,* by Keith Dowd.

code slightly may help the compiler do a better job. If the code still doesn't look good, then send a small piece of source code and the generated assembly language to your compiler vendor so they know what needs to be improved.

Default Optimization Options

Many users keep to the default compiler option of -O. You should understand that this includes different optimizations for each language. In particular, SunPro implements four optimization levels, -O1, -O2, -O3 and -O4. For Sun FORTRAN, the default -O implies -O3, while for Sun C it implies -O2. Unless you are compiling device driver or kernel code, you should try to use -O3 as the default option with C. The issue with device drivers is that the compiler can generate faster code if it assumes that variables do not map onto hardware I/O registers. The -O3 optimizations are safe for normal code, but require that you use the *volatile* keyword correctly in your device driver code.

Automatic Parallelization

With the introduction and shipment of a large number of multiprocessor machines, it becomes cost-effective to recompile applications to utilize several processors on a single UNIX process. SunPro has an automatic parallelizing optimizer available as an option for SPARCompilers 3.0. Its first release supports FORTRAN 77, with support for FORTRAN 90 and C++ planned for later releases. Apogee ships the Kuck and Associates KAP preprocessor as an optional part of their product. This can also be used to parallelize code, although it uses UNIX processes as its unit of concurrency, whereas the SunPro optimizer uses lightweight processes (Solaris 2 threads bound to LWPs) in a single UNIX context to reduce context switching overhead.

Applications vary, and some parallelize better than others. One source of examples is the individual SPECfp92 benchmarks and the recently proposed PAR94 parallel benchmark suite. See the "SPARCserver 1000 and SPARCcenter 2000 Performance Brief" and the "SPARCstation 10 Product Line Technical White Paper."

Effective Use of Provided System Functions

This is a general call to avoid reinventing the wheel. The SunOS libraries contain many high-level functions that have been debugged, tuned, and documented for you to use. If your system hot spot turns out to be in a library routine, then it may be worth looking at recoding it in some streamlined way, but the next release of SunOS or the next generation of hardware may render your homegrown version obsolete. As an example, the common string handling routines provided in the standard SunOS 4.X C library are simple, compiled C code. In Solaris 2, these routines are written in optimized assembler.

Some very powerful library routines seem to be underused, and I provide some pointers to my favorites below.

Mapped Files

SunOS 4.X, Solaris 2.X, and all versions of UNIX System V Release 4 (SVR4) include a full implementation of the `mmap` system call. This call allows a process to map a file directly into its address space without the overhead of copying to and from a user buffer. It also allows shared files, so that more efficient use of memory is possible and interprocess communication can be performed. The shared library system used for dynamic linking uses `mmap` as its basis.

Memory Advice

The `madvise` routine tells the system how you intend to access memory. You can say that you will or won't need everything in a certain range, so that the kernel can prefetch or free the pages; you can say whether access will be sequential or random, so that the kernel can free pages that have already been used sequentially or avoid prefetching extra pages that probably will not be needed.

Asynchronous I/O

Asynchronous I/O is an extension to the normal blocking read and write calls to allow the process to issue nonblocking reads and writes[5].

Memory Allocation Tuning

The standard version of `malloc` in the Sun-supplied `libc` is optimized for good space utilization rather than for fast execution time. A version of `malloc` that optimizes for speed rather than space uses the "BSD malloc" algorithm and is provided in `/usr/lib/libbsdmalloc.a`. Link with the `-lbsdmalloc` option. It is very rare for the CPU time used by `malloc` to be an issue, so don't use the BSD `malloc` unless you are sure you need it.

There are some useful options in the standard version of `malloc`.

- `mallocmap` prints a map of the heap to the standard output.

- `mallinfo` provides statistics on `malloc`.

---

5. Described in the `aioread` and `aiowrite` manual pages.

Note – There is a small block allocation system controlled by the `mallopt` routine. This is not actually implemented in the code of the default version of `malloc` or the BSD `malloc`; the interface is part of SVID but the implementation is vendor-dependent.

In Solaris 2 there are three versions of `malloc`, System V.4 `malloc`, SunOS 4 `malloc` for backward compatibility and BSD `malloc`. When linking with third-party libraries that use `malloc`, take care not to mix implementations. Attempts to allocate a zero-sized section of memory are handled differently by each version.

Linking and Localization of Reference and Libraries

There are two basic ways to link to a library in SunOS and SVR4; static linking is the traditional method used by other systems, and dynamic linking is a runtime link process. With dynamic linking, the library exists as a complete unit that is mapped into the address space of every process that uses it. This saves a lot of RAM, particularly with window system libraries at over a megabyte each. It has several implications for performance tuning, however.

Each process that uses a shared library shares the physical pages of RAM occupied by the library but uses a different virtual address mapping. This implies that the library may end up being cached differently from one run of a program to the next. On machines with physically addressed caches (e.g., SuperSPARC), this difference can cause interactions that increase the variance of benchmark results. The library must also be compiled with position-independent code. Such code is a little less efficient than normal code because every call requires an indirect table jump which is less efficient than a direct call. Static linking is a good thing to use when benchmarking systems, since the performance may be better and the results will have less variance. Production code should normally dynamically link to save memory, particularly to the system interface library `libc`. A mixture can be used; for example, in the following compilation the FORTRAN library is statically linked, but `libc` is dynamically linked.

```
% f77 -fast -o fred fred.f -Bstatic -lF77 -lV77 -lm -Bdynamic -lc
```

This compilation dynamically links in the `libc` library and makes everything else static. The order of the arguments is important. If you are shipping products written in FORTRAN to customers who do not have FORTRAN installed on their systems, you will need to use this trick.

Tuning Shared Libraries

When static linking is used, the library is accessed as an archive of separate object files, and only the files needed to resolve references in the code are linked in. This means that the position of each object module in memory is hard to control or predict. For dynamic linking, the entire library is available at runtime regardless of which routines are used. In fact, the library is demand-paged into memory as it is needed. Since the object modules making up the library are always laid out in memory the same way, a library can be tuned when it is built by reordering it so that modules that call each other often are in the same memory page. In this way, the working set of the library can be dramatically reduced. The window system libraries for SunView™ and OpenWindows™ are tuned in this way since there is a lot of intercalling between routines in the library. Tools to do this automatically on entire programs or libraries are provided as part of the SPARCworks Analyser, using some functionality that is only provided in the Solaris 2 debug interface (/proc), linker, and object file format. The main difference is that the a.out format used in BSD UNIX and SunOS 4 allows only entire object modules to be reordered. The ELF format used in UNIX SVR4 and Solaris 2 allows each function and data item in a single object module to be independently relocated.

A special tool called the Shared Library Interposer can be used to measure and tune the performance of shared libraries. It was developed in particular for tuning graphics and window system libraries. It is not a product, but you can obtain a copy by sending email to the sli-software-request@creek.eng.sun.com alias.

Multithreaded Programming

Solaris 2 supports multithreaded application programs. Each release of Solaris 2 has extended the limits of this support. Multithreaded versions of some major application software packages are now available.

MP Programming with SunOS 4.1.2 and 4.1.3

There is no supported programmer interface to the multiple processors. Multiple UNIX processes must be used.

MP Programming with Solaris 2.0 and 2.1

The programmer's libraries are not present in the Solaris 2.0 and 2.1 releases.

MP Programming with Solaris 2.2

A multithreaded programmer interface is included in the Solaris 2.2 release, and several system libraries have been made reentrant, or MT-safe.

MP Programming with Solaris 2.3

UNIX International (SVR4 ES/MP) and a POSIX standards committee (1003.4a) are defining APIs for multithreaded programming. Solaris 2.3 includes an implementation of the POSIX threads standard that is very close to the latest draft of the standard and has many more MT-safe system libraries.

The SPARCworks 3.0 multithreaded-application-development tools became available soon after Solaris 2.3 shipped.

MP Programming with Solaris 2.4

In Solaris 2.4 almost all the libraries are thread-safe and the rpcgen program can automatically generate the code for a multithreaded RPC server.

Applications

This section discusses what a user running an application on a Sun machine can control or monitor on a program-by-program basis.

Customizing the Execution Environment

Limits

The execution environment is largely controlled by the shell. There is a command which can be used to constrain a program that is hogging too many resources. For `csh` the command is `limit`; for `sh` and `ksh` the command is `ulimit`. A default set of Solaris 2 resource limits is shown in Table 4-1, the SunOS 4 limits are similar.

Users can increase limits up to the hard system limit. The system-wide default limits can only be changed by patching the kernel directly with `adb`. See "Setting Default Limits" on page 221 for details. The limits on *data size* and *stack size* are 2 Gbytes on recent machines with the SPARC Reference MMU, but are limited to 512 Mbytes and 256 Mbytes respectively by the sun4c MMU used in the SPARCstation 1 and 2 families of machines. See "The Sun-4 MMU — sun4, sun4c, sun4e Kernel Architectures" on page 164.

Table 4-1   Resource Limits

Resource Name	Soft User Limit	Hard System Limit
cputime	unlimited	unlimited
filesize	unlimited	unlimited
datasize	524280 – 2097148 Kbytes	524280 – 2097148 Kbytes
stacksize	8192 Kbytes	261120 – 2097148 Kbytes
coredumpsize	unlimited	unlimited
descriptors	64	1024
memorysize	unlimited	unlimited

The most useful changes to the defaults are those made to prevent core dumps from happening when they aren't wanted:.

```
% limit coredumpsize 0
```

To run programs that use vast amounts of stack space:

```
% limit stacksize unlimited
```

To run programs that need to open more than 64 files at a time:

```
% limit descriptors 256
```

The maximum number of descriptors in SunOS 4.X is 256. This was increased to 1024 in the DBE version of SunOS 4 and in Solaris 2, although the standard I/O package still handles only 256. The standards-compliant definition of FILE in `/usr/include/stdio.h` has only a single byte to record the underlying file descriptor index.

If a process exceeds its memory usage limit, then it is more likely to have pages taken from it when the system runs short of memory, and may be swapped out earlier than processes that are within their limits. The *memorysize* limit does not actually prevent a process from exceeding the limit.

Tracing in SunOS 4.X

When tuning or debugging a program, it is often useful to know the system calls that are being made and the parameters that are being passed. This is done by setting a special bit in the process mask via the `trace` command. `trace` then prints out the information that is reported by the kernel's system call interface routines. `trace` can be used for an entire run or can be attached to a running process at any time. No special compiler options are required. In Solaris 2, `trace` has been renamed `truss` and has more functionality.

Here's some SunOS4 `trace` output with commentary added to sort the wheat from the chaff. It also indicates how `cp` uses the `mmap` calls and how the shared libraries start up.

Trace Output	Comments
`% trace cp NewDocument Tuning`	Use **trace** on a **cp** command.
`open ("/usr/lib/ld.so", 0, 04000000021) = 3`	Get the shared library loader.
`read (3, "".., 32) - 32`	Read **a.out** header to see if dynamically linked.
`mmap (0, 40960, 0x5, 0x80000002, 3, 0) = 0xf77e0000`	Map in code to memory.
`mmap (0xf77e0000, 0192, 0x7, 0x00000012, 3, 32768) = 0xf77e8000`	Map in data to memory.
`open ("/dev/zero", 0, 07) = 4`	Get a supply of zeroed pages.
`getrlimit (3, 0xf7fff8b0) = 0`	Read the limit information.
`mmap (0xf7800000, 8192, 0x3, 0x80000012, 4, 0) = 0xf7800000`	Map /dev/zero to the bss?
`close (3) = 0`	Close ld.so.
`getuid () = 1434`	Get user ID.
`getgid () = 10`	Get group ID.
`open ("/etc/ld.so.cache", 0, 05000000021) = 3`	Open the shared library cache.
`fstat (3, 0xf7fff750) = 0`	See if cache is up to date.
`mmap (0, 4096, 0x1, 0x80000001, 3, 0) = 0xf77c0000`	Map it in to read it.
`close (3) = 0`	Close it.
`open ("/usr/openwin/lib", 0, 01010525) = 3`	LD_LIBRARY_PATH contains /usr/openwin/lib,
`fstat (3, 0xf7fff750) = 0`	so look there first.
`mmap (0xf7802000, 8192, 0x3, 0x80000012, 4, 0) = 0xf7802000`	
`getdents (3, 0xf78000d8, 8192) = 1488`	Get some directory entries looking for the right
`getdents (3, 0xf78000d8, 8192) = 0`	version of the library.
`close (3) = 0`	Close /usr/openwin/lib
`open ("/usr/lib/libc.so.1.6", 0, 032724) = 3`	Get the shared libc.
`read (3, "".., 32) = 32`	Check that it's OK.
`mmap (0, 458764, 0x5, 0x80000002, 3, 0) = 0xf7730000`	Map in the code
`mmap (0xf779c000, 16384, 0x7, 0x80000012, 3, 442368) = 0xf779c000`	Map in the data.
`close (3) = 0`	Close libc.
`close (4) = 0`	Close /dev/zero.
`open ("NewDocument", 0, 03) = 3`	Finally! open input file.
`fstat (3, 0xf7fff970) = 0`	Find its size.
`stat ("Tuning", 0xf7fff930) = -1 ENOENT (No such file or directory)`	Try to stat output file.
`stat ("Tuning", 0xf7fff930) = -1 ENOENT (No such file or directory)`	But it's not there.
`creat ("Tuning", 0644) = 4`	Create output file.
`mmap (0, 82, 0x1, 0x80000001, 3, 0) = 0xf7710000`	Map input file.
`mctl (0xf7710000, 82, 4, 0x2) = 0`	Madvise sequential access.
`write (4, "This is a test file for my book".., 82) = 82`	Write out to new file.

Trace Output	Comments
`munmap (0xf7710000, 82) = 0`	Unmap input file.
`close (3) = 0`	Close input file.
`close (4) = 0`	Close output file.
`close (0) = 0`	Close stdin.
`close (1) = 0`	Close stdout.
`close (2) = 0`	Close stderr.
`exit (0) = ?`	Exit program.
`%`	

Tracing in Solaris 2

The `truss` command has many useful features not found in the SunOS 4 `trace` command. It can trace child processes, and it can count and time system calls and signals. Other options allow named system calls to be excluded or focused on, and data structures can be printed out in full. Here is an excerpt showing a fragment of `truss` output with the `-v` option to set verbose mode for data structures, and an example of `truss -c` showing the system call counts.

```
% truss -v all cp NewDocument Tuning
execve("/usr/bin/cp", 0xEFFFFB28, 0xEFFFFB38)  argc = 3
open("/usr/lib/libintl.so.1", O_RDONLY, 035737561304) = 3
mmap(0x00000000, 4096, PROT_READ, MAP_SHARED, 3, 0) = 0xEF7B0000
fstat(3, 0xEFFFF768)= 0
    d=0x0080001E i=29585 m=0100755 l=1  u=2     g=2     sz=14512
  at = Apr 27 11:30:14 PDT 1993  [ 735935414 ]
  mt = Mar 12 18:35:36 PST 1993  [ 731990136 ]
  ct = Mar 29 11:49:11 PST 1993  [ 733434551 ]
  bsz=8192  blks=30     fs=ufs
....
```

```
% truss -c cp NewDocument Tuning
syscall       seconds   calls  errors
_exit            .00       1
write            .00       1
open             .00      10       4
close            .01       7
creat            .01       1
chmod            .01       1
stat             .02       2       1
lseek            .00       1
fstat            .00       4
execve           .00       1
mmap             .01      18
munmap           .00       9
memcntl          .01       1
```

```
% truss -c cp NewDocument Tuning
                  ----      ---    ---
sys totals:       .07       57      5
usr time:         .02
elapsed:          .43
```

Timing

The C-shell has a built-in `time` command that is used when benchmarking or tuning to see how a particular process is running.

```
% time man madvise
...
0.1u 0.5s 0:03 21% 0+168k 0+0io 0pf+0w
%
```

In this case, 0.1 seconds of user CPU and 0.5 seconds of system CPU were used in 3 seconds elapsed time, which accounted for 21 percent of the CPU[1]. The growth in size of the process, the amount of I/O performed, and the number of page faults and page writes are recorded. Apart from the times, the number of page faults is the most useful figure. In this case, everything was already in memory from a previous use of the command. Solaris 2 has a `timex` command that provides much extended functionality. See the manual pages for more details.

The Effect of Underlying Filesystem Type

Some programs are predominantly I/O-intensive or may open and close many temporary files. SunOS has a wide range of filesystem types, and the directory used by the program could be placed onto one of the following types.

UNIX File System (UFS)

The standard filesystem on disk drives is the UNIX File System, which in SunOS 4.1 and on is the Berkeley Fat Fast Filesystem[2]. If your files have more than a temporary existence then this will be fastest. Files that are read stay in RAM until a RAM shortage reuses the pages for something else. Files that are written are sent out to disk, but the file stays in RAM until the pages are reused for something else. There is no special buffer cache

---

1. CPU percentages account for all the processors in system, so 100 percent represents every processor totally busy.

2. The *fat* fast filesystem supports more inodes per filesystem than does the regular BSD FFS.

Databases and Configurable Applications

Examples

Examples of configurable applications include relational databases, such as Oracle®, Ingres™, Informix™, and Sybase™ that have large numbers of configuration parameters and an SQL-based configuration language. Many CAD systems and Geographical Information systems also have sophisticated configuration and extension languages. This chapter concentrates on the Sun-specific database issues at a superficial level; the subject of database tuning is beyond the scope of this book.

Hire an Expert!

For serious tuning, you either need to read all the manuals cover-to-cover and attend training courses or hire an expert for the day. The black box mentality of using the system exactly the way it came off the tape, with all parameters set to default values will get you going but there is no point in tuning the rest of the system if it spends 90 percent of its time inside a poorly configured database. Experienced database consultants will have seen most problems before. They know what to look for and are likely to get quick results. Hire them, closely watch what they do, and learn as much as you can from them.

Use Sun's Database Excelerator Product with SunOS 4.X

Sun has a version of SunOS tuned for use on systems with large amounts of memory running databases. It is called DBE — Database Excelerator. There are versions for each recent release of SunOS 4: DBE 1.2 for SunOS 4.1.2 and DBE 1.3 for SunOS 4.1.3. It is sold at a very low cost for media, manual, and site license, and it dramatically improves the performance of databases, particularly with large numbers of concurrent users. For Solaris 1.1.1 (4.1.3U1) it is distributed on the operating system CD ROM. If used on a system with less than 16 Mbytes of RAM, it is likely to run more slowly than the standard SunOS runs, since several algorithms have been changed to improve speed at the expense of more memory usage. Thirty-two Mbytes is the minimum, practical configuration.

Basic Tuning Ideas

Several times I have discovered untuned database installations, so some basic recommendations on the first things to try may be useful. They apply to most database systems in principle, but I will use Oracle as an example.

Increasing Buffer Sizes

Oracle uses an area of shared memory to cache data from the database so that all Oracle processes can access the cache. It defaults to about 400 Kbytes but it can be increased to be bigger than the entire data set if needed. I would increase it to at least 20 percent of the total RAM in the machine if you are using raw disks to hold the database tables (see the next section). There are ways of looking at the cache hit rate within Oracle, so increase the size until the hit rate stops improving or until the rest of the system starts showing signs of memory shortage. Avoiding unnecessary random disk I/O is one of the keys to database tuning.

Both DBE 1.3 and Solaris 2^3 implement a feature called *intimate shared memory* by which the virtual address mappings are shared as well as the physical memory pages. ISM makes virtual memory operations, and context switching, more efficient when very large, shared memory areas are used. In Solaris 2, ISM is enabled by the application when it attaches to the shared memory region. Oracle 7 and Sybase System 10 both enable ISM automatically by setting the SHM_SHARE_MMU flag in the shmat(2) call.

Using Raw Disk Rather than Filesystems

When installing SunOS you should reserve at least three empty disk partitions, spread across as many different disks and controllers as possible (but avoiding slices zero and two). You can then change the raw devices to be owned by Oracle and, when installing Oracle, specify the raw devices rather than files in the usual filesystem as the standard data, log1, and log2 files. Filesystems incur more CPU overhead than do raw devices and can be much slower for writes due to inode and indirect block updates. Two or three blocks in widely spaced parts of the disk must be written to maintain the filesystem, whereas only one block needs to be written on a raw partition. Oracle often uses 2 Kbytes as its I/O size, and the filesystem uses 8 Kbytes so each 2-Kbyte read or write is always rounded up to 8 Kbytes. The data will be held in the Oracle SGA as well as in the main memory filesystem cache, thus wasting RAM. Improvements in the range of 10-25 percent or more in database performance and reductions in RAM requirements have been reported when moving from filesystems to raw partitions. The prestoserve synchronous write accelerator (usually used with NFS servers) can be used with databases that have to use the filesystem and can be used as a database log file accelerator.

Multiprocessor machines running SunOS 4 have particular problems with filesystems. Anything that increases kernel CPU time is a problem, so the extra layer of UFS code and the rounding up of I/O sizes slow things down. See "Monitoring Processors in SunOS 4.1.3 (Solaris 1.1)" on page 95 for more details of this problem. SunOS 4 also runs the

---

3. Implemented in Solaris 2.2 and later releases.

`update` process every 30 seconds, which causes all changes in the entire filesystem cache in main memory to be written back to disk in a single operation. I heard of one machine, a SPARCserver 690 with 1 Gbyte of RAM, which became unusable for several seconds every 30 seconds because of this effect.

Multiprocessor machines running Solaris 2 don't have these problems, and they can be made to run filesystem resident databases as fast or faster than raw ones. The catch is that you must always configure about 20 percent extra RAM and an NVSIMM or prestoserve, so there is an extra hardware cost to be borne for the same performance.

Fast Raw Backups

Database backups can be performed on small databases by copying the data from the raw partition to a filesystem. Often it is important to have a short downtime for database backups, and a disk-to-disk transfer is much faster than a backup to tape. Compressing the data as it is copied can save on disk space but is very CPU intensive; I recommend compressing the data if you have a high-end multiprocessor machine. For example,

```
# dd if=/dev/rsd1d bs=56k | compress > /home/data/dump_rsd1d.Z
```

Balance the Load over all the Disks

The log files should be on a separate disk from the data. This is particularly important for databases that have a lot of update activity. It also helps to put indexes and temporary tablespace on their own disks or to split the database tables over as many disks as possible. The operating system disk is often lightly used, and on a very small two disk system, I would put the log files on the system disk and put the rest on its own disk. One approach that can be used to balance I/O over a larger number of disks is to stripe them together by using Online: DiskSuite. Also see "Load Monitoring and Balancing" on page 75.

Which Disk Partition to Use

If you use the first partition on a disk as a raw Oracle partition, then you will lose the disk's label. This loss can be recovered by using an option of the `format` command if you are lucky but you should put a filesystem, swap space, Online: DiskSuite state database, or small, unused partition at the start of the disk.

On Sun's 424-Mbyte, 535-Mbyte, 1.05-Gbyte, 1.3-Gbyte, 2.1-Gbyte, and 2.9-Gbyte disks, the first part of the disk is the fastest, so a tiny first partition followed by a database partition covering the first half of the disk is recommended for best performance. See "Zoned Bit Rate (ZBR) Disk Drives" on page 64 for more details and an explanation.

The Effect of Indices

When you look up an item in a database your request must be matched against all the entries in a (potentially large) table. Without an index, a full table scan must be performed, and the database reads the entire table from disk in order to search every entry. If there is an index on the table, then the database looks up the request in the index and knows which entries in the table need to be read from disk. Some well-chosen indexes can dramatically reduce the amount of disk I/O and CPU time required to perform a query. Poorly designed or untuned databases are often underindexed. The problem with indexes is that when an indexed table is updated, the index must be updated as well, so peak update performance can be reduced.

How to Configure for a Large Number of Users

The typical scenario is for the users to interact with the database through an ASCII-forms-based interface. The forms' front end is usually created by means of high-level, application-builder techniques and in some cases can consume a large amount of CPU. This forms front end inputs and echoes characters one at a time from the user over a direct serial connection or via Telnet from a terminal server. Output tends to be in large blocks of text. The operating system overhead of handling one character at a time over Telnet is quite high, and when hundreds of users are connected to a single machine, the UNIX kernel consumes a lot of CPU power moving these characters around one at a time. Work is ongoing to find more efficient ways of supporting large numbers of users. Solaris 2.4 is much more efficient at supporting large numbers of users compared to previous releases, and work is ongoing to move the Telnet and remote login processing into the kernel as streams modules. The standard implementation uses a pair of daemon processes, one for each direction of each connection.

The back end of the forms process connects to the central database server and exchanges SQL calls in a relatively infrequent and efficient manner. To connect a large number of users to a single database, the best approach is to build a central client-server cluster consisting of a large database back-end machine with all the disk storage, and multiple smaller front end machines, each running forms for at most 100—200 active users. By varying the number and type of front-end machines, the primary interactive responsiveness for the users can be controlled. The back-end machine is dedicated to run only the back-end processes.When the forms application generates an SQL call, the back-end does not have to compete with all the other interactive front-end processes for CPU time and thus runs much more efficiently.

The most scalable form of client-server configuration is for each user to have a workstation or a PC running the forms-based application and generating SQL calls directly to the back-end server. These two approaches can be mixed as required.

4

Database Tuning Summary

When tuning databases, it is useful to realize that in many cases the sizing rules that have been developed by database software vendors in the past do not scale well to today's systems. In the mainframe and minicomputer worlds, disk I/O capacity is large, processors are slow, and RAM is expensive. With today's systems, the disk I/O capacity is not keeping pace with the huge increases in CPU power and typical RAM sizes. It is worth trading off a little extra CPU overhead and extra RAM usage for a reduction in I/O requirements, so don't be afraid to experiment with buffer sizes that are much larger than those recommended in the database vendors' documentation.

The next chapter examines the reasons why disk I/O is often the problem.

Disks

The art of tuning modern computer systems is becoming more and more dependent on disk I/O tuning. This chapter tries to clear any confusion over the performance of individual disks, shows how to measure and interpret the disk utilization figures, and suggests ways of improving I/O throughput. Many different types of disk and controllers found on Sun systems are described. The chapter also talks about filesystem tuning and combining disks into stripes and mirrors.

File Access Patterns

There are six different basic access patterns. Read, write, and update operations can either be sequential or randomly distributed. Sequential read and write occur when files are copied and created. Random read and write can occur in indexed database reads or can be due to page-in from an executable or page-out to a file. Update consists of a read-modify-write sequence and can be caused by a database system committing a sequence of transactions in either a sequential or random pattern. When working to understand or improve the performance of your disk subsystem, it is useful to spend some time working out which of these categories you expect to be most important.

Disk Specifications

Disk specifications are commonly reported using the "best case" approach, which is disk-format independent. Some parameters are quoted in the same way by both disk manufacturers and computer system vendors, which can confuse you as they are not measuring the same thing.

What the Disk Makers Specify

The disk manufacturers specify certain parameters for a drive.

- Rotational speed in revolutions per minute (rpm)
- The number of tracks or cylinders on the disk
- The number of heads or surfaces in each cylinder

- The rate at which data is read and written (millions of bytes/s)

- The disk controller interface used (IDE, SCSI, Wide SCSI, IPI)

- The *unformatted capacity* of the drive (millions of bytes)

- The average and single track *seek time* of the disk

When disk makers build the read/write heads, the speed of data transfer is measured in megahertz (MHz), which is converted into megabytes by dividing by eight. All the tracks that can be accessed without moving the heads form a cylinder. The single cylinder seek time is the time taken to move the heads to the next cylinder. On many high performance drives the head assembly is accelerated for the first half of the seek and decelerated for the second half. In this way, a seek of several cylinders in one attempt takes less time than many short steps with stops along the way. The average cylinder-to-cylinder seek time is usually calculated taking all possible seek distances into account. To get to a particular sector on the disk, the disk must rotate until it comes past the heads, so another component of overall access time is the rotational latency of the disk. The average rotational latency is usually quoted as the time taken for half a rotation.

The average seek time quoted by the manufacturer is the average cylinder-to-cylinder seek time. The fastest common disks (and almost all of Sun's current disks) tend to be about 11 ms. The average rotational latency for the common 5400 rpm drives is 5.6 ms so the access time for a single random seek is 16.6 ms plus the time taken to transfer the data. This is shown in Figure 5-1.

Figure 5-1   Average Disk Seek and Rotation Components

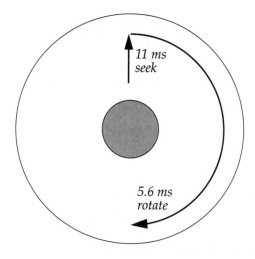

What the System Vendors Specify

The system vendors need to deal with the disk in terms of sectors, each typically containing 512 bytes of data and many bytes of header, preamble and intersector gap. Spare sectors and spare cylinders are also allocated so that bad sectors can be substituted. This reduces the unformatted capacity to what is known as the *formatted capacity*. For example, a 760-Mbyte drive reduces to a 669-Mbyte drive when the format is taken into account. The format command is used to write the sectors to the disk. The file /etc/format.dat contains information about each type of disk and how it should be formatted. The *formatted* capacity of the drive is measured in units of Mbytes = 10^6 = 1,000,000 while RAM sizes are measured in units of Mbytes = 2^{20} = 1,048,576. Confused? You will be! It is very easy to mix these up and make calculations that have a built-in error of 4.8 percent in the time taken to write a block of memory to disk.

What You Must Work Out for Yourself

You will have been told that the disks you bought were a certain size and speed, but the speed will be the peak data rate in Mbyte/s (1,000,000) during a sector and the size will probably be the formatted capacity in Mbytes (1,000,000). For some disks you can work out, using information from /etc/format.dat, the real peak throughput and size in Kbytes (1024) of your disk. The entry for a typical disk is shown in Figure 5-2. In Solaris 2.3 and later releases the format information is read directly from SCSI disk drives by the format command. The /etc/format.dat file entry is no longer required for SCSI disks.

Figure 5-2   /etc/format.dat *Entry for Sun 669-Mbyte Disk*

```
disk_type= "SUN0669" \
        : ctlr= MD21: fmt_time= 4 \
        : trks_zone= 15: asect= 5: atrks= 30 \
        : ncyl=  1614: acyl= 2: pcyl= 1632: nhead= 15: nsect= 54 \
        : rpm= 3600 : bpt= 31410
```

The values to note are:

- rpm = 3600, so the disk spins at 3600 rpm

- nsect = 54, so there are 54 sectors of 512 bytes per track

- nhead = 15, so there are 15 tracks per cylinder

- ncyl = 1614, so there are 1614 cylinders per disk

Since we know that there are 512 bytes per sector, 54 sectors per track, and that a track will pass by the head 3600 times per minute, we can work out the peak sustained data rate and size of the disk.

data rate (bytes/sec) = (nsect * 512 * rpm) / 60 = 1,658,880 bytes/s

size (bytes) = nsect * 512 * nhead * ncyl = 669,358,080 bytes

If we assume that 1 Kbyte is 1024 bytes then the data rate is 1620 Kbytes/s.

The manufacturer (and system vendors) rate this disk at 1.8 Mbytes/s, which is the data rate during a single sector. This is in line with industry practice, but it is impossible to get better than 1620 Kbytes/s for the typical transfer size of between 2 and 56 Kbytes. Large sequential reads on this type of disk tend to run at just over 1500 Kbytes/s which confirms the calculated result.

Standardizing on 1 Kbyte = 1024 is convenient since this is what the disk-monitoring utilities assume; since sectors are 512 bytes, pages are 4096 bytes, and the UFS filesystem uses 8192 byte blocks, it is more useful than 1K = 1000.

Some common Sun disks are listed in Table 5-1 with KB = 2^{10} = 1024. The data rate for ZBR drives cannot be calculated, since the `format.dat` nsect entry is not the real value. A peak measured value for sequential reads of the fastest region has been provided instead.

Table 5-1   Disk Specifications

Disk Type	Bus	MB/s	RPM	Seek	Capacity	Max Data Rate
Sun 207 3.5"	5 MB/s SCSI	1.6	3600	16 ms	203148 KB	1080 KB/s
Sun 424 3.5"	5 MB/s SCSI	2.5-3.0	4400	14 ms	414360 KB	2584 KB/s ZBR
Sun 535 thin 3.5"	10 MB/s SCSI	2.9-5.1	5400	11 ms	522480 KB	3608 KB/s ZBR
Sun 669 5.25"	5 MB/s SCSI	1.8	3600	16 ms	653670 KB	1620 KB/s
CDC 911M 8"	6 MB/s IPI	6.0	3600	15 ms	889980 KB	4680 KB/s
Sun 1.05G 3.5"	10 MB/s SCSI	2.9-5.1	5400	11 ms	1026144 KB	3840 KB/s ZBR
Sun 1.05G thin 3.5"	20 MB/s SCSI	2.9-5.1	5400	11 ms	1026144 KB	3968 KB/s ZBR
Sun 1.3G 5.25"	5 MB/s SCSI	3.25-4.5	5400	11 ms	1336200 KB	3288 KB/s ZBR
Sun 1.3G 5.25"	6 MB/s IPI	3.25-4.5	5400	11 ms	1255059 KB	2610-3510 KB/s
Sun 2.1G 5.25"	10 MB/s DSCSI	3.8-5.0	5400	11 ms	2077080 KB	3952 KB/s ZBR
Sun 2.1G 3.5"	10 MB/s SCSI	3.7-5.2	5400	11 ms	2077080 KB	4022 KB/s ZBR
Sun 2.9G 5.25"	20 MB/s DSCSI	3.7-5.4	5400	11 ms	2841993 KB	4168 KB/s ZBR

Zoned Bit Rate (ZBR) Disk Drives

These drives vary, depending on which cylinder is accessed. The disk is divided into zones with different bit rates; the outer part of the drive is faster and has more sectors per track than the inner part of the drive. This allows the data to be recorded with a constant linear density along the track (bits per inch). In other drives, the peak number of bits per inch that can be made to work reliably is set up for the innermost track, but density is too low on the outermost track, so capacity is wasted. In a ZBR drive, more data is stored on the outer tracks, so greater capacity and higher data rates are possible. The 1.3-Gbyte drive zones mean that peak performance is obtained from the first third of the disk up to cylinder 700. The next third falls off slightly, but the last third of the disk may be as much as 25 percent slower.

Note – When partitioning a ZBR disk, remember that partition "a" or slice 0 will be faster than partition "h" or slice 7.

Table 5-2   1.3-Gbyte IPI ZBR Disk Zone Map

Zone	Start Cylinder	Sectors per Track	Data Rate in Kbytes/s
0	0	78	3510
1	626	78	3510
2	701	76	3420
3	801	74	3330
4	926	72	3240
5	1051	72	3240
6	1176	70	3150
7	1301	68	3060
8	1401	66	2970
9	1501	64	2880
10	1601	62	2790
11	1801	60	2700
12	1901	58	2610
13	2001	58	2610

The `format.dat` entry assumes constant geometry so it has a fixed idea about sectors per track, and the number of cylinders in `format.dat` is reduced to compensate. The number of sectors per track is set to make sure partitions start on multiples of 16 blocks and does not accurately reflect the geometry of the outer zone. The 1.3G-byte IPI drive outer zone happens to match `format.dat`, but the other ZBR drives have more sectors than `format.dat` states.

Sequential versus Random Access

Some people are surprised when they read that a disk is capable of several megabytes per second but they see a disk at 100 percent capacity providing only a few hundred kilobytes per second for their application. Most disks used on NFS or database servers spend their time serving the needs of many users, and the access patterns are essentially random. The time taken to service a disk access is taken up by seeking to the correct cylinder and waiting for the disk to go around. In sequential access, the disk can be read at full speed for a complete cylinder, but in random access, the average seek time quoted for the disk and the average rotational latency should be allowed for between each disk access. The random data rate is thus very dependent on how much data is read on each random access. For filesystems, 8 Kbytes is a common block size, but for databases on raw disk partitions, 2-Kbytes is a common block size. Sybase always issues 2-Kbytes reads, but Oracle tries to cluster 2-Kbyte accesses together whenever possible to get a larger transfer size.

For example, the 2.9 Gbyte disk takes 11 ms for a random seek, waits on average 5.6 ms for the disk to rotate to the right sector, and takes about 0.5 ms for a 2-Kbyte transfer and 2 ms for an 8-Kbyte transfer (ignoring other SCSI bus transfers and software overheads). The data rate for a random seek and a single transfer and the average random service time is thus:

data rate = transfer size / (seek time + (60 / rpm) / 2 + (transfer size / data rate))

2-KB transfer data rate = 118 KB/s @ 17 ms = 2 / (0.011 + 0.0056 + (2 / 4168))

8-KB transfer data rate = 432 KB/s @ 19 ms = 8 / (0.011 + 0.0056 + (8 / 4168))

56-KB transfer data rate = 1864 KB/s @ 30 ms = 56 / (0.011 + 0.0056 + (56 / 4168))

1024-KB transfer data rate = 2834 KB/s @ 262 ms = 1024 / (0.11 + 0.0056 + (1024 / 4168))

These calculations do not include time spent processing the disk request and filesystem code in the operating system (one or two milliseconds); the time spent waiting in a queue for other accesses to be processed and sent over the SCSI bus; and the time spent inside the disk's on-board controller waiting for other accesses to be processed.

Anything that can be done to turn random access into sequential access or to increase the transfer size will have a significant effect on the performance of a system. This is one of the most profitable areas for performance tuning.

IPI Disk Controllers

The I/O performance of a multiuser system depends on how well it supports randomly distributed disk I/O accesses. The ISP-80 disk controller was developed by Sun Microsystems to address this need. It provides much higher performance than the previous generation SMD-based disk subsystems. The key to its performance is the inclusion of a 68020-based, real-time seek optimizer that is fed with rotational position-sensing (RPS) information so that it knows which sector is under the drive's head. It has a 1-Mbyte disk cache organized as 128 x 8 Kbyte disc block buffers and can queue up to

128 read/write requests. As requests are added to the queue, the requests are reordered into the most efficient disk access sequence. The result is that when a heavy load is placed on the system and a large number of requests are queued, the performance is much better than on unoptimized systems. When the system is lightly loaded, the controller performs speculative prefetching of disk blocks to try and anticipate future requests. This controller turns small random accesses into large sequential accesses whenever possible and significantly reduces the average seek time for a disk by seeking to the nearest piece of data in its command queue rather than performing the next command immediately. The 1.3 Gbyte IPI ZBR disk has its zone map stored in the ROM on the ISP-80 controller to allow for the variable geometry.

As long as IPI disks enjoyed a performance advantage over SCSI disks, the extra cost of low-volume IPI specific disks could be justified. Now that SCSI disks are higher capacity, faster, cheaper, and more intelligent, IPI subsystems have become obsolete. Each SCSI disk nowadays contains about as much intelligence and RAM buffer as the entire IPI controller from a few years ago.

An SBus IPI controller is available from Genroco, Inc., so that existing disk subsystems can be migrated to current generation servers.

SCSI Disk Controllers

SCSI Interface Types

SCSI Controllers can be divided into five generic classes. Very old ones only support *Asynchronous SCSI,* old controllers support *Synchronous SCSI,* most recent ones support *Fast Synchronous SCSI;* the latest two types to appear are *Fast And Wide Synchronous SCSI,* and *Fiber Channel SCSI.* Working out which type you have on your Sun is not that simple. The main differences between them are in the number of disks that can be supported on a SCSI bus before the bus becomes saturated and the maximum effective cable length allowed.

The original asynchronous and synchronous SCSI interfaces support data rates up to 5 Mbytes/s on a 6 meter effective cable length. The speed of asynchronous SCSI drops off sharply as the cable length increases, so keep the bus as short as possible.

Fast SCSI increases the maximum data rate from 5 Mbytes/s to 10 Mbytes/s and halves the cable length from 6 meters to 3 meters. By using the latest type of very high quality SCSI cables and active termination plugs from Sun, fast SCSI can be made to work reliably at up to 6 meters.

Fast and Wide SCSI uses a special cable with extra signals to carry 16 bits of data rather than 8 in each clock cycle. This doubles the data rate to 20 Mbytes/s. Fiber Channel SCSI uses a very high speed optical fiber interconnect to carry the SCSI protocol to a disk array. It runs at about 25 Mbytes/s in each direction simultaneously for over a 1000 meters or more.

Differential signaling can be used with Fast SCSI and Fast and Wide SCSI to increase the cable length to 25 meters, but it uses incompatible electrical signals and a different connector so can only be used with devices that have purpose-built differential interfaces. The principle is that instead of a single electrical signal varying between 0V and +5V, the transmitter generates two signals varying between +5V and -5V, where one is the inverse of the other. Any noise pickup along the cable tends to be added to both signals, but in the receiver, it is the difference between the two signals that is used, so the noise cancels out and the signal comes through clearly.

Most of the SCSI disks shown inTable 5-2 on page 65 transfer data at a much slower rate. They do, however, have a buffer built into the SCSI drive that collects data at the slower rate and can then pass data over the bus at a higher rate. With Asynchronous SCSI the data is transferred by means of a handshake protocol that slows down as the SCSI bus gets longer. For fast devices on a very short bus it can achieve full speed, but as devices are added and the bus length and capacitance increases, the transfers slow down. For Synchronous SCSI the devices on the bus negotiate a transfer rate that will slow down if the bus is long, but by avoiding the need to send handshakes, more data can be sent in its place and throughput is less dependent on the bus length. The transfer rate is sometimes printed out by the device driver as a system boots[1] and is usually 3.5 to 5.0 Mbytes/s, but could be up to 10.0 Mbytes/s for a fast SCSI device on a fast SCSI controller.

Tagged Command Queuing Optimizations

TCQ provides optimizations similar to those implemented on IPI controllers described above, but the buffer and optimization occur in each drive rather than in the controller for a string of disks. TCQ is implemented in Solaris 2 only, and is supported on the disks listed in Table 5-3. Sun has spent a lot of time debugging the TCQ firmware in these disks. Since few other vendors use this feature it may be wise to completely disable TCQ, particularly if old third-party disks are configured on a system. Some old third-party drives, when probed, indicate that they support TCQ but fail when it is used. This may be

---

1. With SunOS 4.1.1 and subsequent releases of SunOS 4.X.

an issue when upgrading from SunOS 4 (which never tries to use TCQ) to Solaris 2. In Solaris 2, TCQ is disabled by clearing a scsi_options bit, as described in the next section.

Table 5-3   Advanced SCSI Disk Specifications

Disk Type	Tagged Commands	On-board Cache
Sun 424 3.5"	None	64 KB
Sun 535 thin 3.5"	64	256 KB
Sun 1.05G 3.5"	64	256 KB
Sun 1.05G thin 3.5"	64	256 KB
Sun 2.1G 5.25"	16	256 KB
Sun 2.1G 3.5"	64	256 KB
Sun 2.9G 5.25"	64	512 KB

Setting the SCSI Options Variable

A kernel variable called *scsi_options* is used to globally enable or disable several SCSI features. To see the option values, look at the values defined in the file (for Solaris 2) /usr/include/sys/scsi/conf/autoconf.h. The default value for the kernel variable *scsi_options* is 0x1F8, which enables all options except wide SCSI. To disable tagged command queuing, set it to 0x178. If the 2.9-Gbytes wide SCSI disks are being used with Solaris 2.3, then /etc/system should have the command set scsi_options=0x3F8 added. This is set by default in Solaris 2.4.

Figure 5-3   SCSI Options Bit Definitions

```
#define SCSI_OPTIONS_DR      0x8     Global disconnect/reconnect
#define SCSI_OPTIONS_LINK    0x10    Global linked commands
#define SCSI_OPTIONS_SYNC    0x20    Global synchronous xfer capability
#define SCSI_OPTIONS_PARITY  0x40    Global parity support
#define SCSI_OPTIONS_TAG     0x80    Global tagged command support
#define SCSI_OPTIONS_FAST    0x100   Global FAST scsi support
#define SCSI_OPTIONS_WIDE    0x200   Global WIDE scsi support
```

Sun's SCSI Controller Products

The original SPARCstation 1 and the VME-hosted SCSI controller used by the SPARCserver 470 do not support Synchronous SCSI. In the case of the SPARCstation 1, this is due to SCSI bus noise problems that were solved for the SPARCstation 1+ and subsequent machines. If noise occurs during a Synchronous SCSI transfer, then a SCSI reset happens, and, although disks will retry, tapes will abort. In versions of SunOS before SunOS 4.1.1, the SPARCstation 1+, IPC, and SLC have Synchronous SCSI disabled as well. The VME SCSI controller supports a maximum of 1.2 Mbytes/s while the original SBus SCSI supports 2.5 Mbytes/s because it shares its unbuffered DMA controller bandwidth with the Ethernet.

The SPARCstation 2, IPX, and ELC use a higher-performance, buffered-SBus DMA chip than the SPARCstation 1, 1+, SLC and IPC, and they can drive sustained SCSI bus transfers at 5.0 Mbytes/s. The original SBus SCSI add-on cards and the built-in SCSI controller on the SPARCstation 330 and the original SPARCserver 600 series are also capable of this speed. The SPARCserver 600 spawned the first combined SCSI/Buffered Ethernet card, the SBE/S; one is integrated into the CPU board.

The SPARCstation 10 introduced the first fast SCSI implementation from Sun, together with a combined fast SCSI/Buffered Ethernet SBus card, the FSBE/S. The SPARCserver 600 series was upgraded to have the fast SCSI controller built in at this time.

A differential version of the fast SCSI controller with buffered Ethernet, the DSBE/S, was then introduced to replace the IPI controller in the high-end, rack-based systems. The DSBE/S is used together with a 2.1-Gbyte differential fast SCSI drive, which comes in a rack-mount package of up to six disks.

All the above SCSI controllers are relatively simple DMA bus master devices that are all supported by the `esp` driver in Solaris 2.

The replacement for the DSBE/S is the DWI/S, which is a differential wide SCSI interface with no Ethernet added. The wide SCSI interface runs at twice the speed and can support twice as many SCSI target addresses. The matching disk is the latest 2.9-Gbyte drive, which has the differential wide interface built in; it comes in the same rack-mount package as the 2.1-Gbyte disk but the controller can connect to two packs of six disks. The DWI/S is a much more intelligent SCSI controller and has a new `isp` device driver. The `isp` driver is much more efficient than the `esp` driver and uses fewer interrupts and less CPU power to do an I/O operation.

Table 5-4   SCSI Controller Specifications

Controller	Bus Interface	Speed	Type
Sun SCSI-II	VME	1.2 MB/s	Asynchronous
SPARCserver 330	Built-in	5.0 MB/s	Synchronous
SPARCstation 1	Built-in SBus	2.5 MB/s	Asynchronous[1]
SPARCstation 1+ SPARCstation IPC SPARCstation SLC	Built-in SBus	2.5 MB/s	Synchronous
SPARCstation 2 SPARCstation ELC SPARCstation IPX	Built-in SBus	5.0 MB/s	Synchronous
SBus SCSI X1055	SBus Add-on	5.0 MB/s	Synchronous

Table 5-4   SCSI Controller Specifications

Controller	Bus Interface	Speed	Type
Early SPARCserver 600	Built-in SBus	5.0 MB/s	Synchronous
SBE/S X1054	Sbus Add-on	5.0 MB/s	Synchronous
SPARCstation 10 SPARCclassic SPARCstation LX SPARCstation 5 SPARCstation 20	Built-in SBus	10.0 MB/s	Fast
Late model SPARCserver 600	Built-in SBus	10.0 MB/s	Fast
FSBE/S X1053	SBus Add-on	10.0 MB/s	Fast
DSBE/S X1052	SBus Add-on	10.0 MB/s	Differential fast
SPARCserver 1000	Built-in SBus	10.0 MB/s	Fast
DWI/S X1062	SBus Add-on	20.0 MB/s	Differential wide
SPARCstorage Array SOC	SBus Add-on	25+25MB/s	2 x Fiber Channel
SPARCstorage Array Internal	Built-in SBus	20.0 MB/s	Wide

1. Synchronous SCSI is disabled by the kernel due to noise problems on the original SPARCstation 1 only.

The SPARCstorage Disk Array

The latest SCSI-based interface from Sun is the SPARCstorage™ Disk Array. The architecture of this subsystem is shown in Figure 5-4. It connects to a system using the SCSI protocol over a Fiber Channel link. A single SBus Fiber Channel card (the SBus Optical Channel) supports two separate connections so that two disk arrays can be connected to a single SBus slot. Since each array holds up to 30 1.05-Gbyte disks, over 60 Gbytes of disk can be connected to one SBus slot.

Figure 5-4   SPARCstorage Disk Array Architecture

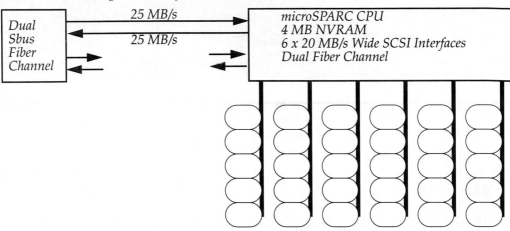

30 x 1.05 GB Low-Profile Wide SCSI Disk Drives

Each Fiber Channel interface contains two fibers that carry signals in opposite directions at up to 25 Mbytes/s. This is unlike normal SCSI where the same set of wires is used in both directions, and it allows concurrent transfer of data in both directions. Within the SPARCstorage Disk Array there is a microSPARC™ processor that connects to a dual Fiber Channel interface, allowing two systems to share a single array for high availability configurations. There is a 4-Mbyte nonvolatile RAM buffer to store data that is on its way to disk. Since it has a battery backup, writes can safely be acknowledged as soon as they are received, before the data is actually written to disk. The microSPARC processor also controls six separate Fast and Wide SCSI channels, each connected to five 1.05-Gbyte disks at 20 Mbytes/s. The software/hardware combination supports any mixture of mirroring, disk striping and RAID5 across the drives.

This system can sustain over 2000 I/Os per second (IOPS). The Fiber Channel interface is faster than any other SCSI controller interface and supports simultaneous transfer in both directions, unlike a conventional SCSI bus. The large NVRAM store provides a very fast turnaround for writes. Read latency is not as good as a directly connected wide SCSI disk but is comparable to any other SCSI controller. The provision of up to 30 disks in a very compact package (the same size as a SPARCserver 1000 chassis) also makes it easier to configure a large number of independent disks for good I/O performance. Each disk is a new type of low-profile 1 inch thick form-factor drive, holding 1.05 Gbytes with a wide SCSI interface running at 20 Mbytes/s. The SPARCstorage Manager software provided with the array has a GUI that helps you keep track of all the disks, monitors performance, and makes it easy to allocate space within the array.

This product provides a very convenient way to configure a large number of independent disks, using a single SBus interface and a single enclosure. A shortage of independent disks is one of the biggest causes of performance problems, so this is a very significant step in the right direction. Figures 5-5 and 5-6 illustrate the graphical user interface.

Figure 5-5   SPARCstorage Array Manager Configuration Display

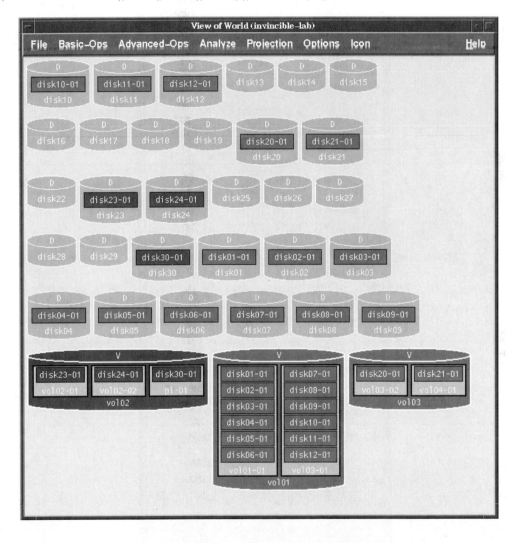

Figure 5-6   SPARCstorage Array Monitoring Display Screen Shot

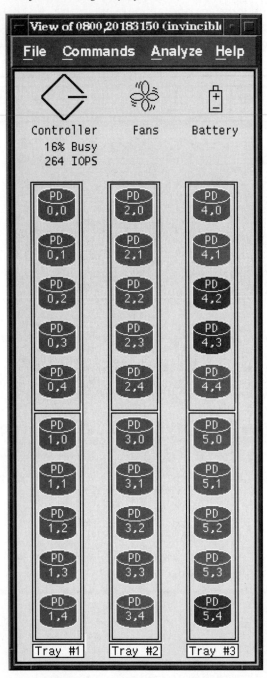

Load Monitoring and Balancing

If a system is under a heavy I/O load, then the load should be spread across as many disks and disk controllers as possible. To see what the load looks like use the `iostat` command. A rule-based summary of how to use the results of iostat can be found in "Disk I/O Rules" on page 228.

Iostat in SunOS 4.X

The `iostat` command produces output in two forms. One form looks at the total throughput of each disk in KB/s (`bps`), the average seek time in milliseconds (`msps`), and number of transfers per second (`tps`). The other form looks at the number of read (`rps`) and write (`wps`) transfers separately and gives a percentage utilization (`util`) for each disk. Both forms show the number of characters per second of terminal I/O (`tin`, `tout`) and the CPU loading (`user`, `niced`, `system`, `idle`).

```
% iostat 5
        tty            sd0            sd1            sd3            cpu
tin tout bps tps msps  bps tps msps  bps tps msps  us ni sy id
  0    0   1   0 0.0     0   0 0.0     0   0 0.0    15 39 23 23
  0   13  17   2 0.0     0   0 0.0     0   0 0.0     4  0  6 90
  0   13 128  24 0.0     0   0 0.0    13   3 0.0     7  0  9 84
  0   13  88  18 0.0     0   0 0.0    48  10 0.0    11  0 11 78
  0   13 131  24 0.0     0   0 0.0    15   3 0.0    21  0 20 59
  0   13  85  17 0.0     0   0 0.0    13   3 0.0    17  0 11 72
```

```
% iostat -tDc 5
        tty            sd0            sd1            sd3            cpu
tin tout rps wps util  rps wps util  rps wps util  us ni sy id
  0    0   0   0  0.6     0   0 0.0     0   0 0.1   15 39 23 23
  0   13   0   2  4.9     0   0 0.0     0   0 0.0   12  0  8 79
  0   13   1   0  4.0     0   0 0.0     0   0 0.0   35  0 11 54
  0   13   7   0 23.1     0   0 0.0     2   0 7.6   21  0 11 68
  0   13   6   4 33.5     0   0 0.0     2   1 7.7    6  0  6 89
  0   13  11   1 32.3     0   0 0.0     0   0 0.8   12  0 11 77
```

The second form, `iostat -D`, was introduced in SunOS 4.1 and continues unchanged in Solaris 2. The above output shows paging activity on a SPARCstation 1 with Quantum 104-Mbyte disks; the SCSI device driver does not collect seek information, so the `msps` field is always zero. The `iostat-D` command can be used with SMD and IPI disks to see whether the disk activity is largely sequential (less than the rated seek time) or largely random (equal to or greater than the rated seek time). The first line of output shows the average activity since the last reboot.

The util field is the most useful. In SunOS 4, all the disks are sampled by the 100 Hz clock interrupt to see if they were busy, and util is calculated. In Solaris 2 the device driver issues commands to the drive and measures how long it takes to respond and how much time the disk is idle between commands to produce a more accurate util measure. A 100 percent busy disk is one that has no idle time before the next command is issued. Disks that sustain over 35 percent busy during a 30-second interval are probably causing performance problems. SunOS 4 provides only throughput and utilization measures; it doesn't provide latency, which make it harder to decide if a disk is responding slowly.

iostat in Solaris

Solaris 2 has three forms of iostat output: one is the same -D option described above for SunOS 4.X, the other two are described below. The default output with no options has changed to show some new values in a similar layout. For each disk, the same values as before are reported for kilobytes per second (now labelled Kps rather than bps) and transfers per second. A new value of service time in milliseconds is also reported. The service time is the average time taken to service a complete I/O request, including time spent waiting for preceding requests in the I/O queue to finish. Nice CPU has been dropped in favor of time spent blocked waiting for I/O. Unlike SunOS 4.X, floppy disk activity is reported in Solaris 2.

```
% iostat 5
        tty          fd0            sd0            sd1            sd3           cpu
 tin tout Kps tps serv  Kps tps serv  Kps tps serv  Kps tps serv  us sy wt id
   0    1   0   0    0    3   0   50    2   0   51    2   0   63  18  7  2 73
   0   16   0   0    0   23   4   43    0   0    0    0   0    0  19  9 13 60
   0   15   0   0    0   99  16   38    0   0    0    0   0    0  32 17 49  2
   0   16   0   0    0   93  15   37    0   0    0    0   0    0  43 17 40  0
   0   16   0   0    0  111  17   40    0   0    0    0   0    0  41 17 41  1
   0   16   0   0    0  117  17   36    0   0    0    0   0    0  40 22 37  1
   0   16   0   0    0  103  18   50    0   0    0    0   0    0  29 18 51  2
   0   16   0   0    0    6   1   85    0   0    0    8   1  116  20  7  0 73
```

The new variant iostat -x provides extended statistics and is easier to read when a large number of disks are being reported, since each disk is summarized on a separate line. The values reported are the number of transfers and kilobytes per second, with read and write shown separately; the average number of commands waiting in the queue; the average number of commands actively being processed by the drive[2]; the service time described above; and the percentage of the time that commands were waiting in the queue; and commands active on the drive.

---

2. This will be less than 1.0 unless the drive uses the IPI controller or is a SCSI drive with tagged command queuing support.

```
% iostat -txc 5
                               extended disk statistics        tty          cpu
 disk    r/s  w/s   Kr/s    Kw/s wait actv  svc_t  %w  %b  tin tout us sy wt id
 fd0     0.0  0.0   0.0     0.0  0.0  0.0    0.0    0   0    0   77 42  9  9 39
 sd0     0.0  3.5   0.0    21.2  0.0  0.1   41.6    0  14
 sd1     0.0  0.0   0.0     0.0  0.0  0.0    0.0    0   0
 sd3     0.0  0.0   0.0     0.0  0.0  0.0    0.0    0   0
                               extended disk statistics        tty          cpu
 disk    r/s  w/s   Kr/s    Kw/s wait actv  svc_t  %w  %b  tin tout us sy wt id
 fd0     0.0  0.0   0.0     0.0  0.0  0.0    0.0    0   0    0   82 38 17 44  2
 sd0     0.0 14.8   0.0    90.9  0.0  0.6   38.6    0  56
 sd1     0.0  0.0   0.0     0.0  0.0  0.0    0.0    0   0
 sd3     0.0  0.0   0.0     0.0  0.0  0.0    0.0    0   0
                               extended disk statistics        tty          cpu
 disk    r/s  w/s   Kr/s    Kw/s wait actv  svc_t  %w  %b  tin tout us sy wt id
 fd0     0.0  0.0   0.0     0.0  0.0  0.0    0.0    0   0    0   84 37 17 45  1
 sd0     0.0 16.8   0.0   102.4  0.0  0.7   43.1    2  61
 sd1     0.0  0.0   0.0     0.0  0.0  0.0    0.0    0   0
 sd3     0.0  1.0   0.0     8.0  0.0  0.1  114.3    2   4
```

How to Decide that a Disk Is Overloaded

The key value to watch is the service time (svc_t). This is the time taken to service an I/O request to this drive, including time spent waiting in the queue because other requests were being processed. At very light loads, spurious large service times can occur, so a threshold load level is also important. From various sources, particularly the NFS server LADDIS benchmark, it is generally recognized that I/O service times of more than 50 ms are considered too slow. Disks that are over 20 percent busy averaged over a 30- second period should have their service times checked. A script that can be used to monitor either the local machine or a remote server is shown in Figure 5-7. It runs iostat -x 30 on the machine being monitored and runs a nawk script on the local machine. When started, it goes into the background; when it sees a busy disk, it prints a warning message to the console and plays an audio file to attract the user's attention (by default, the sound indicates that "performance just went down the toilet").

Figure 5-7   `iomon` - *Disk Monitoring Script for Solaris 2*

```
#!/bin/csh
# Adrian.Cockcroft@corp.sun.com 4th Nov 1993
# requires Solaris 2 specific version of iostat
# warn the operator that a disk is overloaded
# cmdline argument is optional server name for remote monitoring
#
# hardwired arguments:
# 30 second monitoring interval for iostat
# monitor disks that contain sd in the name to avoid floppies
# look for disks over 20% busy with more than 50.0ms service time
# play an appropriate sound to indicate performance just went down
# the toilet, /usr/demo/SOUND/sounds/flush.au needs SUNWaudmo pkg
# print out message to the local system console
#
if ($1 == "") then
    set CMD="iostat -x 30"
    set HOST='hostname'
else
    set CMD="rsh $1 exec iostat -x 30"
    set HOST=$1
endif
#                                   disk            %b              svc_t
exec $CMD | nawk -v host=$HOST '$1 ~ "sd" {if ($10 > 20 && $8 \ > 50
> 50.0) { printf("%s: ", host); print; system("audioplay \
/usr/demo/SOUND/sounds/flush.au"); }}' >/dev/console &
```

The output doesn't include the `iostat` header line, but it is easy to get a reminder if it is needed. Here is an example of starting and testing `iomon`.

```
% iomon
[2] 18220 18221
% mkfile 50M /var/tmp/JUNK; rm /var/tmp/JUNK
hostname: sd3        1.9 25.8     9.4 1195.3  4.8  2.9  280.8  95 100
% iostat -x 1 1
                              extended disk statistics
disk      r/s  w/s   Kr/s   Kw/s wait actv  svc_t  %w  %b
...
```

Multiple Disks on One Controller

If the controller is busy talking to one disk, then another disk has to wait; the resulting contention increases the latency for all the disks on that controller. Tests have shown that on a 5-Mbytes/s SCSI bus there should be at most two heavily loaded disks per bus for peak performance. IPI controllers can support at most three heavily loaded disks. As the data rate of one disk approaches the bus bandwidth, the number of disks is reduced. The 10-Mbytes/s fast SCSI bus can actually transfer data over the bus at about 7.5 Mbytes/s when the SCSI protocol overhead is accounted for.

For sequential accesses, there is an obvious limit on the aggregate bandwidth that can be sustained by a number of disks. For random accesses, the bandwidth of the SCSI bus is much greater than the aggregate bandwidth of the transfers, but queuing effects increase the latency of each access as more disks are added to each SCSI bus. For best performance, configure three or four active disks per 10-Mbytes/s SCSI bus and six to eight active disks per 20 Mbytes/s wide SCSI bus (the recommended maximum). If you have too many disks on the bus, you will tend to see high wait values in iostat -x output. The commands queue in the device driver as they wait to be sent over the SCSI bus to the disk.

Tuning Filesystems

The UFS filesystem code was extensively tuned for SunOS 4.1.1 with the introduction of an I/O clustering algorithm, which groups successive reads or writes into a single large command to transfer up to 56 Kbytes rather than lots of 8-Kbyte transfers. The change allows the filesystem layout to be tuned to avoid sector interleaving and allows filesystem I/O on sequential files to get close to its theoretical maximum[3].

If a disk is moved from a machine running an earlier release of SunOS to one running SunOS 4.1.1, then its sectors will be interleaved and the full benefit will not be realized. It is advisable to back up the disk, rerun newfs on it, and restore the data.

The UFS filesystem layout parameters can be modified by means of tunefs[4]. By default, these parameters are set to provide maximum overall throughput for all combinations of read, write, and update operations in both random and sequential access patterns. For a single disk, the gains that can be made by optimizing disk layout parameters with tunefs for one kind of operation over another are small.

The clustering algorithm is controlled by the tunefs parameters, rotdelay and maxcontig. The default rotdelay parameter is zero, meaning that files are stored in contiguous sectors. Any other value disables clustering. The default maxcontig parameter is 7; this is the maximum transfer size supported on all machines, and it gives a good compromise for performance with various access patterns.

---

3. "Extent-like Performance from a UNIX File System," L. McVoy and S. Kleiman.

4. See the manual page and "The Design and Implementation of the 4.3BSD UNIX Operating System," Leffler, McKusick, Karels and Quarterman for details of the filesystem implementation.

The only situation in which I recommend tuning the filesystem is when a small interlace stripe of many disks is being used. In SunOS 4.X, desktop machines can increase this to 14 for better sequential performance, but poorer random access performance. In Solaris 2, higher values can be configured and can be useful when working with Online: DiskSuite stripes or RAID disk subsystems that have a disk interleave of less than 56 Kbytes. In this case, a single clustered write to disk will be broken down into multiple smaller writes; for better sequential performance set `maxcontig` to seven times the number of disks in the stripe, so that each disk gets a 56-Kbyte block of data to transfer. A small interlace is most effective for sequential transfers.

For example, a six-disk stripe with 16-Kbyte interlace and a *maxcontig* value of 48 8-Kbyte blocks will cause a 384-Kbyte sequential access cluster that is broken down by the stripe into six 64-Kbyte transfers from each individual disk. This helps only large sequential reads and writes and may reduce performance for other access patterns slightly.

Eagle DiskPak

A product from Eagle Software, Inc. called DiskPak™ has some novel features that can improve throughput for heavily used filesystems. The product reorganizes the layout of data blocks for each file on the disk to make all files sequential and contiguous and to optimize the placement of the UFS partial block fragments that occur at the end of files. It also has a filesystem browser utility that gives a visual representation of the block layout and free space distribution of a filesystem. The most useful capability of this product is that it can sort files based on several criteria, to minimize disk seek time. The main criteria are access time, modification time, and size. If a subset of the files is accessed most often, then it helps to group them together on the disk. Sorting by size helps separate a few large files from more commonly accessed small files. According to the vendor, speedups of 20 percent have been measured for a mixed workload. DiskPak is available for both SunOS 4.X and Solaris 2.X. The current release can only manage filesystems less than 2 Gbytes in size, but future versions should remove this limitation. The phone number for Eagle Software is 913-823-7257 in the USA.

Combining Physical Disks

Disks can be combined in several ways. There are also two different software packages that can be used to combine disks. Since they use different terminology, I will discuss them one at a time.

RAID and Disk Arrays

The SPARCstorage Array appears to the system as 30 disks on a single controller that are then combined by means of software. Many RAID disk subsystems combine their disks by using a fixed-configuration, hardware RAID controller so it appears as one very big disk. The term RAID was coined to stand for *Redundant Array of Inexpensive Disks*, several levels have been defined to cover the possible configurations. The parity-based RAID configurations are a solution to the problem of low cost, high availability, but do not give as good performance as lots of independent mirrored disks. Here is a useful quote.

> *Fast, cheap, safe; pick any two.*

This book is about performance, so if I start with *fast*, then to be *fast and cheap*, I just use lots of disks; and to be *fast and safe*, I use twice as many and mirror them.

Online: DiskSuite Performance Hints

Sun's Online: DiskSuite product includes a software driver for disk mirroring. When a write occurs, the data must be written to both disks together, and this can cause a bottleneck for I/O. The two mirrored disks should be on completely separate IPI disk controllers or SCSI buses so that the write can proceed in parallel. If this advice is not followed, the writes happen in sequence and the disk-write throughput is halved. Putting the drives on separate controllers also improves the system's availability, since disk controller and cabling failures will not prevent access to both disks.

SPARCstorage Manager Performance Hints

By default, SPARCstorage Manager numbers disks sequentially, on each SCSIbus in turn. When you request that a multi-disk stripe be created, SSM automatically allocates space from disks in sequence. This will probably allocate all the striped disks from one SCSIbus, which is slower than striping across SCSIbuses. Manually select the disks that you want the stripe to use before you create the stripe.

Configuration and Capacity Planning for Solaris by Brian Wong contains more information on the SPARCstorage Array. The terminology differs between Online: DiskSuite and SPARCstorage Manager as shown in Table 5-5.

Table 5-5   Terminology Differences between SPARCstorage Manager and Online: DiskSuite

SPARCstorage Manager	Online: DiskSuite
disk	physical disk
subdisk	partition

Table 5-5 Terminology Differences between SPARCstorage Manager and Online: DiskSuite

SPARCstorage Manager	Online: DiskSuite
plex	metapartition
volume	top-level metapartition
disk group	[no equivalent]

Filesystem Tuning Fix

The Online: DiskSuite 1.0 product was developed at about the time filesystem clustering[5] was implemented, and it doesn't set up the tuning parameters correctly for best performance. After creating a filesystem but before mounting it, run the following command on each metapartition.

```
# tunefs -a 7 -d 0 /dev/mdXX
```

The -a option controls the *maxcontig* parameter. This parameter specifies the maximum number of blocks, belonging to the same file, that will be allocated contiguously before inserting a rotational delay.

The -d option controls the rotdelay parameter. This specifies the expected time (in milliseconds) to service a transfer completion interrupt and initiate a new transfer on the same disk. It is used to decide how much rotational spacing to place between successive blocks in a file. For drives with track buffers, a *rotdelay* of zero is usually the best choice.

Note – Online: DiskSuite 2.0 runs on Solaris 2 and does not need this fix.

Metadisk Options

Several options can be used in the metadisk configuration file to control how mirroring operates.

Writes always go to both disks, so the only option is whether to issue two write requests and wait for them both to finish or to issue them sequentially. The default is simultaneous issue, which is what is wanted in most cases.

Reads can come from either disk. There are four options.

---

5. See "File Access Patterns" on page 61 and the tunefs manual page.

　　　　　　　　Sun Performance and Tuning

- Reads can be issued to each disk simultaneously, canceling the second when the first read completes. This option aims to provide the fastest response but generates extra work and does not work well in a heavily loaded system.

- Reads can be made alternately from one disk and then the other, balancing the load but not taking advantage of any sequential prefetching that disks may do.

- Reads can be made to come from one disk only (except on failure), which can be useful if two separate, read-intensive, mirrored partitions share the same disk. Each partition can be read from a different disk.

- The last option is to geometrically divide the partition in two and to use the first disk to service reads from the first half of the partition, using the second disk to service reads from the second half. For a read-intensive load, the heads will seek only half as far, thus reducing the effective average seek time and providing better performance for random accesses.

Networks

The subject of network configuration and performance has been extensively covered by other writers[1]. For that reason, this chapter concentrates on Sun-specific networking issues, such as the performance characteristics of the many network adapters and operating system releases.

Different Ethernet Interfaces and How They Compare

Three main types of Ethernet interface are used on Sun machines: the Intel `ie`, AMD LANCE `le`, and the `qe` interface used in the latest designs. This classification is further complicated by the way that the Ethernet chip is interfaced to the CPU — it may be built into the CPU board or interfaced via SBus or VMEbus.

SBus Interfaces — `le` and `qe`

The `le` interface is used on all SPARC desktop machines. This built-in Ethernet interface shares its DMA connection to the SBus with the SCSI interface but has higher priority, so heavy Ethernet activity can reduce disk throughput. This can be a problem with the original DMA controller used in the SPARCstation 1, 1+, SLC, and IPC, but subsequent machines have enough DMA bandwidth to support both. The add-on SBus Ethernet card uses exactly the same interface as the built-in Ethernet but has an SBus DMA controller to itself. The more recent buffered Ethernet interfaces used in the SPARCserver 600, the SBE/S, the FSBE/S, and the DSBE/S have a 256-Kbyte buffer to provide a low-latency source and sink for the Ethernet. This cuts down on dropped packets, especially when many Ethernets are configured in a system that also has multiple CPUs consuming the memory bandwidth. The disadvantage is increased CPU utilization as data is copied between the buffer and main memory. The most recent and efficient `qe` Ethernet interface uses a buffer but has a DVMA mechanism to transfer data between the buffer and memory. This interface is found in the SQEC/S quadruple Ethernet SBus card and the 100-Mbit 100baseT Ethernet interface SBus card.

---

1. In particular, see *Managing NFS and NIS* by Hal Stern.

Built-in Interface — `le0`

The `le0` interface is built into the CPU board on the SPARC system 300 range and provides similar throughput to the SBus interface.

Built-in Interface — `ie0`

The `ie0` interface is built into the CPU board on the Sun4/110, Sun4/200 range, and SPARC system 400 range. It provides reasonable throughput but is generally slower than the `le` interface.

VMEbus Interface — `ie`

The `ie` VMEbus interface is the usual board provided on SPARCsystem 400 series machines to provide a second, third, or fourth Ethernet as `ie2`, `ie3`, and `ie4`. It has some local buffer space and is accessed over the VMEbus. It is not as fast as the on-board `ie` interface, but it does use 32-bit VMEbus transfers. The SPARCserver 400 series has a much faster VMEbus interface than other Sun machines have which helps this board perform better.

Multibus Interface — `ie`

The `ie` multibus interface board is an older board that uses a Multibus-to-VME adapter so all VME transfers happen at half speed as 16-bit transfers and are rather slow. It tends to be configured as `ie1`, but it should be avoided if a lot of traffic is needed on that interface.

VMEbus Interface NC400 — `ne`

The `ne` interface is an intelligent board that performs Ethernet packet processing up to the NFS level. It can support about twice as many NFS operations per second as the built-in `ie0` interface on a SPARCserver 490. It actually supports fewer NFS operations per second than `le` interfaces do but off-loads the main CPU so that more networks can be configured. There are no performance figures for routing throughput. It accelerates only the UDP protocol used by NFS; TCP is still handled by the main CPU. This board is not needed on Solaris 2, since the NFS code is multithreaded and better NFS server performance is obtained by using a multiprocessor SPARC machine.

Routing Throughput

Table 6-1 shows throughput between various interfaces on SPARCstation 1 and Sun-4™ /260 machines. The Sun-4/260 figures are taken from an internal Sun document; the SPARCstation figures are taken from the SPARCstation 2 Performance Brief. Since a 100 percent busy Ethernet can have a maximum of less than 15,000 packets per second, with the minimum packet size of 64 bytes, it is apparent that a SPARCstation 2 can effectively route almost a full load between two Ethernets.

Table 6-1   *Ethernet Routing Performance*

Machine	From	To	64-byte packets/sec
Sun-4/260	On-board ie0	Multibus ie1	1813
Sun-4/260	Multibus ie1	On-board ie0	2219
Sun-4/260	On-board ie0	VMEbus ic2	2150
Sun-4/260	VMEbus ie2	On-board ie0	2435
SPARCstation1	On-board le0	SBus le1	6000
SPARCstation 2	On-board le0	SBus le1	12000

Faster Interfaces

Two FDDI interfaces have been produced by Sun, and several third-party VMEbus and SBus options are available as well. FDDI runs at 100 Mbits/s so has ten times the bandwidth of standard Ethernet. Two more recent interfaces are the 100-Mbit Fast Ethernet and the 155-Mbit ATM SBus cards.

Dual Attach VMEbus FDDI/DX

The original Sun FDDI board, Dual Attach VMEbus FDDI/DX, was one of the first available in the industry in 1989. It is bottlenecked by both the VMEbus interface and the on-board 68020 that runs the station management protocol. A peak throughput of about 30 Mbits/s can be expected. The FDDI/DX has a class A dual attach interface, which connects directly into the FDDI rings.

SBus FDDI/S 2.0 — bf

The bf interface is the original Sun SBus FDDI board and driver. It is a single-width SBus card that provides single-attach only.

SBus FDDI/S 3.0 — nf

FDDI/S 3.0 software supports a range of SBus FDDI cards, including both single- and dual-attach types. These are OEM products from Network Peripherals Inc. — Sun's internal development resources are now concentrated on ATM. The FDDI 3.0 cards are lower cost than FDDI 2.0 cards and are slightly more efficient. The nf_stat command provided in /opt/SUNWconn/SUNWnf may be useful for monitoring the interface.

SBus 100baseT Fast Ethernet Card — be

The 100baseT standard takes the approach of requiring shorter and higher-quality, shielded, twisted pair cables, then running the normal Ethernet standard at ten times the speed. Performance is similar to FDDI, but with the Ethernet characteristic of collisions under heavy load. It is most useful to connect a server to a hub, which converts the 100baseT signal into many conventional 10baseT signals for the client workstations.

SBus ATM 155 Mbit Asynchronous Transfer Mode Cards

There are two versions of the SBus ATM 155 Mbit Asynchronous Tranfer Mode card: one uses a fiber interface, the other uses twisted pair cables like the 100baseT card. The ATM standard allows isochronous connections to be set up (so audio and video data can be piped at a constant rate), but the AAL5 standard used to carry IP protocol data makes it behave like a slightly faster FDDI or 100baseT interface for general purpose use. The cost of ATM switches is high, but systems can be connected back-to-back with just a pair of ATM cards and no switch (if you only need two systems).

Using NFS Effectively

The NFS protocol itself limits throughput to about 3 Mbytes/s per active client-side process because it has limited prefetch and small block sizes. The upcoming NFS version 3 protocol allows larger block sizes and other changes that improve performance on high speed networks.   This limit doesn't apply to the aggregate throughput if you have many active client processes on a machine.

First, some references:

* *Managing NFS and NIS* by Hal Stern — essential reading!

* *SMCC NFS Server Performance and Tuning Guide*

The *Solaris 2.3 SMCC NFS Server Performance and Tuning Guide* is part of the SMCC hardware-specific manual set. It contains a good overview of how to size an NFS server configuration, but its tuning recommendations should be considered a first draft, as there are many errors and inconsistencies. It actually covers SunOS 4.1.3/Solaris 1.1 NFS server tuning as well as Solaris 2, but sometimes confuses the two. The Solaris 2.4 version of this manual has been completely rewritten and is now up-to-date and accurate. I helped review it as it was rewritten, and I think you will find it much more useful.

How Many NFS Server Threads?

In SunOS 4, the NFS daemon nfsd is used to service requests from the network, and a number of nfsd daemons are started so that a number of outstanding requests can be processed in parallel. Each nfsd takes one request off the network and passes it to the I/O subsystem. To cope with bursts of NFS traffic, a large number of nfsds should be configured, even on low-end machines. All the nfsds run in the kernel and do not context switch in the same way as user level processes do, so the number of hardware contexts is not a limiting factor (despite folklore to the contrary!). If you want to "throttle back" the NFS load on a server so that it can do other things, the number could be reduced. If you configure too many nfsds some may not be used, but it is unlikely that there will be any adverse side effects as long as you don't run out of process table entries. Some high-end LADDIS results use over 300 nfsds. Take the highest number you get by applying the following three rules:

- Two NFS threads per active client process

- 32 NFS threads on a SPARCclassic server, 64 NFS threads per SuperSPARC processor

- 16 NFS threads per Ethernet, 160 per FDDI

What Is a Typical NFS Operation Mix?

There are characteristic NFS operation mixes for each environment. The LADDIS mix is based on the load generated by slow diskless workstations with a small amount of memory doing intensive software development. It has a large proportion of writes compared to the typical load mix from a modern workstation. If workstations are using the cachefs option, then many reads will be avoided, so the total load is less, but the percentage of writes is more like the LADDIS mix. Table 6-2 summarizes the information.

Table 6-2   The LADDIS NFS Operation Mix

NFS Operation	Mix	Comment (Possible Client Command)
getattr	13%	Get file attributes (ls -l)
setattr	1%	Set file attributes (chmod)
lookup	34%	Search directory for a file and return handle (open)
readlink	8%	Follow a symbolic link on the server (ls)
read	22%	Read an 8KB block of data
write	15%	Write an 8KB block of data
create	2%	Create a file
remove	1%	Remove a file (rm)
readdir	3%	Read a directory entry (ls)
fsstat	1%	Get filesystem information (df)

How to Understand and Use the `nfsstat` Command

NFS Servers

The `nfsstat -s` command shows operation counts for the components of the NFS mix. This section is based upon the *Solaris 2.4 SMCC NFS Server Performance and Tuning Guide*. Figure 6-1 illustrates the results of an `nfsstat -s` command.

Figure 6-1   NFS Server Operation Counts

```
% nfsstat -s

Server rpc:
calls        badcalls    nullrecv    badlen      xdrcall
2104792      0           0           0           0

Server nfs:
calls        badcalls
2104792      5
null         getattr     setattr     root        lookup       readlink    read
10779  1%    966412 46%  13165  1%   0  0%       207574 10%   572  0%     686477 33%
wrcache      write       create      remove      rename       link        symlink
0  0%        179582  9%  5348  0%    9562  0%    557  0%      579  0%     32  0%
mkdir        rmdir       readdir     statfs
120  0%      386  0%     12650  1%   10997  1%
```

The meaning and interpretation of the measurements is as follows:

- calls — the total number of remote procedure (RPC) calls received. NFS is just one RPC application.

- badcalls — the total number of RPC calls rejected, the sum of badlen and xdrcall. If this value is nonzero, then RPC requests are being rejected. Reasons include having a user in too many groups, attempts to access an unexported file system, or an improper secure RPC configuration.

- nullrecv — the number of times an RPC call was not there when one was thought to be received.

- badlen — the number of calls with length shorter than the RPC minimum.

- xdrcall — the number of RPC calls whose header could not be decoded by the external data representation (XDR) translation.

- readlink — if this value is more than 10 percent of the mix, then client machines are making excessive use of symbolic links on NFS-exported filesystems. Replace the link with a directory, perhaps using a loopback mount on both server and clients.

- getattr — if this value is more than 60 percent of the mix, then check that the attribute cache value on the NFS clients is set correctly. It may have been reduced or set to zero. See the `mount_nfs` command and the `actimo` option.

- null — if this value is more than 1 percent then the automounter time-out values are set too short. Null calls are made by the automounter to locate a server for the filesystem.

- writes — if this value is more than 5 percent, then configure a Prestoserve™ option on the server.

NFS Clients

On each client machine, use `nfsstat -c` to see the mix. The example shown in Figure 6-2 was taken on Solaris 2.4, and it makes a point of distinguishing NFS version 2 from the upcoming NFS version 3 protocol. Solaris 2.4 contains the infrastructure to support NFS V2 and NFS V3 side-by-side, but NFS V3 is not provided as a standard part of Solaris 2.4.

Figure 6-2   NFS Client Operation Counts (Solaris 2.4 Version)

```
% nfsstat -c

Client rpc:
calls       badcalls    retrans     badxids     timeouts    waits       newcreds
1121626     61          464         15          518         0           0
badverfs    timers      toobig      nomem       cantsend    bufulocks
0           442         0           0           0           0


Client nfs:
calls       badcalls    clgets      cltoomany
1109675     6           1109607     0
Version 2:  (1109678 calls)
null        getattr     setattr     root        lookup      readlink    read
0 0%        345948 31%  4097 0%     0 0%        375991 33%  214 0%      227031 20%
wrcache     write       create      remove      rename      link        symlink
0 0%        112821 10%  3525 0%     3120 0%     290 0%      54 0%       0 0%
mkdir       rmdir       readdir     statfs
370 0%      45 0%       10112 0%    26060 2%
```

- calls — the total number of calls sent.

- badcalls — the total number of calls rejected by RPC.

- retrans — the total number of retransmissions.

- badxid — the number of times that a duplicate acknowledgment was received for a single NFS request. If it is approximately equal to timeout and above 5 percent, then look for a server bottleneck.

- timeout — the number of calls that timed out waiting for a reply from the server. If the value is more than 5 percent, then RPC requests are timing out. A badxid value of less than 5 percent indicates that the network is dropping parts of the requests or replies. Check that intervening networks and routers are working properly; consider reducing the NFS buffer size parameters (see `mount_nfs rsize` and `wsize`), but reducing the parameters will reduce peak throughput.

- wait — the number of times a call had to wait because no client handle was available.

- newcred — the number of times authentication information had to be refreshed.

- null — if this value is above zero by a nontrivial amount, then increase the automount timeout parameter `timeo`.

You can also view each mount point by using the `nfsstat -m` command on a client, as shown in Figure 6-3.

Figure 6-3   NFS Operation Response Times Measured by Client

```
% nfsstat -m
/home/username from server:/export/home3/username
 Flags:    vers=2,hard,intr,down,dynamic,rsize=8192,wsize=8192,retrans=5
 Lookups: srtt=7 (17ms), dev=4 (20ms), cur=2 (40ms)
 Reads:   srtt=16 (40ms), dev=8 (40ms), cur=6 (120ms)
 Writes:  srtt=15 (37ms), dev=3 (15ms), cur=3 (60ms)
 All:     srtt=15 (37ms), dev=8 (40ms), cur=5 (100ms)
/var/mail from server:/var/mail
 Flags:    vers=2,hard,intr,dynamic,rsize=8192,wsize=8192,retrans=5
 Lookups: srtt=8 (20ms), dev=3 (15ms), cur=2 (40ms)
 Reads:   srtt=18 (45ms), dev=6 (30ms), cur=5 (100ms)
 Writes:  srtt=9 (22ms), dev=5 (25ms), cur=3 (60ms)
 All:     srtt=8 (20ms), dev=3 (15ms), cur=2 (40ms)
```

This output shows the smoothed round trip times (srtt), the deviation or variability of this measure (dev), and the current time-out level for retransmission (cur). Values are converted into milliseconds and are quoted separately for read, write, lookup, and all types of calls.

The system will seem slow if any of the round trip times exceed 50 ms. If you find a problem, watch the `iostat -x` measures on the server for the disks that export the slow filesystem, as described in "How to Decide that a Disk Is Overloaded" on page 77. If the write operations are much slower than the other operations you may need a prestoserve, assuming that writes are an important part of your mix.

≡ 6

NFS Server Not Responding

If you see the "not responding" message on clients and the server has been running without any coincident downtime, then you have a serious problem. Either the network connections or the network routing is having problems or the NFS server is completely overloaded.

How to Understand and Use the Netstat Command

Several options to the netstat command show various parts of the TCP/IP protocol parameters and counters. The most useful options are the basic netstat command that monitors a single interface and the netstat -i command that summarizes all the interfaces.

Figure 6-4   Netstat -i Output Showing Multiple Network Interfaces

```
% netstat -i
Name  Mtu   Net/Dest      Address        Ipkts   Ierrs Opkts  Oerrs Collis Queue
lo0   8232  loopback      localhost      1247105 0     1247105 0     0      0
bf0   4352  labnet-fddi   testsys-fddi   5605601 0     1266263 0     0      0
le1   1500  labnet-71     testsys-71      738403 0      442941 0     11485  0
le2   1500  labnet        testsys-lab    4001566 1     3141510 0     47094  0
le3   1500  labnet-tpt    testsys        4140495 2     6121934 0     70169  0
```

From a single measurement, you can calculate the collision rate since boot time; from noting the difference in the packet and collision counts over time, you can calculate the ongoing collision rates as Collis * 100 / Opkts for each device. In this case lo0 is the internal loopback device, bf0 is an FDDI so has no collisions, le1 has a 2.6 percent collision rate, le2 has 1.5 percent, and le3 has 1.2 percent.

Processors 7≣

Previous chapters have looked at the disk and network components of a system. This chapter covers the processor component. The details of particular processors are dealt with later. This chapter explains the measurements that each version of Solaris makes. It provides guidelines for you to decide how much spare capacity you have and when more or faster CPUs are needed to support your workload.

Monitoring Processors in SunOS 4.1.3 (Solaris 1.1)

Processor Monitoring Tools Provided with SunOS 4.1.3

The load average displayed by the `perfmeter`, `uptime`, and `w` commands is the primary indicator of processor loading on servers. It is described in "Understanding and Using the Load Average" on page 97 and is the same in SunOS 4 and Solaris 2. The `vmstat` command is the most useful monitoring tool.

Two "MP-aware" commands are provided on MP capable machines only. `/usr/kvm/mpstat` breaks down the CPU loading for each processor and provides a total. `/usr/kvm/mps` is the same as `ps(1)`, in that it lists the processes running on the machine, except that it includes a column to say on which CPU each process was last scheduled.

Understanding **vmstat** on a Multiprocessor

`vmstat` provides a convenient summary of performance on a multiprocessor system. If there are two processors, then a CPU load (`us` + `sy`) of 50 percent means that one processor is completely busy. If there are four processors, then a CPU load of 25 percent means that one processor is completely busy. Refer to Figure 7-1 to see the column headers printed by `vmstat`.

Figure 7-1   Sample vmstat *Output*

```
% vmstat 5
 procs     memory            page            disk          faults      cpu
 r b w   swap  free  re  mf pi po fr de sr f0 s3 s5 s6   in   sy   cs us sy id
 0 0 0  56360  1308   0   5  3  1  3  0  2  0  1  0  0   50  129   84  7  3 91
```

The first column of output is the average number of runnable processes. To actually use two or four processors effectively, this number must average more than two or four. On a multiuser time-sharing or database server, this figure can be quite large. If you currently have a uniprocessor or dual processor system and are trying to decide whether an upgrade to two or four processors would be effective this is the first thing you should measure. If you have a compute server that runs only one job, then it may use 100 percent of the CPU on a uniprocessor but will only show one runnable process. On a dual processor, this workload would only show 50 percent CPU busy. If several jobs are running, then it may still show 100 percent CPU busy, but the average number of runnable processes will be shown and you can decide how many CPUs you should get for that workload. The `vmstat` command is described in more detail in "Understanding vmstat and sar Output" on page 194.

The number of involuntary context switches is often reduced on a multiprocessor as you increase the number of CPUs. For some workloads, this reduction can increase the overall efficiency of the machine. One case when the context switch rate will not be reduced can be illustrated by considering a single Oracle database batch job. In this case an application process is issuing a continuous stream of database queries to its Oracle back-end process via a socket connection between the two. Two processes are running flat out and context switch rates can be very high on a uniprocessor. If a dual processor is tried, it will not help. The two processes never try to run at the same time, one is always waiting for the other one, so on every front-end to back-end query, there will be a voluntary context switch, regardless. The relationship between window-system applications and the X server process is different because the application doesn't wait for completion and dual CPUs do provide some acceleration.

The number of interrupts, system calls, and the system CPU time are the most important measures from a tuning point of view. When a heavy load is placed on a SPARCserver 600MP the kernel may bottleneck on system CPU time of 50 percent on a two-processor system or 25 percent on a four-processor system. The number of interrupts and system calls and the time taken to process those calls must be reduced to improve the throughput. Some kernel tweaks to try are increasing *maxslp* to prevent swap outs and reducing *slowscan* and *fastscan* rates. These parameters are described in "The Paging Algorithm in SunOS 4" on page 202. Reducing the use of system-call-intensive programs like `find` or moving a database file from a filesystem to a raw partition, also helps. Patch 100575 for SunOS 4.1.2 reduces spinning by making disk I/O more efficient (reducing the system time) and allows some kernel block copies to occur outside the mutex lock, so that more than one CPU can be productive. The problem is fixed in SunOS 4.1.3.

It is hard to see how much time each CPU spends spinning, waiting for the kernel lock. The total productive system CPU time will never exceed one processor's worth, so any excess CPU time will be due to spinning. On a four-processor machine reporting a sustained 75 percent system CPU time, 25 percent is productive (one CPU's worth) and 50 percent is spent waiting for the kernel lock (two CPUs worth that might as well not be configured). Conversely, a two processor machine that often has system CPU time over 50 percent will not benefit from the addition of two more processors and may actually slow down. It is possible to patch a kernel so that it will ignore one or more CPUs at boot time. This patch allows testing on variable numbers of processors without having to physically remove the module. The *okprocset* kernel variable needs to be patched in a copy of vmunix by using adb, then the system must be rebooted using the patched kernel. These values assume that CPU #1 is in control and *okprocset* controls the additional CPUs that will be started. Check how many you have with mpstat. Table 7-1 summarizes the abd command required to control the number of CPUs.

Table 7-1   Disabling Processors in SunOS 4.1.X

Number Of CPUs	adb -w /vmunix.Ncpu
1	okprocset?W0x1
2	okprocset?W0x3
3	okprocset?W0x7
4	okprocset?W0xf

Monitoring Processors in Solaris 2

CPU Control Commands — psrinfo and psradm

Some new commands were implemented in Solaris 2.2. Psrinfo tells you which CPUs are in use and when they were last enabled or disabled. Psradm actually controls the CPUs. Note that clock interrupts always go to CPU 0[1], even if it is disabled. Solaris 2.3 reintroduces a more useful version of mpstat.

Understanding and Using the Load Average

The load average is the sum of the run queue length and the number of jobs currently running on CPUs. In Solaris 2.0 to 2.2 the load average did not include the running jobs but this bug was fixed in Solaris 2.3. The three figures given are averages over the last 1, 5, and 15 minutes. They can be used as an average run queue length indicator with the rules described in Appendix A, "Rules and Tunables Quick Reference Tables," to see if more CPU power is required.

```
% uptime
  11:40pm  up 7 day(s),  3:54,  1 user,  load average: 0.27, 0.22, 0.24
```

---

1. On SPARCserver 1000 and SPARCcenter 2000 machines the system CPU defaults to CPU 0 but can be configured. See which board has the console connected to it. A CPU on that board will be taking the clock interrupt.

Using mpstat to Monitor Interrupts and Mutexes

The mpstat output shown below was measured on a 16-CPU SPARCcenter 2000 running Solaris 2.4 and with about 500 active time-shared database users. One of the key measures is smtx, the number of times the CPU failed to obtain a mutex immediately. If it is more than about 200 per CPU, then usually system time begins to climb. The exception is the master CPU that is taking the 100 Hz clock interrupt[2], normally CPU 0 but in this case CPU 4. I'm not sure why, but it seems to have a larger number (1000 or more) of very short mutex stalls that don't hurt performance.

Figure 7-2   Monitoring All the CPUs with mpstat

CPU	minf	mjf	xcal	intr	ithr	csw	icsw	migr	smtx	srw	syscl	usr	sys	wt	idl
0	45	1	0	232	0	780	234	106	201	0	950	72	28	0	0
1	29	1	0	243	0	810	243	115	186	0	1045	69	31	0	0
2	27	1	0	235	0	827	243	110	199	0	1000	75	25	0	0
3	26	0	0	217	0	794	227	120	189	0	925	70	30	0	0
4	9	0	0	234	92	403	94	84	1157	0	625	66	34	0	0
5	30	1	0	510	304	764	213	119	176	0	977	69	31	0	0
6	35	1	0	296	75	786	224	114	184	0	1030	68	32	0	0
7	29	1	0	300	96	754	213	116	190	0	982	69	31	0	0
9	41	0	0	356	126	905	231	109	226	0	1078	69	31	0	0
11	26	0	0	231	2	805	235	120	199	0	1047	71	29	0	0
12	29	0	0	405	164	793	238	117	183	0	879	66	34	0	0
15	31	0	0	288	71	784	223	121	200	0	1049	66	34	0	0
16	71	0	0	263	55	746	213	115	196	0	983	69	31	0	0
17	34	0	0	206	0	743	212	115	194	0	969	69	31	0	0

Cache Affinity Algorithms

When a system that has multiple caches is in use, a process may run on a CPU and load part of itself into that cache, then stop running for a while. When it resumes, the UNIX scheduler must decide which CPU to run it on. To reduce cache traffic, the process must preferentially be allocated to its original CPU, but that CPU may be in use or the cache may have been cleaned out by another process in the meantime. The cost of migrating a process to a new CPU depends on the time since it last ran, the size of the cache, and the speed of the central bus. A delicate balance must be struck; a general purpose algorithm that adapts to all kinds of workloads has been developed. In the case of the SPARCcenter 2000, this algorithm manages up to 40 Mbytes of cache and has a significant effect on performance. The algorithm works by moving jobs from the central run queue to a

---

2. Interrupt distribution is explained in "SBus Interrupt Processing" on page 147.

private run queue for each CPU. The job stays on a CPU's run queue, unless another CPU becomes idle, looks at all the queues, finds a job that hasn't run for a while on another queue, and migrates the job to its own run queue.

Vmstat Run Queue Differences in Solaris 2

It is important to note that vmstat in SunOS 4.X reports the number of jobs in the run queue, including the jobs that are actually running. Solaris 2 reports only the jobs that are waiting to run. The difference is equal to the number of CPUs in the system. A busy four-CPU system might show six jobs in the run queue on SunOS 4.1.3 and only two jobs on Solaris 2 even though the two systems are behaving identically. If vmstat reports zero jobs in Solaris 2, then there may be one, two, three, or four jobs running; you have to work it out for yourself from the CPU percentages.

Multiprocessors

Multiprocessor machines introduce yet another dimension to performance. Sun has been shipping multiprocessor servers for some time, but the introduction of Solaris 2 and the desktop multiprocessor SPARCstation range has brought multiprocessing into the mainstream both for end-users and application developers. This section provides a brief description of how multiprocessor machines work. The section "Vmstat Run Queue Differences in Solaris 2" on page 99, explains how to measure the utilization of multiple processors to see if the existing processors are working effectively, and to see if adding more processors would provide a worthwhile improvement.

Basic Multiprocessor Theory

Why Bother with More Than One CPU?

At any point in time, there exist CPU designs that represent the best performance that can be obtained with current technology at a reasonable price. The cost and technical difficulty of pushing the technology further means that the most cost-effective way of increasing computer power is to use several processors. There have been many attempts to harness multiple CPUs and, today, there are many different machines on the market. Software has been the problem for these machines. It is hard to design software that will be portable across a large range of machines, and few of these machines sell in large numbers, so the market for multiprocessor software has been small and fragmented. This situation is now changing, since Sun has now shipped many multiprocessor UNIX machines and leading software vendors have brought out multiprocessor versions of their applications.

The most common applications that can use multiprocessors are time-shared systems and database servers. These have been joined by multithreaded versions of CPU-intensive programs like MCAD finite element solvers and EDA circuit simulation packages. For graphics-intensive applications where the X server uses a lot of the CPU power on a desktop machine, configuring a dual CPU system will help — the X protocol allows buffering and batching of commands with few commands needing acknowledgments. The application sends X commands to the X server and continues to run without waiting for them to complete, in most cases. One CPU runs the application, and the other runs the X server and drives the display hardware.

Multiprocessor Classifications

Two classes of multiprocessor machines have some possibility of software compatibility and both have SPARC-based implementations. Descriptions of each class are found in Figures 7-3 and 7-4.

Distributed Memory Multiprocessors

Figure 7-3   Typical Distributed Memory Multiprocessor with Mesh Network

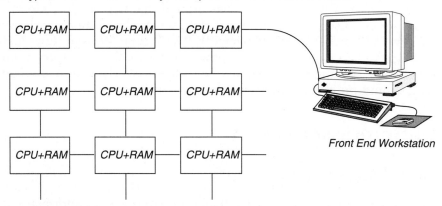

Distributed memory multiprocessors can be thought of as a network of uniprocessors packaged into a box. Each processor has its own memory, and data must be explicitly copied over the network to another processor before it can be used. The benefit of this is that there is no contention for memory bandwidth to limit the number of processors. Moreover, if the network is made up of point-to-point links, then the network throughput increases as the number of processors increase. There is no theoretical limit to the number of processors that can be used in a system of this type, but there are problems finding algorithms that scale with the number of processors, thus limiting their usefulness for general purpose computing.

The most common examples of this architecture are the Meiko CS2, which has SuperSPARC processors running Solaris 2 on each node; the Thinking Machines CM-5, which has SPARC processors; the NCube system; and the Intel iPSC Hypercube, which has Intel processors, and a myriad of Inmos Transputer-based machines. The SPARCcluster 1 can also be placed in this category[3]. Most of the named systems have vector units to provide high-peak, floating-point performance for very fast running of specially written numerical programs. Some have also been used to run databases, in particular, the Oracle Parallel Server product. There is no software compatibility across these machines, and there is no dominant operating system for this type of computer (although there is a trend toward providing various forms of UNIX compatibility). They are sometimes interfaced to a front-end Sun workstation that provides a user interface, development environment, disk storage, and network interface for the machine.

Shared Memory Multiprocessors

Figure 7-4   Typical Small Scale Shared Memory Multiprocessor

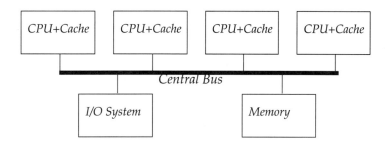

A shared memory multiprocessor is much more tightly integrated than a distributed memory multiprocessor and consists of a fairly conventional starting point of CPU, memory and I/O subsystem, with extra CPUs added onto the central bus. This configuration multiplies the load on the memory system by the number of processors, and the shared bus becomes a bottleneck. To reduce the load, caches are always used and very fast memory systems and buses are built. If more and faster processors are added to the design, the cache size must increase, the memory system must be improved, and the bus throughput must be increased. Most small-scale MP machines support up to four processors. Larger ones support a few tens of processors. With some workloads, the bus or memory system will saturate before the maximum number of processors has been configured.

---

3. See "SPARCcluster 1" on page 149 for more details.

Special circuitry snoops activity on the bus at all times so that all the caches can be kept coherent. If the current copy of some data is in more than one of the caches, then it will be marked as being shared. If it is updated in one cache, then the copies in the other caches are either invalidated or updated automatically. From a software point of view, there is never any need to explicitly copy data from one processor to another, and shared memory locations are used to communicate values among CPUs. The cache-to-cache transfers still occur when two CPUs use data in the same cache line, so such transfers must be considered from a performance point of view, but the software does not have to worry about it.

There are many examples of shared memory mainframes and minicomputers. SPARC-based UNIX multiprocessors include four-processor Sun SPARCserver 600 and SPARCstation 10 models, various ICL DRS6000s and machines from Solbourne, the eight-processor SPARCserver 1000, the 20-processor SPARCcenter 2000, and the 64-processor Cray® SuperServer CS6400.

The high-end machines often have multiple I/O subsystems and multiple memory subsystems connected to the central bus, allowing more CPUs to be configured without causing bottlenecks in the I/O and memory systems. The SPARCcenter 2000 takes this approach further by having dual buses with a 256-byte interleave, and the Cray CS6400 has quadruple buses.

Similarities and Future Convergence

Although the two types of MP machines started out as very different approaches, the most recent examples of these types are starting to converge.

The shared memory machines all have large caches for each CPU. For good performance, it is essential for the working set of data and instructions to be present in the cache. The cache is now analogous to the private memory of a distributed memory machine, and many algorithms that have been developed to partition data for a distributed memory machine are applicable to a cache-based shared, memory machine.

The latest distributed memory machines have moved from a software-or DMA-driven point-to-point link, to an MMU-driven, cache-line-based implementation of distributed shared memory. This is used in the Thinking Machines CM-5, the Meiko CS-2, and in an experimental interconnect called S3.MP[4], developed at Sun. With this system, the hardware is instructed to share a region of address space with another processor, and cache coherence is maintained over a point-to-point link. As the speed of these links approaches the speed of a shared memory backplane, the distributed memory system can be used to run shared memory algorithms efficiently. The Meiko CS-2 runs each point-to-

---

4. Described at the IEEE Hot Interconnects Conference, August 1993.

point link at about 50 Mbytes/s, while S3.MP runs at up to 200 Mbytes/s. These speeds are comparable to the low end of shared memory backplane speeds, although they typically have much higher latency. The extra latency is due to the physical distances involved and the use of complex switching systems to interconnect large numbers of processors. It should also be noted that large, shared memory systems also tend to have higher latency than smaller ones.

UNIX on Shared Memory Multiprocessors

Critical Regions

The UNIX kernel has many critical regions, or sections of code where a data structure is being created or updated. These regions must not be interrupted by a higher-priority interrupt service routine. The uniprocessor UNIX kernel manages these regions by setting the interrupt mask to a high value during the region. On a multiprocessor, there are other processors with their own interrupt masks, so a different technique must be used to manage critical regions.

The Spin Lock or Mutex

One key capability in shared memory, multiprocessor systems is the ability to perform interprocessor synchronization using atomic load/store or swap instructions. All SPARC chips have an instruction called LDSTUB, which means load-store-unsigned-byte. It reads a byte from memory into a register, then writes 0xFF into memory in a single indivisible operation. The value in the register can then be examined to see if it was already 0xFF, which means that another processor got there first, or if it was 0x00, which means that this processor is in charge. This instruction is used to make *mutual exclusion locks* (known as mutexes) which make sure that only one processor at a time can hold the lock. The lock is acquired through LDSTUB and cleared by storing 0x00 back to memory. If a processor does not get the lock, then it may decide to *spin* by sitting in a loop and testing the lock until it becomes available. By checking with a normal load instruction in a loop before issuing an LDSTUB, the spin is performed within the cache, and the bus snooping logic watches for the lock being cleared. In this way, spinning causes no bus traffic, so processors that are waiting do not slow down those that are working. A spin lock is appropriate when the wait is expected to be short. If a long wait is expected, the process should sleep for a while so that a different job can be scheduled onto the CPU.

Code Locking and SunOS 4.1.X

The simplest way to convert a UNIX kernel that is using interrupt levels to control critical regions for use with multiprocessors, is to replace the call that sets interrupt levels high with a call to acquire a mutex lock. At the point where the interrupt level was lowered, the lock is cleared. In this way, the same regions of code are locked for exclusive access. This method has been used to a greater or lesser extent by most MP UNIX implementations, including SunOS 4.1.2 and SunOS 4.1.3 on the SPARCserver 600MP machines[5]. The amount of actual concurrency that can take place in the kernel is controlled by the number and position of the locks.

In SunOS 4.1.2 and SunOS 4.1.3, there is effectively a single lock around the entire kernel. The reason for using a single lock is to make these MP systems totally compatible with user programs and device drivers written for uniprocessor systems. User programs can take advantage of the extra CPUs, but only one of the CPUs can be executing kernel code at a time.

When code locking is used, there are a fixed number of locks in the system; this number can be used to characterize how much concurrency is available. On a very busy, highly configured system, the code locks are likely to become bottlenecks so that adding extra processors will not help performance and may actually reduce performance.

Data Locking and Solaris 2.0

The problem with code locks is that different processors often want to use the same code to work on different data. To allow this use to happen, locks must be placed in data structures rather than in code. Unfortunately, this requires an extensive rewrite of the kernel — one reason why Solaris 2 took several years to create[6]. The result is that the kernel has a lot of concurrency available and can be tuned to scale well with large numbers of processors. The same kernel is used on uniprocessors and multiprocessors, so that all device drivers and user programs must be written to work in the same environment and there is no need to constrain concurrency for compatibility with uniprocessor systems. The locks are still needed in a uniprocessor, since the kernel can switch between kernel threads at any time to service an interrupt.

With data locking, there is a lock for each instance of a data structure. Since table sizes vary dynamically, the total number of locks grows as the tables grow, and the amount of concurrency that is available to exploit is greater on a very busy, highly configured

---

5. The multiprocessor features are described in *"New Technology for Flexibility, Performance and Growth, The SPARCserver 600 Series."*

6. See *"Solaris 2.0 Multithread Architecture White Paper"* and *"Realtime Scheduling in SunOS 5.0"*, by Sandeep Khanna, Michael Sebrée, John Zolnowsky.

system. Adding extra processors to such a system is likely to be beneficial. Solaris 2 has over 150 different data locks and multiplied by the number of instances of the data there will typically be several thousand locks in existence on a running system. As Solaris 2 is tuned for more concurrency, some of the remaining code locks are turned into data locks, and "large" locks are broken down into finer-grained locks. Tools exist to monitor the lock contention in the kernel, but access to kernel source code is required to make sense of the results. If mutex access routines appear at the top of the list of a kernel profile, then contention may be occurring[7]. There is a trade-off between having lots of mutexes for good MP scalability and few mutexes for reduced CPU overhead on uniprocessors.

---

7. See kgmon on page 220.

≡ 7

Sun Performance and Tuning

System Architectures 8 ☰

This chapter describes the architecture of recent SPARC-based systems and explores the performance trade-offs that are made throughout the range. The appropriate SPEC benchmarks are listed for each machine. The uniprocessor SPARC machines are described first, then the multiprocessor machines are described in detail. Subsequent chapters describe the components that make up these systems in more depth. I would have liked to have a whole chapter to explain the benchmarks, but this book is already overdue!

Uniprocessors

Uniprocessor SPARC systems are relatively simple. In this section they are grouped into four generations of system designs.

SPARC Uniprocessor VMEbus Systems

At the time SPARC was introduced, it was positioned at the high end of the product line. These systems are built using many components on large-format VMEbus cards. Each member of this family implemented different variations on a common theme, with a single CPU, 128-Kbyte cache to hold both data and instructions (apart from the Sun-4/100), Sun-4 MMU[1], single large memory system, some on-board I/O devices, and a single VMEbus for expansion. This forms the "sun4" kernel architecture, and a single version of the kernel code can run on any of these systems. The Sun-4 range is now obsolete and relatively small volumes were produced, their many variations are not discussed in great detail.

Table 8-1   SPEC89 Benchmark Results for SPARC Uniprocessor VME bus Systems

Machine	MHz	SPECmark89	Compiler
Sun4/110 and Sun4/150	14	6.1 (est)	SunPro 1.0
Sun4/260 and Sun4/280	16.6	8.1	SunPro 1.0
Sun4/330, Sun4/370 and Sun4/390	25	13.4	SunPro 1.0
Sun4/470 and Sun4/490	33	19.4	SunPro 1.0

---

1. See "The Sun-4 MMU — sun4, sun4c, sun4e Kernel Architectures" on page 164.

The First Generation of SPARC Uniprocessor Desktop Systems

This family of systems conforms to a set of kernel-to-hardware interfaces known as the "sun4c" kernel architecture. The key design goal was to keep the cost down, so all main memory accesses and I/O are carried by a single 32-bit SBus. A small set of very highly integrated chips was used to implement these machines, so they all share a great many architectural details. Compared to the earlier Sun-4 machines, they have a smaller 64-Kbyte cache, a simplified version of the Sun-4 MMU, and smaller main memory system. The I/O bus changes from VME to SBus, and unlike previous systems, the SBus is also used to carry all the CPU to memory system traffic. The CPU boards are much smaller than before, despite the inclusion of more I/O options as standard. See Figure 8-1.

In earlier machines (the SS1, 1+, IPC, and SLC), there is a single clock rate for the whole system, and main memory can only provide data at half speed, so there is a wait cycle on the SBus between each cycle of data transfer from memory. The SBus DMA interface on these machines performed only single-word transfers on the SBus, and the overhead of acquiring the bus and sending the address for every word severely limited DMA transfer rates.

In later machines (the SS2, IPX, ELC), the CPU Integer Unit (IU), Floating Point Unit (FPU), Memory Management Unit (MMU), and Cache are clocked at twice the speed of the SBus, and the memory system uses faster DRAM to transfer data on every cycle. A newer version of the SBus DMA, called DMA+, transferred up to four words at a time on the Sbus, for much better performance.

Figure 8-1   The SPARCstation 1, 1+, IPC, SLC, 2, IPX, and ELC Family System Architecture

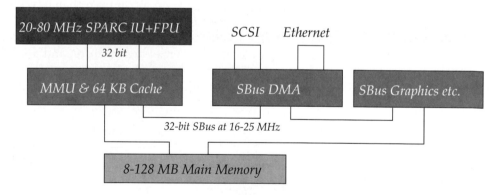

An upgrade for the SPARCstation IPX and SPARCstation 2 is available from Weitek and is called the PowerUP™. It consists of a plug-in replacement CPU chip that runs at 80 MHz internally, using a 16-Kbyte instruction cache and an 8-Kbyte data cache. It uses the external 64-Kbyte cache as a second level. Generally, the rest of the system hardware and software doesn't need to know that anything is different, so it is quite compatible and substantially faster.

I have had to provide two sets of benchmark results for these machines, shown in Tables 8-2 and 8 3, as results for the early machines were only published using SPEC89. Later ones were published using SPEC92 as well; those results are quoted for the remainder of the systems in this chapter.

Table 8-2   SPEC89 Benchmark Results for First Generation SPARC Desktops

Machine	MHz	SPECmark89	Compiler
SPARCstation 1	20	8.8	SunPro 1.0[1]
SPARCstation SLC	20	8.8	SunPro 1.0
SPARCstation 1+ (old compiler)	25	11.8	SunPro 1.0
SPARCstation 1+ (new compiler)	25	13.5	SunPro 2.0[2]
SPARCstation IPC	25	13.5	SunPro 2.0
SPARCstation ELC	33	20.3	SunPro 2.0
SPARCstation IPX	40	24.4	SunPro 2.0
SPARCstation 2	40	25.0	SunPro 2.0

1. The SunPro 1.0 code generator was used by C 1.1 and F77 1.4

2. The SunPro 2.0 code generator was used by C 2.0 and F77 2.0

Table 8-3   SPEC92 Benchmark Results for First Generation SPARC Desktops

Machine	MHz	SPECint92	Compiler	SPECfp92	Compiler
SPARCstation 1	20	N/A		N/A	
SPARCstation SLC	20	N/A		N/A	
SPARCstation 1+	25	13.8	SunPro 2.0	11.1	SunPro 2.0
SPARCstation IPC	25	13.8	SunPro 2.0	11.1	SunPro 2.0
SPARCstation ELC	33	18.2	SunPro 2.0	17.9	SunPro 2.0
SPARCstation IPX	40	21.8	SunPro 2.0	21.5	SunPro 2.0
SPARCstation 2	40	21.8	SunPro 2.0	22.7	SunPro 2.0
SPARCstation 2 PowerUP	80	32.2	SunPro 2.0	31.1	SunPro 2.0

Second Generation Uniprocessor Desktop SPARC Systems

The design goal was to provide performance comparable to that of the SPARCstation 2, but at the lowest possible cost, using the highest levels of integration. The resulting pair of machines were the SPARCclassic and the SPARCstation LX. A large number of chips from the previous designs were combined, and the highly integrated microSPARC CPU was used. microSPARC has a much smaller cache than the SPARCstation 2, but compensates with a higher clock frequency and a faster memory system to get slightly higher overall performance. The 6-Kbyte cache is split into a 4-Kbyte instruction cache and a 2-Kbyte data cache[2]. Unlike previous designs, the sun4m kernel architecture is used along with a SPARC Reference Memory Management Unit (SRMMU)[3]. The memory bus is 64-bits wide rather than 32, and main memory traffic does not use the same data path as SBus I/O traffic, which improves performance for both memory-intensive and I/O-intensive applications. The SBus DMA controller is integrated along with SCSI, Ethernet, and high-speed parallel ports into a single chip. The difference between the two machines is that the SPARCstation LX adds a GX graphics accelerator, ISDN interface and CD quality audio to the basic SPARCclassic design. Figure 8-2 illustrates the architecture; Table 8-4 summarizes the benchmark results.

Figure 8-2   The SPARCstation LX and SPARCclassic Family System Architecture

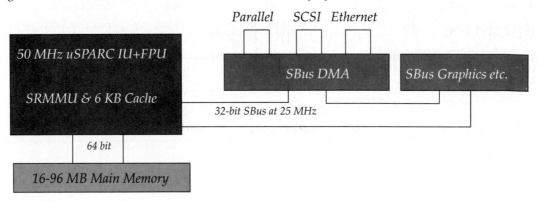

Table 8-4   SPEC Benchmark Results for Second Generation SPARC Desktops

Machine	MHz	SPECint92	Compiler	SPECfp92	Compiler
SPARCclassic	50	26.3	SunPro 3.0	20.9	Apogee 0.82
SPARCstation LX	50	26.3	SunPro 3.0	20.9	Apogee 0.82

2. See "On-chip Caches" on page 158 for more details.

3. See "The SPARC Reference MMU — sun4m and sun4d Kernel Architectures" on page 167.

Third Generation Uniprocessor Desktop SPARC Systems

Following the SPARCclassic and the SPARCstation LX, a much faster version of the microSPARC processor called microSPARC II has been developed, and is used in the SPARCstation 5 and SPARCstation™ Voyager™. The main differences are that microSPARC II has a much larger cache, runs at higher clock rates, and has a special graphics interface on the memory bus to augment the usual SBus graphics cards. As in the original microSPARC, the sun4m kernel architecture is used along with the SPARC Reference MMU. The SPARCstation™ Voyager™ is a nomadic system, and it has an integrated driver for a large LCD, flat-screen display, power management hardware, and a PCMCIA bus interface via the SBus. The speed of the SBus is either 1/3, 1/4, or 1/5 of the processor speed, since the SBus standard specifies a maximum of 25 MHz. This gives rise to some odd SBus rates at the 70 and 85 MHz clock rates used in the two versions of the SPARCstation 5. I have shown 125 MHz as the maximum clock rate, since this is the maximum speed that can be divided down into a standard SBus specification. Figure 8-3 illustrates the architecture; Table 8-5 summarizes the benchmark results.

Figure 8-3   The SPARCstation Voyager and SPARCstation 5 Family System Architecture

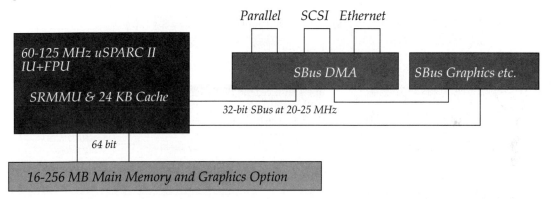

Table 8-5   SPEC Benchmark Results for Third Generation SPARC Desktops

Machine	MHz	SPECint92	Compiler	SPECfp92	Compiler
SPARCstation Voyager	60	47.5	Apogee 2.951	40.3	Apogee 2.951
SPARCstation 5	70	57.0	Apogee 2.951	47.3	Apogee 2.951
SPARCstation 5	85	64.1	Apogee 2.951	54.6	Apogee 2.951

Entry-level Multiprocessor-capable Desktop

The SPARCstation 10 and SPARCstation 20 are often used as uniprocessors, particularly since SunOS 4 is not supported on multiprocessor configurations. These machines are multiprocessor capable since the SPARC modules can be upgraded and a second module can be added. The diagram shown in Figure 8-4 is rather complex, but later sections will refer to this diagram as the details are explained. The entry-level models do not include the 1 Mbyte SuperCache, so the processor is directly connected to the MBus and takes its clock signal from the bus. The SX option shown in the diagram is supported only on the SPARCstation 10SX and all SPARCstation 20 models. These models also have a 64-bit SBus interface, although it is not supported until Solaris 2.4, and the only 64-bit SBus device available is the FiberChannel SOC/S used with the SPARCstorage Array.

Figure 8-4   SPARCstation 10 Model 30, 40, and SPARCstation 20 Model 50 Organization

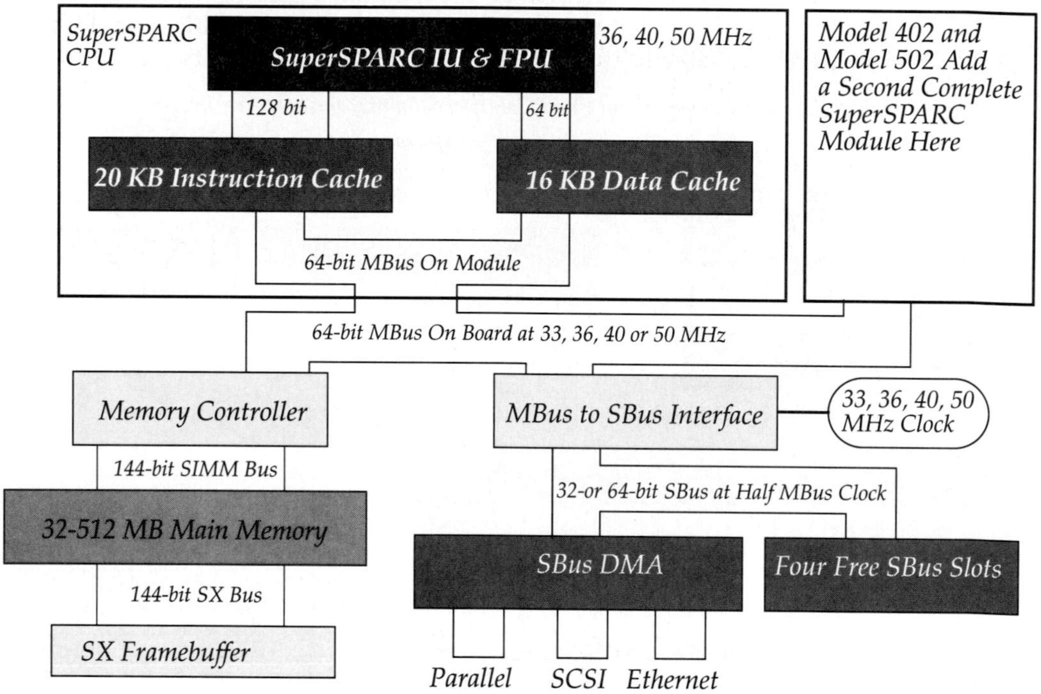

Table 8-6   SPEC Benchmark Results for Entry-level MP-capable Desktops

Machine	MHz	SPECint92	Compiler	SPECfp92	Compiler
SPARCstation 10 Model 30	36	45.2	SunPro 3.0α	54.0	Apogee 1.059
SPARCstation 10 Model 40	40	50.2	SunPro 3.0α	60.2	Apogee 1.059
SPARCstation 20 Model 50	50	69.2	Apogee 2.3	78.8	Apogee 2.3

Multiprocessor-capable Desktop and Server

The SPARCserver 600 was the first machine to use multiprocessor-capable architecture. It has a VMEbus interface coming off the SBus as shown in Figure 8-5. It also uses a different memory controller and SIMM type that gives more RAM capacity by using extra boards; there is no SX interface or parallel port. The SPARCstation 10 and 20 are as described in the previous section except for the addition of a SuperCache controller and 1 Mbyte of cache RAM. There are now two clocks in the machine, the SPARC module clock and the system clock. In the performance table both are shown as "module/system."

Figure 8-5   SPARCsystem 10, 20, and 600 Model 41, 51, and 61 Organization

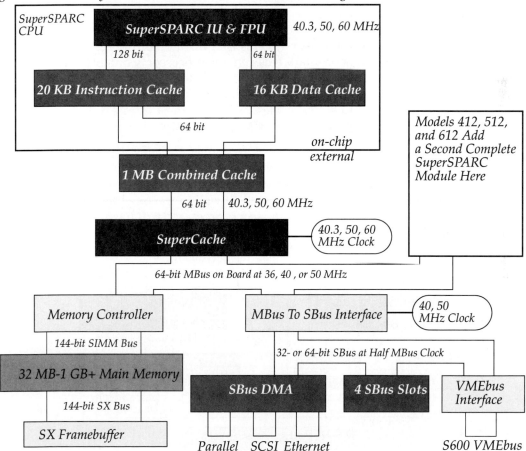

Table 8-7   SPEC Benchmark Results for High-end MP-capable Desktops and Servers

Machine	MHz	SPECint92	Compiler	SPECfp92	Compiler
SPARCserver 600 Model 41	40.33/40	53.2	SunPro 3.0α	67.8	Apogee 1.059
SPARCstation 10 Model 41	40.33/40	53.2	SunPro 3.0α	67.8	Apogee 1.059
SPARCstation 10 Model 51	50/40	65.0	SunPro 3.0α	83.0	Apogee 2.3
SPARCstation 20 Model 51	50/40	73.6	Apogee 2.3	84.8	Apogee 2.3
SPARCstation 20 Model 61	60/50	88.9	Apogee 2.3	102.8	Apogee 2.3

Adding More Processors

The benchmark used for multiprocessor systems is SPECrate; for the results shown, one copy of the standard SPEC92 benchmark was run per processor. Contention for memory reduces the multiprocessor results. The result is scaled into units of jobs per unit time, but there is a constant scale factor of 23.72 for all uniprocessor results between the SPECint92 and SPECrate_int92 values, and between the SPECfp92 and SPECrate_fp92 values. A summary showing scaling ratios is given in "Desktop Multiprocessor Scalability Summary" on page 116.

In the SPARCstation 10 Model 402MP and the SPARCstation 20 Model 502MP, two SuperSPARC+ processors are directly connected to the memory, as shown in Figure 8-6. If one processor is running a program that doesn't fit well in the on-chip caches and it makes heavy use of main memory, then the second processor will have to wait longer for its memory accesses to complete and will not run at full speed. This diagram has been simplified to show only the SPARC modules and the memory system.

Figure 8-6   SPARCstation 10 Model 402MP and SPARCstation 20 Model 502MP Cache[4] Organization

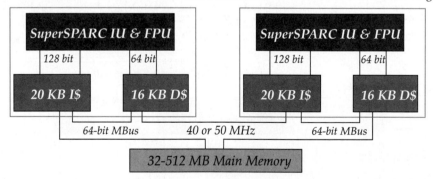

---

4. The symbol "$" is commonly used as an abbreviation for the word "cache" (cash).

Table 8-8   SPEC Rate Benchmark Results for Entry-level Multiprocessor Desktops

Machine	MHz	Rate_int92	Compiler	Rate_fp92	Compiler
SPARCstation 10 Model 40	40	1191	Apogee 2.3	1427	Apogee 2.3
SPARCstation 10 Model 402	40	2112	Apogee 2.3	2378	Apogee 2.3
SPARCstation 20 Model 50	50	1641	Apogee 2.3	1869	Apogee 2.3
SPARCstation 20 Model 502	50	2833	Apogee 2.3	2995	Apogee 2.3

In the Model 412MP, Model 512MP, Model 612MP, and Model 514MP, each processor has its own SuperCache™ as shown in Figure 8-7. This reduces the number of references to main memory from each processor so that there is less contention for the available memory bandwidth. The 60 MHz processors run hotter than the 50 MHz ones and cooling limits in the package prevent a Model 614MP from being configured. When the 50 MHz parts are used in the SPARCstation 20, it automatically senses and reduces its MBus clock rate from 50 MHz to 40 MHz, this maintains the clock rate difference required for synchronization, but it is unfortunate that the system that needs the fastest possible MBus doesn't get it.

Figure 8-7   The SPARCsystem 10, 20, and 600 Model 514MP Cache Organization

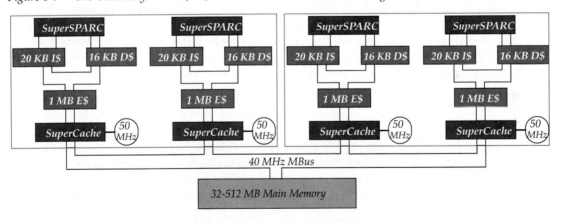

Table 8-9   SPEC Rate Benchmark Results for SuperSPARC Desktops

Machine	MHz	Rate_int92	Compiler	Rate_fp92	Compiler
SPARCstation 10 Model 51	50/40	1731	Apogee 2.3	1995	Apogee 2.3
SPARCstation 10 Model 512	50/40	2950	Apogee 2.3	3744	Apogee 2.3
SPARCstation 20 Model 61	60/50	2109	Apogee 2.3	2438	Apogee 2.3
SPARCstation 20 Model 612	60/50	3903	Apogee 2.3	4645	Apogee 2.3
SPARCstation 20 Model 514	50/40	6142	Apogee 2.3	6812	Apogee 2.3

Desktop Multiprocessor Scalability Summary

Table 8-10 Summary Showing Multiprocessor Scalability Ratios

Machine	Rate int92	Rate / 23.72	MP Scale	Rate fp92	Rate / 23.72	MP Scale
SPARCstation 10 Model 40	1191	50.2	1.00	1427	60.2	1.00
SPARCstation 10 Model 402	2112	89.1	1.77	2378	100.3	1.67
SPARCstation 20 Model 50	1641	69.2	1.00	1869	78.8	1.00
SPARCstation 20 Model 502	2833	119.5	1.73	2995	126.3	1.60
SPARCstation 10 Model 51	1731	73.0	1.00	1995	84.1	1.00
SPARCstation 10 Model 512	2950	124.4	1.70	3744	157.9	1.88
SPARCstation 20 Model 61	2109	88.9	1.00	2438	102.8	1.00
SPARCstation 20 Model 612	3903	164.6	1.85	4645	195.9	1.91
SPARCstation 20 Model 51	1748	73.7	1.00	2011	84.8	1.00
SPARCstation 20 Model 514	6142	259.0	3.51	6812	287.3	3.39

In this table I start with the SPECrate value, divide down to more familiar units of "times faster than a VAX 11/780," and calculate the scale factor between the uniprocessor and multiprocessor versions of the same CPU type. The usual benchmark caveat applies here — your own workload is unlikely to be multiple copies of SPEC92 and will probably scale differently. What is interesting is to see that the addition of the 1-Mbyte cache improves the scalability significantly, especially for the floating-point benchmarks.

When used with an external cache on each processor the memory system has more headroom to support the four processor Model 514MP. The point at which the main memory system becomes saturated is application-and operating system-dependent. Later releases of Solaris 2 use much less backplane bandwidth than do earlier releases on multiprocessor machines. Further tuning is in progress both to make the kernel use the cache more efficiently and to reduce the cache footprint of shared libraries and applications.

SPARC-based Multiprocessor Hardware

There are two classes of multiprocessor machines based on SPARC architecture: 1-to 4-processor MBus-based systems; and high-end systems with up to 8, 20, or 64 processors. Their system architectures are quite different and both are quite complex. Before I summarize the performance of the high end server range we will take a more in-depth look at SuperSPARC, the MP architectures, and the differences between the two classes.

This material is based on parts extracted from two white papers that I wrote, *"SPARCstation 10 Product Line Technical White Paper"* and *"A Scalable Server Architecture for Department to Enterprise — The SPARCserver 1000 and the SPARCcenter 2000."* The second of these was in turn partly based upon *"The SPARCcenter 2000 Architecture and Implementation White Paper"* by Brian Wong.

Bus Architectures Overview

There are two things to consider about bus performance. The peak data rate is easily quoted, but the ability of the devices on the bus to source or sink data at that rate for more than a few cycles is the real limit to performance. The second consideration is whether the bus protocol includes cycles that do not transfer data, thus reducing the sustained data throughput.

Older buses like VMEbus usually transfer one word at a time so that each bus cycle includes the overhead of deciding which device will access the bus next (arbitration) as well as setting up the address and transferring the data. This is rather inefficient, so more recent buses like SBus and MBus transfer data in blocks. Arbitration can take place once per block, then, a single address is set up and multiple cycles of data are transferred. The protocol gives better throughput if more data is transferred in each bus transaction. For example, SPARCserver 600MP systems are optimized for a standard transaction size of 32 bytes by providing 32-byte buffers in all the devices that access the bus and using a 32-byte cache line. The SPARCcenter 2000 is optimized for 64-byte transactions.

Circuit-switched Bus Protocols

One class of bus protocols effectively opens a circuit between the source and destination of the transaction and holds on to the bus until the transaction has finished and the circuit is closed. This protocol is simple to implement, but when a transfer from a slow device like main memory to a fast device like a CPU cache (a cache read) occurs, there must be a number of wait states to let the main memory DRAM access complete in the interval between sending the address to memory and the data returning. These wait states reduce cache read throughput, and nothing else can happen while the circuit is open. The faster the CPU clock rate, the more clock cycles are wasted. On a uniprocessor this just adds to the cache miss time, but on a multiprocessor the number of CPUs that a bus can handle is drastically reduced by the wait time. Note that a fast device like a cache can write data with no delays to the memory system write buffer. MBus uses this type of protocol and is suitable for up to four CPUs.

Packet-switched Bus Protocols

To make use of the wait time, a bus transaction must be split into a request packet and a response packet. This protocol is hard to implement because the response must contain some identification and a device on the bus such as the memory system may have to queue up additional requests coming in while it is trying to respond to the first one.

A protocol called XBus, extends the basic MBus interface to implement a packet-switched protocol in the SuperCache controller chip used with SuperSPARC. This extension provides more than twice the throughput of MBus and is designed to be used in larger multiprocessor machines that have more than four CPUs on the bus. The SPARCcenter 2000 uses XBus within each CPU board and multiple, interleaved XBuses on its interboard backplane. The backplane bus is called XDBus. On the SPARCserver 1000 there is a single XDBus, and on the SPARCcenter 2000 there is a twin XDBus. On the Cray Superserver CS6400 there is a quadruple XDBus running at a higher clock rate.

Table 8-11 SPARC Multiprocessor Bus Characteristics

Bus Name	Clock	Peak Bandwidth	Read Throughput	Write Throughput
Solbourne KBus	16 MHz	128 Mbytes/s	66 Mbytes/s	90 Mbytes/s
ICL HSPBus	16 MHz	128 Mbytes/s	66 Mbytes/s	90 Mbytes/s
MBus	40 MHz	320 Mbytes/s	90 Mbytes/s	200 Mbytes/s
XBus	40 MHz	320 Mbytes/s	250 Mbytes/s	250 Mbytes/s
Single XDBus	40 MHz	320 Mbytes/s	250 Mbytes/s	250 Mbytes/s
Dual XDBus	40 MHz	640 Mbytes/s	500 Mbytes/s	500 Mbytes/s
Quad XDBus	55 MHz	1760 Mbytes/s	1375 Mbytes/s	1375 Mbytes/s

MP Cache Issues

In systems that have more than one cache on the bus, a problem arises when the same data is stored in more than one cache and the data is modified. A cache coherency protocol and special cache tag information are needed to keep track of the data. The basic solution is for all the caches to include logic that watches the transactions on the bus (known as snooping the bus) and look for transactions that use data that is being held by that cache[5]. The I/O subsystem on Sun's multiprocessor machines has its own MMU and

---

5. This is described very well in the *SPARCserver 10 and SPARCserver 600 Performance Brief*.

cache, so that full bus snooping support is provided for DVMA[6] I/O transfers. The coherency protocol that MBus defines uses invalidate transactions that are sent from the cache that owns the data when the data is modified. This procedure technique invalidates any other copies of that data in the rest of the system. When a cache tries to read some data, the data is provided by the owner of that data, which may not be the memory system, so cache-to-cache transfers occur. An MBus option that is implemented in Sun's MBus-based system is that the memory system grabs a copy of the data as it goes from cache to cache and updates itself[7].

The cache coherency protocol slows down the bus throughput slightly compared to a uniprocessor system with a simple uncached I/O architecture (reflected in extra cycles for cache miss processing). This slowdown is a particular problem with the Ross CPU module used in the first generation SPARCserver 600 systems. The cache is organized as a 32-bit-wide bank of memory, whereas the MBus transfers 64-bit-wide data at the full cache clock rate. A 32-byte buffer in the 7C605 cache controller takes the data from the MBus, then passes it onto the cache. This extra level of buffering increases cache miss cost but makes sure that the MBus is freed early to start the next transaction. This also makes cache-to-cache transfers take longer. The SuperSPARC with SuperCache module has a 64-bit-wide cache organization, so the intermediate buffer is not needed. This extra efficiency helps the existing bus and memory system cope with the extra load generated by CPUs that are two to three times faster than the original Ross CPUs and future SuperSPARC modules that may double performance again.

MBus Machines with Up to Four CPUs

There are three generations of machines in this category: the SPARCserver 600 range, the SPARCstation 10, and the SPARCstation 20. They are so similar, yet there are so many model options, that it is best to concentrate on just the common parts of the implementation. The SPARCstation 600 was the first implementation; if its VMEbus interface is removed, then it is almost identical to the SPARCstation 10. The SPARCstation 20 reworks a higher clock rate version of the SPARCstation 10 into a lower-cost package.

To help you understand the architecture, I will take an inside look at the SPARCstation 10 Model 40 and Model 41 to see what goes on and how the caches fit into the picture; omitting the more complex details of the implementation [8]. Refer to Figure 8-4 on page 112 and Figure 8-5 on page 113 for block diagrams of the architecture.

---

6. DVMA stands for Direct Virtual Memory Access. It is used by intelligent I/O devices that write data directly into memory, using virtual addresses, for example, the disk and network interfaces.

7. This is known as *reflective memory*.

8. An in-depth description can be found in *"The SuperSPARC Microprocessor Technical White Paper."* A more rigorous technical explanation of caches can be found in *Computer Architecture - A Quantitative Approach*, by Hennessy and Patterson.

The Model 40 SuperSPARC processor runs at 40 MHz. Another way of looking at this is to say that one clock cycle takes 25 nanoseconds. During that one clock cycle, the SuperSPARC processor can execute three instructions, including a load or store of one piece of data. Each instruction is a 32-bit value and the data can be up to 64 bits, so in each cycle the SuperSPARC processor can access up to five 32-bit words. If any of these five words takes longer than 25 nanoseconds to access, then the processor will stop processing for a number of clock cycles and wait until the access is completed.

The main memory on the SPARCstation 10 consists of 32 Mbytes (or more) of RAM. The RAM chips themselves are rated at 80 nanoseconds, but this is only part of the access time, and it takes many clock cycles to read or write main memory. The memory is connected to the processors via MBus, which is a 64-bit-wide bus also running at 40 MHz.

The main memory cannot provide more than two 32-bit words in each clock cycle over the MBus, and it also takes several clock cycles between the processor specifying the memory address and the access completing. Since the SuperSPARC processor needs to have five words immediately available in every clock cycle to run at full speed, a small amount of very fast CPU cache memory is used.

The idea behind a cache is that programs often spend a large amount of time in a small amount of program code, such as a loop. They also tend to keep accessing a small number of data locations repeatedly. The code and the data values can be held in the cache where access times are one cycle. A cache works because *on average* memory locations that are close together will be accessed at about the same time. Memory locations tend to be accessed repeatedly in a short period of time so the whole program does not need to be held in the cache. It is possible to construct programs that do not behave in this way, and get poor performance on machines that have caches. For the last few years, *every* new machine in the industry has been built with a cache, but most software is still written without taking the cache into account. These issues are described in more detail in "Cache Tutorial" on page 151.

The SuperSPARC processor has its cache built onto the chip, the cache being the largest part of the chip, taking approximately half the total number of transistors. SuperSPARC is one of the largest CPU chips on the market, with over 3 million transistors, and several years after introduction, it still has more on-chip cache than any of its competitors.

The cache is split in two, with 20 kilobytes dedicated to feeding instructions into the processor and another 16 Kbytes used to hold data. The 20-Kbyte instruction cache is 128 bits wide, and four instructions can be read from the cache in a single clock cycle. The 16-Kbyte data cache is 64 bits wide and can be read or written in one clock cycle. Both caches can be accessed in the same clock cycle, so are able to keep the SuperSPARC processor running at full speed.

Cache Block Transfers

A method is needed for keeping track of what's in the cache as well as for transferring code and data from memory to the cache and back. The processor will stall if it tries to access data that is not in the cache, and it will continue when the data arrives from main memory. The best performance is obtained by minimizing the number of times that the processor stalls (known as a cache miss) and minimizing the time taken to get the data into the cache (known as the cache miss cost). The cache hit rate is the percentage of the time that the processor found the data in the cache.

On the SPARCstation 10, the memory system is designed to work with 32-byte blocks of memory; the cache also uses 32 bytes (8 words) as its cache block size. The amount of data loaded into the cache from memory is always 32 bytes, even if the processor only tried to access one byte. On average, memory locations that are adjacent are often used at about the same time, so the extra data or instructions that are loaded are quite likely to be used, reducing the number of cache misses. If they are not used, then extra, unproductive work has been performed. On a SPARCstation 10 Model 40, the SuperSPARC processor takes approximately 10 clock cycles the first time a memory location is accessed, but subsequent accesses to that location and accesses to the rest of the 32-byte cache block take one cycle.

The cache hardware keeps track of each block of data by remembering its memory address. It also notes whether the data in the cache has been written to, and in multiprocessor machines, it notes whether the same block of data is in a cache on another processor, since shared data must be handled specially. Every 4-Kbyte page of memory maps directly to the caches, so the hardware only has to remember which page the cache block was from. The data cache holds 16 Kbytes so there are four possible places to put each cache block; the instruction cache holds 20 Kbytes, so there are five possible places to put each cache block[9]. When several blocks are loaded at the same page address (e.g., the first word in several different pages is accessed at about the same time), each cache block is loaded into a different part of the cache. After four different data accesses at the same part of a page, the next different access at that address will overwrite the least recently used block. If the block had been written to, then it is written back to memory before the new line is loaded. Figure 8-8 illustrates these principles.

---

9. The number of places data can be put into a cache is known as the "associativity" of the cache.

Figure 8-8   Main Memory and Data Cache Mapping

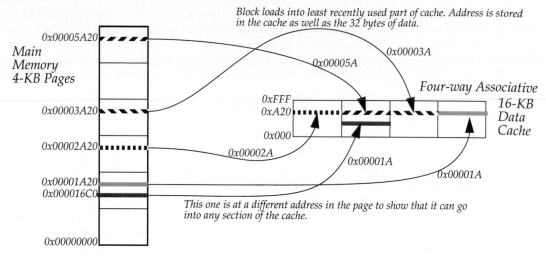

SuperSPARC has a much more complex and efficient on-chip cache than most other systems have. The type of on-chip cache used in other processors usually allows only one possible location for each cache block. Thus, if two blocks that are being used intensively try to use the same cache line the hardware caches only one of them at a time, and the processor wastes time stalled in cache misses.

Adding a Second-level Cache

The SPARCstation 10 Model 41 contains everything that is in a SPARCstation 10 Model 40. It runs the CPU module at 40.33 MHz and the MBus at 40.0 MHz. Since there are two independent clocks, they synchronize more quickly if there is a slight clock speed difference. It also contains a SuperCache controller and 1 Mbyte of extra cache RAM. This cache holds both instructions and data and is direct mapped[10], so there is only one location where a cache line can be loaded. Each megabyte of physical memory is mapped directly onto the one megabyte cache. Due to the virtual memory system, the arrangement of 4-Kbyte pages in use by a program usually maps to the 1 Mbyte differently each time the program is run, so it is important to run simple benchmarks multiple times. This section explains where the external 1 Mbyte cache fits and how it affects the behavior of the system. See Figure 8-5 on page 113.

---

10. The on-chip caches are four-way and five-way associative; the off-chip cache is one-way associative or direct mapped.

The external cache is located between the on-chip cache and the main memory. The SuperCache controller provides the interface to memory via the MBus at a fixed 40 MHz clock rate, but a clock crystal is used to set the speed of the SuperSPARC, its on-chip caches, and the external 1-Mbyte cache to a higher clock rate. The Model 41 actually runs at 40.3 MHz; the slight speed mismatch is used to obtain synchronization between the CPU module clock and the motherboard system clock. The Model 51 runs its caches and CPU at 50 MHz, and the SPARCstation 20 Model 61 runs its MBus at 50 MHz and its CPU at 60 MHz.

The effect of the external 1-Mbyte cache is that the time taken to load a block of 32 bytes into the on-chip cache is halved, from approximately 10 cycles to 5 cycles, as long as the data is already in the 1-Mbyte cache. For programs that do not fit into 36 Kbytes but that do not intensively access more than 1 Mbyte the cache doubles the effective speed of main memory on the Model 41. For the Model 51, 61, and future machines that run at even higher clock rates, the 1 Mbyte of cache speeds up with the processor, whereas the main memory does not, and this becomes more important. The SPARCstation 20 has a higher MBus speed and a faster memory system using 60-ns SIMMs rather than 80-ns SIMMs, but both the SPARCstation 10 and the SPARCstation 20 are designed to last a long time as a desktop chassis, with successive generations of module upgrades going to 100 MHz or above, and the external cache becomes more and more important as the clock rate rises.

If the data is not in either cache, then there is extra work to do. First the on-chip cache must be checked, the data is not found, so the external cache is checked, the data is still not found, so main memory is asked for the data. The data returns and is loaded into the external cache, it is then copied into the on-chip cache, and finally the processor can continue. Main memory access takes about four times longer on a Model 41 than it does on a Model 40.

The comparison between the Model 40 and Model 41 can fall three ways.

- The Model 41 will sometimes work within its on-chip cache and will perform at the same level as a Model 40, so the external cache is irrelevant and performance will be similar to that of a Model 40.

- The Model 41 will sometimes exceed the capacity of the 36 Kbytes of on-chip cache, but work within the external 1 Mbyte cache. Its cache miss costs will be halved compared to a Model 40, so performance will be better than that of a Model 40.

- The Model 41 will sometimes exceed the capacity of the 1-Mbyte cache. Its cache miss costs will be quadrupled, so performance will be lower than that of a Model 40.

Programs spend a varying proportion of their execution time in all of the above modes. Caches work on a statistical basis, and, on average, a 1-Mbyte cache is big enough for most applications.

The SuperCache controller also implements in hardware some extra functions that can be used by the kernel to perform block copies and block zeroes of memory without passing the data through the cache.The controller can keep track of the number of references made by the CPU to the 1-Mbyte cache, as well as the number of cache misses, where it had to access main memory. A special device driver can extract this information but is not provided as a standard part of the operating system.

A Scalable Server Architecture for High-end MP

The high-end server marketplace is a particularly challenging one to design for with several conflicting trade-offs to be made. In particular, there is a wide range of capacity and performance requirements, but relatively low production volumes compared to the workstation marketplace. For most vendors, this leads to a product line that includes many low-volume machines, each spanning a small performance range, and with high upgrade costs for users moving up the range. The design costs for each model are amortized over a relatively small production run, the manufacturing process is less automated, and the pricing is correspondingly higher than for volume workstation products.

Sun has been moving into the server marketplace for some time, using the high-volume economics of the workstation production process to push commodity pricing into the low end and mid-range server markets. After launching the multiprocessor SPARCserver 600MP range in 1991, Sun became the number one vendor of multiprocessor UNIX servers by both unit shipments and installed base during 1992, surpassing several companies that had been specializing in this type of machine for many years.

The Scalable SPARC server architecture brings this approach to the high end of the server marketplace. Two packages are used to deliver the architecture; one low-cost package that can sit on or beside a desk in an office environment, and one package which maximizes expansion capacity, for the data center. These two packages contain scaled versions of the same architecture, and the investment in IC designs and operating system porting and tuning is shared by both machines. The same architecture is used by Cray Research SuperServers, Inc. in their much larger CS6400 package.

A key theme of this SPARC server architecture is that it is built from a small number of highly integrated components that are replicated to produce the required configuration. Several of these components, including processor modules and SBus I/O cards, are identical to those used in the high volume workstation product line, which reduces per-processor costs and provides a wide choice of I/O options. The system design that connects processors, I/O, and memory over multiple, high-speed buses is implemented in a small number of complex ASICs, which reduces the number of ICs on each board, easing manufacture, reducing cost, and increasing reliability.

Compared to an MBus system, with one to four processors connected to one memory bank and one SBus, the additional throughput of the SPARCserver 1000 and SPARCcenter 2000 comes from the use of many more processors interconnected via substantially faster buses to multiple, independent memory banks and multiple SBuses, as summarized in Table 8-12.

Table 8-12 SPARCserver System Expansion Comparisons

Machine	SS 10, 20	SS 1000	SC 2000	CS6400
SuperSPARC Clock Rate	40, 50, 60 MHz	50 MHz	50 MHz	60 MHz
CPU External Cache	Optional 1 MB	1 MB	1 MB or 2 MB	2 MB
Max Number of CPUs	4	8	20	64
Total Memory	32–512 MB	32–2048 MB	64–5120 MB	128 MB–16 GB
Memory Banks	1 512 MB	4 x 512 MB	20 x 256 MB	64 x 256 MB
SBus I/O Slots	4 at 20–25 MHz	12 at 20 MHz	40 at 20 MHz	64 at 25 MHz
Independent SBuses	1@40–100 MB/s	4@50 MB/s	10@50 MB/s	16@60 MB/s
Interconnect	MBus	XDBus	2 x XDBus	4 x XDBus
Speed and Width	40, 50 MHz, 64 bits	40 MHz, 64 bits	40 MHz, 64 bits	55 MHz, 64 bits
Interconnect Throughput	105 MB/s	250 MB/s	500 MB/s	1500 MB/s
Internal Disk Capacity	2 x 2.1 GB	4 to 16^2 x 535 MB	18 x 2.9 GB	
Maximum Disk Capacity[1]	250 GB	750 GB	2 TB	3 TB

1. Assuming two SPARCstorage Arrays at 30 GB each on most available SBus slots.

2. Four are packaged; additional internal disks take the place of system boards.

Architectural Requirements

A server architecture must have high ultimate capacity. Even when a small configuration is used, there must be room to expand as the workload increases. The system must be optimized for throughput. The ability to process a large number of concurrent jobs or transactions is the top priority. Applications running on servers are often a critical part of the infrastructure of a company, so reliability and high availability must be designed into the architecture.

Capacity

The architecture consists of multiple, high-performance SuperSPARC CPUs connected to multiple memory controllers and many independent SBuses for I/O. The primary limitations to the capacity of an implementation are the physical constraints of available board area and package dimensions; the SPARCcenter 2000 implementation is the largest configuration that can be fitted into a standard Sun rack-mount cabinet.

Throughput

There are multiple, high-capacity, packet-switched XDBuses connecting the functional units in the architecture. To keep the throughput of the system in balance with the number of CPU and I/O buses, systems can be implemented with one, two, or four XDBuses. Memory banks are interleaved across multiple XDBuses to balance the workload and to improve performance by distributing sequential requests across multiple memory banks. An XDBus is usually configured to support approximately ten SuperSPARC CPUs and five SBuses. To manage the throughput of the hardware, the multithreaded Solaris 2 kernel allows all CPUs to share the interrupt load and I/O processing requirements.

Reliability and Availability

Throughout the design, the use of highly integrated components provides exceptional reliability. A novel, transmission line technology called GTL is used on all buses, allowing much higher clock rates and better noise immunity than the usual CMOS allows. The architecture provides error correction code (ECC) protected memory with parity protection on all buses for both the data path and control signals to detect errors. On power-up, or after the system detects an error and reboots, an advanced system testing and configuration process is used. Failed components can be identified and configured out of the system, enabling continued operation for high-availability applications.

Architectural Overview

Building Blocks

The architecture is based on a small number of building blocks, which are combined in three configurations to produce the SPARCserver 1000, SPARCcenter 2000, and CS6400. This section looks at the individual blocks; the next section examines the combinations used to build each system board and the way in which system boards are connected. One key feature of the design is the unprecedented level of integration of the circuitry. In most cases, a single ASIC implements the complete functionality of a major subsystem, and there is virtually no support logic or "glue" in the design. The effect of compressing a huge amount of functionality into a very small space can be seen in the compact dimensions of the SPARCserver 1000 and the high capacity of the full size SPARCcenter 2000 rack. Figure 8-9 illustrates these building blocks.

Figure 8-9   The CPU, I/O, and Memory Building Blocks of the SPARCserver 1000

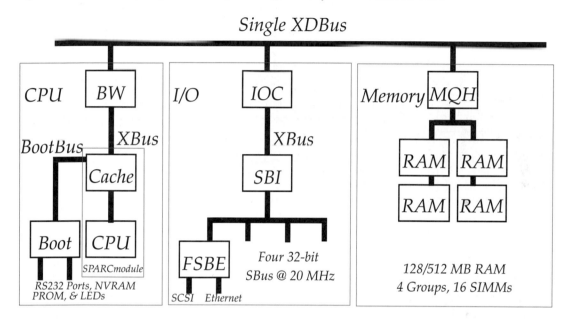

XDBus System Interconnect

At the heart of the SPARCserver 1000 is an XDBus — a high-speed, packet-switched, backplane bus that provides very high data transfer bandwidth. A single instance of this bus has a nominal bandwidth of 320 Mbytes/s. In addition, its packet-switched design means the bus will be able to deliver a high proportion of this bandwidth, typically sustaining 250 Mbytes/s. By comparison, typical circuit-switched buses can provide only a fraction of their peak bandwidths under load. The SPARCcenter 2000 uses twin interleaved XDBuses that provide even higher bandwidth and higher availability, since the SPARCcenter 2000 can continue to operate even when one of its XDBuses has failed. In practice, the paired buses provide overall throughput of approximately 500 Mbytes/s. The architecture supports up to four XDBuses in a single machine; and the Cray SuperServer CS6400 pushes the technology further by running its four XDbuses at 55 MHz to get a total of about 1500 Mbytes/s throughput. Figure 8-10 illustrates the building blocks of the SPARCcenter 2000.

Figure 8-10 The CPU, I/O and Dual Memory Building Blocks of the SPARCcenter 2000

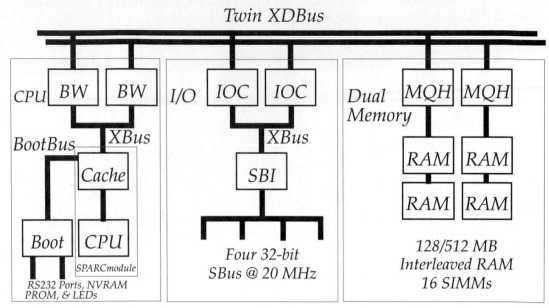

CPU Building Blocks

Attached to the XDBus to form a symmetric, shared-memory multiprocessor are a number of CPUs. These are packaged in removable SPARCmodules identical to those used in the high-end workstation product line, containing a 50 or 60 MHz SuperSPARC, SuperCache controller,[11] and 1 Mbyte of external cache. The module detects which type of machine it is plugged in to and uses a more advanced XBus packet-switched interface protocol that can take advantage of the full XDBus bandwidth. A large ASIC, called the bus watcher (BW), connects each CPU to each XDBus. A special feature of the SPARCcenter 2000 is support for a unique SPARCmodule with 2 Mbyte of cache that requires two bus watchers per CPU to operate. Systems can be extended in the field by adding SPARCmodules or upgrading them to higher clock rates.

---

11. The SuperCache controller is also known as the MXCC, or MBus/XBus cache controller. XBus is used within the system board, it is similar to a single XDBus.

I/O Building Blocks

Each I/O block implements an industry-standard SBus interface that is accessed via the XDBus. A single, large ASIC implements the SBus interface (SBI), and the SBI is connected to each XDBus via an I/O Cache ASIC (IOC). Each SBI delivers over 50 Mbytes/s throughput on the SBus at 20 MHz and supports four slots.

Memory Building Blocks

Main memory is configured with two levels of interleave. Accesses from multiple CPUs and I/O devices are processed in parallel by multiple memory banks, and each memory bank can also queue multiple requests and process them in parallel on different groups of SIMMs. Memory is managed and connected to one XDBus only by a single large ASIC called the Memory Queue Handler (MQH). The access time is the same for all of memory, no matter where it is physically located on the XDBus. The memory address space and interleave is configured automatically by the power-on self-test (POST) code in the boot PROM in order to optimize performance and program around missing or failed memory.

Reliability, Availability, and Serviceability

The system contains an extensive power on self-test (POST) capability that uses multiple processors to test and configure all functional units in the system. In this way, the time taken to do the testing does not increase unduly for the largest configurations. The concept of a "minimum hot core" is used. If a single SPARCmodule is working, it can read the POST PROM from its directly connected BootBus, set LEDs to indicate any problems, and send messages to a serial port, all using the BootBus. It then explores the rest of the system, and units that pass the test are attached to the XDBus and configured into the address space. Probing and configuration use the IEEE JTAG interface (normally used in IC testing during manufacture), so that full internal testing of the main ASICs in the system is done independently of the XDBus interconnect.

If a component fails, this fact is logged into nonvolatile memory, and the operator is notified. The system can configure around failed components, including a failed or nonexistent XDBus; there is essentially no difference between a SPARCserver 1000 and a SPARCcenter 2000 that has configured out one XDBus due to a failure. If neither XDBus is available, the system reverts to a single board mode, using only the local part of the XDBus to access memory and the SBus. Unlike most other systems, this architecture ensures that the system can always reboot very quickly after a failure and has a very high availability rating. In the past dual systems with shared disks have been used to provide high availability, but a single SPARCserver 1000 or SPARCcenter 2000 can be configured to provide better inherent reliability and a comparable availability rating in a single system, without the complexity of a dual machine.

SPARCserver 1000 System Implementation Overview

The design objective for the SPARCserver 1000 was to take the architecture into an office environment and to introduce a low-cost entry point into the range. This goal was achieved by using a very compact package, about the same size as an office laser printer, that can be put on a desktop, stacked on the floor, or rack-mounted.

Taking the three basic building blocks already described, the SPARCserver 1000 system board contains twin CPU blocks sharing a single BootBus, a single SBus I/O block, including an integrated FSBE/S interface, and a single memory bank on one XDBus. The backplane accepts up to four system boards for a total of 8 CPUs, 16 SBus slots, and 2048 Mbytes of RAM. Figure 8-11 illustrates the configuration and Tables 8-13 and 8-14 summarize the benchmark results.

Figure 8-11   SPARCserver 1000 Configuration

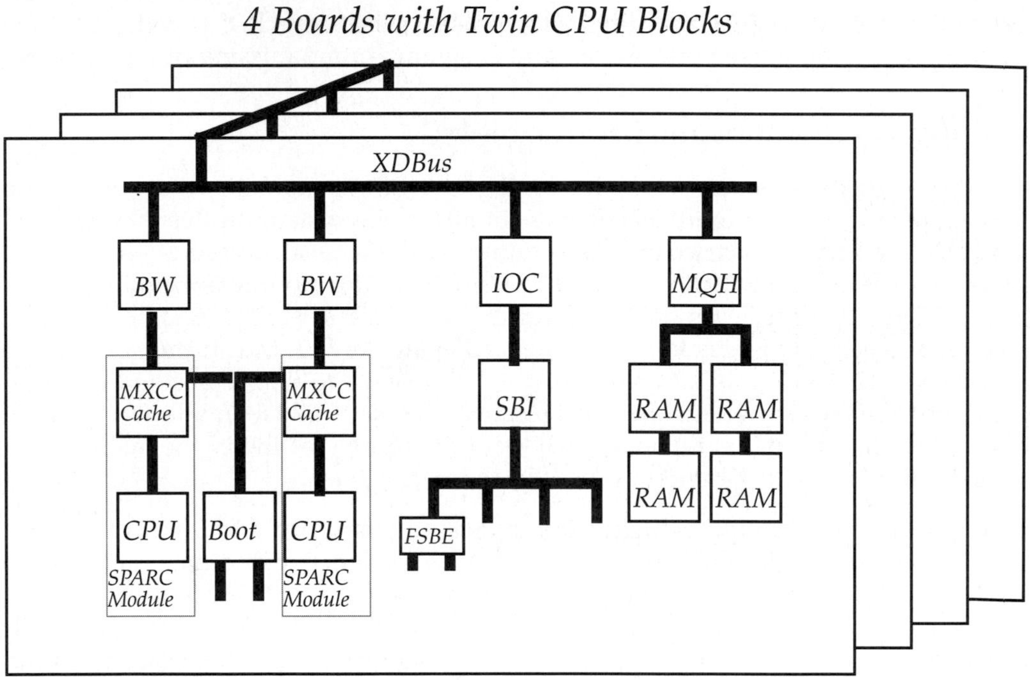

4 Boards with Twin CPU Blocks

Table 8-13 NFS and Database Server Benchmark Results

Machine	LADDIS	TPC A	TPC C
SPARCserver 1000 4 CPU	1410 @ 42.3/ms		
SPARCserver 1000 8 CPU	2106 @ 49.8/ms	400.5 @ $5068/tpsA	1079.4 @ $1032/tpmC

For these machines it only makes sense to use SPECrate measures. See "Server Multiprocessor Scalability Summary" on page 134 for more comparisons.

Figure 8-12 illustrates the layout of the SPARCserver 1000. Table 8-14 summarizes benchmark results for SuperSPARC desktops.

Table 8-14 SPEC Rate Benchmark Results for SuperSPARC Desktops

Machine	MHz	Rate_int92	Compiler	Rate_fp92	Compiler
SPARCserver 1000 1 CPU	50	1422	SunPro 3.0α	1884	Apogee 1.059
SPARCserver 1000 2 CPU	50	2730	SunPro 3.0α	3681	Apogee 1.059
SPARCserver 1000 4 CPU	50	5318	SunPro 3.0α	7076	Apogee 1.059
SPARCserver 1000 8 CPU	50	10113	SunPro 3.0α	12710	Apogee 1.059

Figure 8-12 Physical Layout of the SPARCserver 1000 System Board

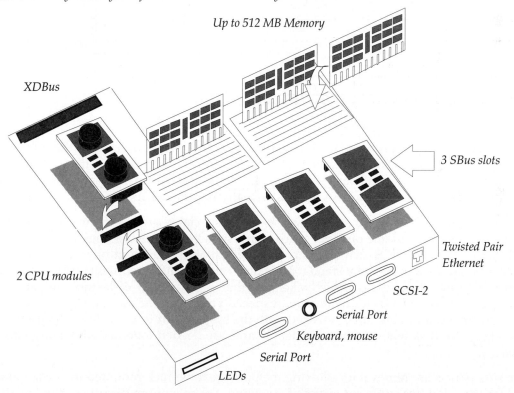

The system board acts as an infrastructure to support plug-in components. The memory subsystem uses the same SIMMs as used in the SPARCcenter 2000. The I/O subsystem uses the same SBus cards used in the rest of Sun's product line, and the CPU modules are the same as those used in the SPARCstation 10 model 51. Actually, the modules used in the SS1000 have a different part number and are supported in both MBus and XDBus systems. Modules with the SPARCstation 10 part number are not tested in XDBus systems. When the time comes to upgrade the server modules to a higher speed, the existing modules can be used to upgrade low-end SPARCstation 10s. Figure 8-13 illustrates the SPARCserver 1000 package.

Figure 8-13   The SPARCserver 1000 Package

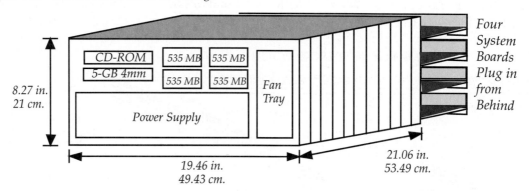

The package is extremely compact; four system boards lie flat and make up the full height and width of the box. The disks, DAT tape, and CD-ROM fit in front of the XDBus backplane, and the system board is L-shaped to fit around them. The power supply and fan tray squeeze into the gaps, so there is virtually no unused space.

To provide more flexibility in the same package, a special board containing low-profile disk drives fits in the same physical space as a system board. The package contains four 1 inch high 535-Mbyte SCSI drives and connects to an SBus SCSI controller mounted on a system board. In this way, the standard package can be configured with a single system board and three disk boards, which taken together with the four disks mounted at the front provides over 8 Gbytes of storage. A special version of the package that leaves out the front-mounted items can be stacked with the system unit to provide external mountings for disk boards if more system boards are needed together with a large disk capacity.

The side panels are removable, allowing the package to be rack-mounted in any standard 19 inch rack that has sufficient airflow for cooling. For maximum directly connected disk capacity, the rack-mounted disk units used in the SPARCserver 2000 can be configured, with the SPARCserver 1000 sitting inside or on top of the mass storage rack. These racks take eight trays of six 2.9-Gbyte disks, and two trays can be configured on each fast/wide

SCSI controller. The best-matched I/O subsystem is the SPARCstorage Array, as the package dimensions of the SPARCserver 1000 and the SPARCstorage Array are the same and they stack together in an office environment.

SPARCcenter 2000 System Implementation Overview

Taking the three basic building blocks already described, the SPARCcenter 2000 system board contains a dual-up CPU block sharing a single BootBus, a single SBus I/O block and a single memory bank on each XDBus. The entire system board contains only 19 highly integrated ASICs: 9 large 100K gate ASICs and 10 much smaller chips. The backplane accepts up to 10 system boards for a total of 20 CPUs, 40 SBus slots, and 5120 Mbytes of RAM. The SPARCcenter 2000 uses a modified form of the Sun rack-mount server packaging that was used on the previous generation SPARCserver 690. Figure 8-14 illustrates the configuration.

Figure 8-14   SPARCcenter 2000 System Board Configuration

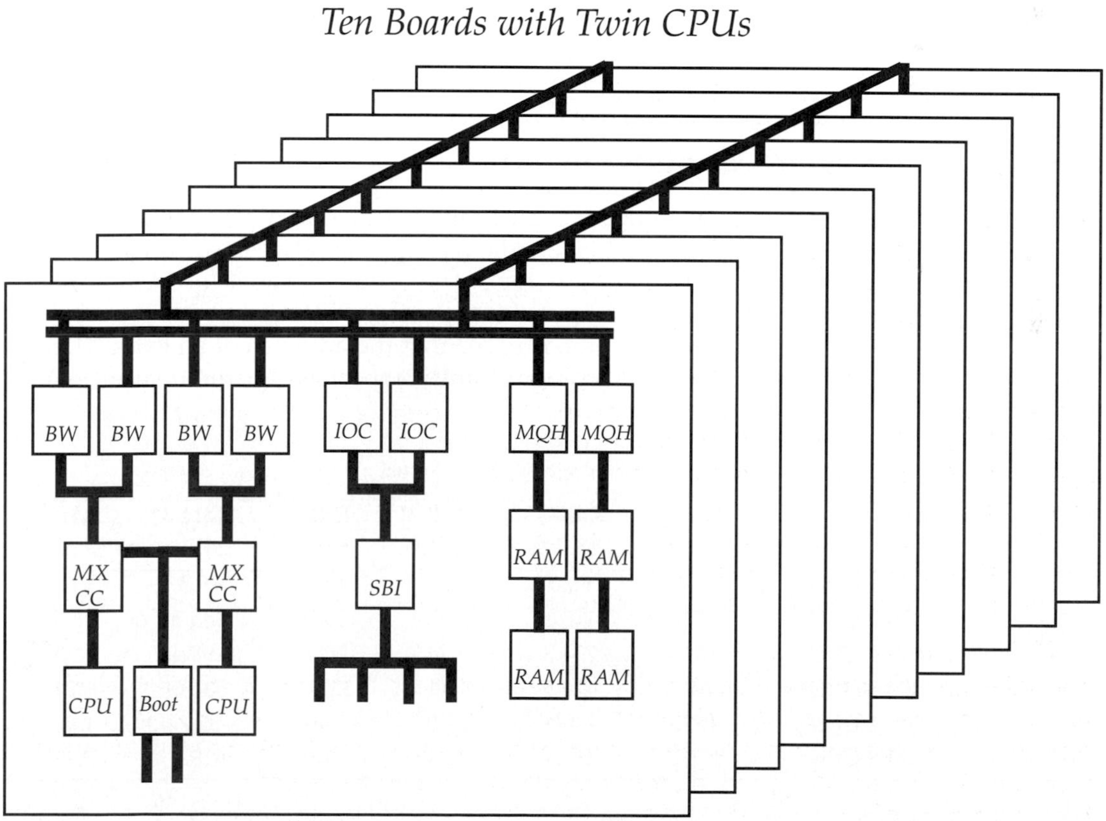

Ten Boards with Twin CPUs

The benchmark results in Table 8-15 are taken from "SPARCserver 100 & SPARCcenter 20000 Performance Brief," March 1994.

Table 8-15 NFS and Database Server Benchmark Results for SPARCcenter 2000

Machine	LADDIS	TPC A	TPC C
SPARCcenter 2000 8 CPU	2575 @ 48.9ms		
SPARCcenter 2000 12 CPU		734.1 @ $5346/tpsA	

The larger cache and dual XDBus give a useful improvement over the SPARCserver 1000, as shown in Table 8-16.

Table 8-16 SPEC Rate Benchmark Results for SPARCcenter 2000 with 2-Mbyte Caches

Machine	MHz	Rate_int92	Compiler	Rate_fp92	Compiler
SPARCcenter 2000 1 CPU	50	1523	SunPro 3.0α	1963	Apogee 1.059
SPARCcenter 2000 8 CPU	50	11177	SunPro 3.0α	14689	Apogee 1.059
SPARCcenter 2000 12 CPU	50	16272	SunPro 3.0α	21464	Apogee 1.059
SPARCcenter 2000 16 CPU	50	21196	SunPro 3.0α	28064	Apogee 1.059
SPARCcenter 2000 20 CPU	50	24864	SunPro 3.0α	31922	Apogee 1.059

Server Multiprocessor Scalability Summary

In Table 8-17, I again start with the SPECrate value, divide down to more familiar units of "times faster than a VAX 11/780," and calculate the scale factor between the uniprocessor and multiprocessor versions of the same CPU type. The usual benchmark caveat applies here — your own workload is unlikely to be multiple copies of SPEC92 and will probably scale differently. What is interesting this time is to see that the addition of an extra XDBus and 2-Mbyte cache improves the scalability significantly, especially for the floating-point benchmarks.

Table 8-17 Summary Showing Multiprocessor Server Scalability Ratios

Machine	Rate int92	Rate / 23.72	MP Scale	Rate fp92	Rate / 23.72	MP Scale
SPARCserver 1000 1 CPU	1422	60.0	1.00	1884	79.5	1.00
SPARCserver 1000 2 CPU	2730	115.1	1.92	3681	155.2	1.95
SPARCserver 1000 4 CPU	5318	224.3	3.74	7076	298.4	3.75
SPARCserver 1000 8 CPU	10113	426.5	7.11	12710	536.0	6.74
SPARCcenter 2000 1 CPU	1523	64.2	1.00	1963	82.8	1.00
SPARCcenter 2000 8 CPU	11177	471.3	7.34	14689	619.4	7.48

Table 8-17 Summary Showing Multiprocessor Server Scalability Ratios

Machine	Rate int92	Rate / 23.72	MP Scale	Rate fp92	Rate / 23.72	MP Scale
SPARCcenter 2000 12 CPU	16272	686.2	10.68	21464	905.1	10.93
SPARCcenter 2000 16 CPU	21196	893.8	13.92	28064	1183.4	14.29
SPARCcenter 2000 20 CPU	24864	1048.5	16.33	31922	1346.1	16.26

The SunPro release 3.0 FORTRAN compiler can be used to automatically parallelize code. When it is applied to the SPECfp92 set of benchmarks some of them parallelize well, and others not at all, as summarized in Table 8-18. The combined overall improvement is indicative of the minimum improvement you might find if you try the compiler on a large collection of programs and get partial parallelization. At the other extreme, the Linpack DP1000 benchmark shows how many MFLOPS you can get by parallelizing the code. It actually shows super-linear speedup. The code does not fit into the cache on a uniprocessor, but when it is parallelized, the size per processor is reduced and the improved cache hit rate gives a boost. At the high end, the overhead of splitting the work into 20 parts starts to dominate, as the work done by each CPU is now only 5 percent of the uniprocessor case. If the problem size is increased, better high-end scalability can usually be obtained.

Table 8-18 Summary Showing Multiprocessor Server, Parallelized Code Ratios

Machine	SPEC fp92	MP Scale	Linpack DP1000	MP Scale
SPARCserver 1000 1 CPU	79.9	1.00	25.3	1.00
SPARCserver 1000 2 CPU	92.3	1.16	53.2	2.10
SPARCserver 1000 4 CPU	112.8	1.41	106.8	4.22
SPARCserver 1000 8 CPU	123.1	1.54	197.5	7.81
SPARCcenter 2000 1 CPU			27.9	1.00
SPARCcenter 2000 8 CPU			223.1	8.00
SPARCcenter 2000 12 CPU			295.3	10.58
SPARCcenter 2000 16 CPU			333.0	11.94
SPARCcenter 2000 20 CPU			331.7	11.89

SPARC Server Architecture and Implementation Details

This section may be skipped. If you don't want to know the details go to "Using /usr/kvm/prtdiag to Show the Configuration" on page 147.

Multiple XDBuses

The XDBus is a packed-switched, parity-protected, high-performance interconnect. A packet-switched bus, unlike the typical circuit-switched bus, eases the implementation of interleaved memory and allows the connection of slow devices without overall performance degradation.

The unique advantage of the XDBus is its "packet-switched" design. A packet-switched bus permits substantially greater overall throughput than comparable circuit-switched buses by separating bus requests from their corresponding replies. A requester arbitrates for the bus, sends a request packet that specifies the target address, and then releases the bus to make it available for other activity. While the request is being serviced, the bus is free to perform other activities. All packets on the bus are tagged so that a request can be associated with its reply. There is an added efficiency when multiple, interleaved XDBuses are used, since activity on each bus is completely independent. The interleave is 256 bytes, which is four consecutive cache lines. One CPU can make a request on XDBus 0, and, while the reply is being transferred another CPU can make a request on XDBus 1. The effect is a single bus with twice the bandwidth.

Although packet-switched implementations are more complex than circuit-switched buses of similar specifications, they provide greater effective throughput. For example, the 40 MHz implementation of the MBus has a peak bandwidth of 320 Mbytes/s and an effective speed of about 105 Mbytes/s. The XDBus implementation in the SPARCcenter 2000 also operates at 40 MHz, and its peak bandwidth is also 320 Mbytes/s. Because arbitration for one packet is overlapped with actual transmission of the previous packet, it is possible to achieve much higher efficiency, and 250 Mbytes/s is often observed.

The SPARCcenter 2000 system has a pair of XDBuses. Should one bus fail, the system is capable of operating in a degraded mode with only one functioning XDBus. In this mode only 1 Mbyte of cache can be used, and the half of the main memory attached to the failed XDBus is not accessible. The remaining parts of the system are operational.

The Cray Superserver CS6400 has four interleaved XDBuses. By providing extra cooling, restricting the operating temperature range and using 60 MHz CPU modules, they are able to run a larger XDBus with more devices at 55 MHz. The combined throughput is over 1.2 Gbytes/s.

XDBus Arbitration and Flow Control

With many devices competing to use the bus, some arrangement must be made to permit each device to make appropriate use of the bus. The XDBus is hierarchically arbitrated, using a central arbiter on the backplane itself and local arbitration for each segment. Each XDBus has an arbiter that grants requests to use the bus on a priority basis. Within each priority level, the arbiter guarantees fair service to all devices. Bus allocation is non-preemptive since all packets are of fixed, small size.

The arbitration scheme is designed to maximize performance. The bus request and grant lines are implemented on dedicated lines, permitting transmission of one packet to be overlapped with arbitration for the next. This makes it possible to completely fill the bus with packets, even though arbitration is required for every packet. Additionally, a device may make multiple requests before the first is granted, permitting a single device to use the bus to its maximum potential. The arbiter provides for a number of outstanding requests to each device in order to avoid resorting to explicit flow control whenever possible.

XBus and Cache Coherency

In a system of multiple processors, data coherency becomes a problem. If processors are caching the same data, then it is important to provide a cache coherency protocol among them. The SPARC server architecture implements a bus watcher mechanism on the XDBus. These bus watchers implement a cache coherency protocol that keeps all the caches synchronized with one another. In addition, a bus, called the XBus, interfaces each of the caches to its bus watchers. The XBus, like the XDBus, is packet-switched, allowing for asynchronous operation between the processor units and the bus watchers. The difference is that it is never interleaved and has a few extra transaction types that are used to synchronize the cache tags in the SuperCache with the duplicate tags in the bus watcher.

The family supports cache coherency in one of three ways: write-invalidate, write-broadcast, and competitive caching, a hybrid of the first two. The caching method is configured by the operating system software and selected based on expected workloads. Write-invalidate works well when there is little write-sharing among the processors. Write-broadcasts works well when there is a lot of write-sharing among the processors. Competitive caching is a method for adapting between these two extremes.

Solaris 2 currently uses the write-invalidate mechanism, but a future version of Solaris may permit the use of the other protocols to optimize performance for specific work loads.

Processors and Symmetric Multiprocessing

The first processor module incorporated into the SPARCcenter 2000 included a 40 MHz SuperSPARC processor. This was upgraded to 50 MHz when higher-speed parts became available, and an optional version with 2 Mbytes of cache per processor has been added to the product line. The first module incorporated into SPARCserver 1000 is the 50 MHz SuperSPARC processor. In the future, higher performance modules will become available and will simply plug in to the existing machines. 60 MHz modules should become available by the time this book is published. One restriction is imposed by current Solaris

2 releases, all CPUs are assumed to be identical, and mixed clock rate modules are not supported in a single machine with Solaris 2.3. The main issue is the expensive test and support implications of allowing a much larger range of system configurations.

SPARCmodule Caches

In addition to controlling the cache, the SuperCache provides hardware support for accelerated block copy (bcopy) and block zero (bzero) operations. The bcopy/bzero accelerator is crucial to the design of systems with high-capacity I/O subsystems. In such systems, the most common usage of bcopy is to copy whole I/O buffers between system and user space. Bzero is often used to create blank memory pages when memory is allocated. The SuperCache cooperates with the bus watchers to implement the XDBus cache coherency algorithms. The 60 MHz modules include a new revision of the SuperCache controller (MXCC version 3). This revision reduces the number of cycles needed to perform many of the cache-related operations.

Interrupts

One of the crucial features in a symmetric multiprocessing system is the management of interrupts. Many SMP systems use a specialized mechanism to distribute interrupts. The SPARC server architecture uses the XDBus for most interrupt distribution; avoiding specialized mechanisms, an interrupt is merely transported as a specific kind of XDBus packet. This arrangement dramatically simplifies the system's overall implementation while imposing very few demands upon the system backplane.

Most interrupts come from peripheral devices on an SBus that do not have direct access to the processor units. An XDBus device that wants to interrupt a processor simply prepares an interrupt packet and places it onto the XDBus. SBus devices can be programmed to direct their interrupts to specific processors.

When a device wants to interrupt, it sends an appropriate XDBus packet to the destination processor, a specific processor, or a broadcast to all processors. All bus watchers watch for interrupt packets addressed to their processor. When a bus watcher detects such an interrupt packet, it generates an XBus packet describing the interrupt source to the associated SuperCache controller. When the SuperCache controller receives this packet, it sets the appropriate bit in its pending interrupt register. At the end of each instruction cycle, the SPARC processor examines this pending interrupt register and takes appropriate action.

One useful consequence of using the standard XDBus as the interrupt transmission mechanism is that the interrupted processor always knows the source of the interrupt: The originator's XDBus device ID is part of the transmitted packet. This eliminates polling to determine the identity of the interrupting device, resulting in a significant increase in overall interrupt processing efficiency.

Interrupt Distribution Tuning

On the SPARCserver 1000 and SPARCcenter 2000, there are up to 10 independent SBuses, and there is hardware support for steering the interrupts from each SBus to a specific processor. See "SBus Interrupt Processing" on page 147.

The algorithm used in Solaris 2.2 permanently assigns the clock interrupt to a CPU to obtain good cache hit rates in a single cache. The clock presents a relatively light and fixed load at 100 Hz, so this does not significantly unbalance the system. To balance the load across all the other CPUs, a round-robin system is used, whereby all interrupts are directed to one CPU at a time. When the CPU takes the first interrupt, it sends a special broadcast command over the XDBus to all the SBus controllers to direct the next interrupt to the next CPU. This scheme balances the load but, when there is a heavy interrupt load from a particular device, it is less efficient from the point of view of cache hit rate.

The algorithm can be switched to a static interrupt distribution, whereby each SBus device is assigned to a different CPU. For some I/O-intensive workloads, this scheme has given better performance, and it is the default in Solaris 2.3 and later releases.

The kernel variable that controls interrupt distribution is called *do_robin*, and it defaults to 1 in the sun4d kernel architecture of Solaris 2.2, and to 0 in 2.3 and later releases. If it is set to 0 in /etc/system, then the static interrupt distribution algorithm is used.

Console Terminal and Clock Interrupt Issues

Since Solaris expects to have a single console terminal, the board that the console is connected to is designated as the master CPU during the first power-on boot. One of the CPUs on this board always takes the 100 Hz clock interrupt. If the system ever finds it has no master at boot time, then it selects the lowest numbered board that has a working CPU. It is best to keep this as board zero, because the file /etc/iu.ap only has autopush stream entries for the ports on this board, and the installation is hard to use on a raw stream device. The commands to manually push streams (if you find that you have no echo on the console in single-user boot mode) are shown in Figure 8-15. The first line must be typed blind with a control-J terminator. This sounds obscure, but it took me ages to work out why an SC2000 with the console on board two did this, so it is worth sharing!

Figure 8-15   How to Manually Push Streams on an Alternative Console Port

```
# strchg -h ldterm^J
# strchg -h ttcompat
```

Memory

In the current implementation, a memory bank consists of up to 16 SIMMs. SIMMs hold either 8 Mbytes or 32 Mbytes of RAM each, so the maximum capacity is either 128 Mbytes or 512 Mbytes of RAM per bank. The architecture supports next generation capacities as well, but DRAM technology has not gone far enough to get 128 Mbytes on one SIMM. The SPARCserver 1000 system board has a single full-bank of 16 SIMMs, and the SPARCcenter 2000 system board has two half-banks of 8 SIMMs, so the maximum capacity of a single board is 512 Mbytes in both cases. The Cray CS6400 has four half-banks of SIMMs on larger boards for 1 Gbyte of RAM per board. A fully configured SPARCserver 1000 has a memory capacity of 2048 Mbytes or 2 Gbytes. In the SPARCcenter 2000 with configurations of ten system boards, the memory capacity is 5120 Mbytes, or 5 Gbytes. The Cray CS6400 goes up to 16 Gbytes on 16 system boards. Furthermore, the memory system is flexible enough to accommodate non-volatile RAM SIMMs (NVSIMMs), which are used as a prestoserve synchronous disk write accelerator. The NVSIMM is more efficient than the SBus prestoserve because it operates at full memory speeds rather than at SBus I/O speeds.

You may wonder how a 32-bit processor architecture can support more than 4 Gbytes of RAM. The answer is that the SPARC Reference MMU translates a 4 Gbytes virtual address space into a 64 Gbytes physical address space. Any one process can use a maximum of 4 Gbytes of RAM, but on a multiprocessor system several processes can use different parts of the physical memory. See "The SPARC Reference MMU — sun4m and sun4d Kernel Architectures" on page 167.

Memory Structure

Each bank of memory in the family is an array of DRAMs controlled by an ASIC, called the Memory Queue Handler (MQH). The MQH implements address decoding, ECC error correction, XDBus access, and memory control in a single chip. It only transfers full blocks of 64 bytes. Figures 8-16 and 8-17 illustrate the structures.

Figure 8-16 SPARCserver 1000 Memory Unit Structure

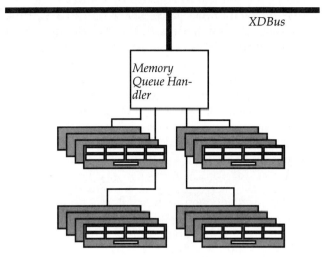

Figure 8-17 SPARCcenter 2000 Memory Unit Structure

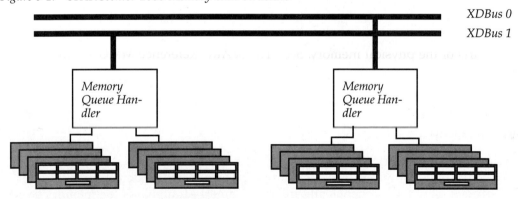

Each memory bank is assigned a base address under software control. This allows the software to configure around missed or failed memory, as well as being able to handle heterogeneous memory, such as NVRAM.

Memory Accesses

Memory requests come in from multiple CPUs more quickly than main memory DRAMs can respond. Interleaved memory helps reduce the cost of memory access by distributing sequential requests from multiple CPUs across all the memory banks in the system and permitting multiple memory components to operate in parallel.

A single bank consists of one to four groups of four SIMMs. When a request for data arrives at an MQH, it dispatches the request to a group of 4 SIMMs that in turn fetch or store data from the 18 DRAMs on each SIMM. Each SIMM has an 18-bit interface, so the group of four provides 72 bits (64 bits of data plus ECC). The 18 DRAMs on each SIMM provide four bits in each DRAM cycle, which is loaded into crossbar ASIC on the SIMM, such that the 4 bits are in successive words. After one DRAM cycle, the MQH loads four complete 72 bit words from the crossbars on the 4 SIMMs, while the DRAMs cycle again to produce another four words. Without a break, the next four words are loaded into the crossbar and read out by the MQH. The MQH reads the eight words out of the SIMMs at the same 40 MHz rate that the words are transferred over the XDBus; it also arranges for the address that was requested to be transferred as the first word in the block. This allows the CPU to start processing as soon as the first word arrives, rather than waiting for all eight.

A single XDBus interleaves addresses between memory banks on 64-byte boundaries, so the maximum interleave on the SPARCserver 1000 is four-way. The XDBuses used in the SPARCcenter 2000 are interleaved on 256-byte boundaries, producing an eight-way interleave of the memory banks.

The interleaving not only reduces the latency for accesses to blocks of memory, but, on average, the access pattern of all the CPUs and I/O subsystems will be distributed uniformly across all the memory banks, minimizing the chance that a block sequential access from one device will conflict with the access from another. Specifically, within an MQH, the multiple SIMMs and DRAMs reduce latency for accessing a subblock. Interleaving addresses across MQHs and across XDBuses balances the load and helps avoid hot spots.

Error Correction

ECC is implemented in the MQH chip. Within a 64-bit memory word, it is able to detect and correct all single-bit errors, to detect all two-bit errors, and to detect three-bit and four-bit errors if all of the erroneous bits are in the same 4-bit nibble of the memory word. The SIMM crossbar ASIC orders memory bits so that each bit of a 64-bit memory word is in a different DRAM chip, so the failure of a chip causes a series of single-bit correctable errors. In such an event, the ECC fault handler can take appropriate action. Single-bit errors are written back to memory as the corrected data is delivered, ensuring that errors do not build up in memory. The MQH provides ECC for the entire memory subsystem, including the MQH itself, the memory crossbar on each SIMM, and on the DRAMs themselves.

Prestoserve Nonvolatile Memory (NVRAM)

One of the most expensive operations for systems operating in an I/O-intensive environment is the synchronous disk write. Disk operations are performed synchronously, when data integrity is paramount, such as NFS write operations, updates to file system directory entries, and updates to a database management system's log file. Synchronous writes are posted immediately, then the invoking process is blocked until a successful completion is verified. These synchronous operations are expensive because they cause a process to wait while data is written to the physical disk drive and acknowledged. This process has much higher latency than the buffered write-behind scheme used by UNIX. With the optional nonvolatile memory, the operation can be done in two phases: the data can be committed to the NVRAM, where it will survive a system crash, even one involving a power failure. Later, the data is physically written to the disk drive, improving responsiveness as well as reducing peak disk utilization levels.

Two types of memory SIMMs are supported: standard DRAMs and battery-backed NVRAMs. Both DRAM and NVRAM are implemented on the same SIMM form factor. However, they cannot be mixed within a single bank. The NVRAM SIMM consists of an array of 1-Mbit SRAMs and a small lithium battery.

SIMMs must be configured in groups of four on the SPARCserver 1000 and eight on the SPARCcenter 2000 (one group of four in each bank is required to maintain the XDBus interleave). The batteries of each group of NVRAM SIMMs are wired in parallel. Sufficient power in each group is available to guarantee that no data will be lost even if one battery fails while the system is not in operation. Each NVRAM SIMM provides a battery status indicator. In the event of a battery failure during system operation, the operating system can force an immediate update of the disks and reconfigure the marginal NVRAM group out of the system.

Configuring Memory Interleave on the SPARCcenter 2000

The SC2000 has up to ten system boards with two memory banks on each board. Each bank is connected to one of the XDBuses. At boot time the system configures its physical memory mappings so that the memory systems on each XDBus are interleaved together on 64-byte boundaries as well as the 256-byte interleave of the dual XDBus itself. The maximum combined interleave occurs when eight memory banks are configured, with four on each XDBus. This is a minimum of 512 Mbytes of RAM, and higher performance can be obtained by using eight 64-Mbyte banks rather than two 256-Mbyte banks. The effect of the interleave can be considered for the common operation of a 4-Kbyte page being zeroed. The first four 64-byte cache lines are passed over the first XDBus to four different memory banks; the next four 64-byte cache lines are passed over the second XDBus to four more independent memory banks. After the first 512 bytes have been written, the next write goes to the first memory bank again, which has had plenty of time to store the data into one of the special SIMMs. On average, the access pattern of all the CPUs and I/O subsystems will be distributed randomly across all (up to twenty) of the memory banks. The interleave prevents a block sequential access from one device from hogging all the bandwidth in any one memory bank.

In summary, use more system boards with 64-Mbyte memory options on the SC2000 to give better performance than fewer 256-Mbyte memory options and install the memory banks evenly across the two XDBuses as far as possible.

I/O Subsystem

Each system supports multiple, industry-standard SBus I/O subsystems conforming to IEEE P1496 and SBus revision B.0. Each SBus delivers over 50 Mbytes/s sustained throughput; on a fully configured SPARCcenter 2000, the total SBus capacity (10 times 50 Mbytes/s) is matched to the internal XDBus capacity (500 Mbytes/s). All peripheral devices are connected to the SBus. An I/O unit (IOC) provides buffering or a bridge between the SBus, its peripherals, and the XDBus. The IOC is composed of cache chips and page tables. See Figure 8-18.The SPARCserver 1000 only uses one I/O Cache ASIC, because it only has to connect to a single XDBus.

In the case of the SPARCcenter 2000, each system board has an SBus with four SBus slots. With a maximum of ten system boards in one system, I/O capacity can be distributed over10 SBuses, with 40 Ethernets and 40 SCSI buses. Each SCSI bus runs at 10 Mbytes/s and each Ethernet runs at just over 1 Mbytes/s so the maximum aggregate throughput during DMA I/O transfers is approximately 450 Mbytes/s.

In the SPARCserver 1000, each system board has an SBus with three free SBus slots and one built-in FSBE/S combined fast SCSI and Ethernet board. Therefore, with a maximum of 4 system boards per system, I/O capacity can be distributed over 4 SBuses, 16 Ethernets, and 16 SCSI buses, with a maximum aggregate throughput during DMA I/O transfers of approximately 180 Mbytes/s.

SBus Interface Details

The SBus implements all burst sizes from 4 bytes to 64 bytes and parity support. The SBus operates at 20 MHz, independently of the system clock, so that the XDBus frequency can be set without affecting the SBus. Parity support can be enabled on a per-slot basis, permitting the use of peripherals that do not support the parity extension. However, all Sun peripherals do currently support parity, including the DSBE/S Differential Fast SCSI/Buffered Ethernet board (the primary disk and Ethernet interface on the SPARCserver 2000), the FSBE/S (used to interface tapes and CD on the SPARCcenter 2000 and the main interface on the SPARCserver 1000), the FDDI/S network interface board and the SOC/S FiberChannel interface used with the SPARCstorage Array.

Figure 8-18   SBus I/O Unit Structure

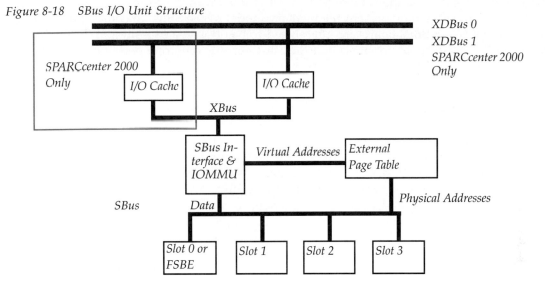

SBus Transfer Modes

The SBus implementation provides three transfer modes:

- Programmed I/O
- Consistent mode direct virtual memory access (DVMA)
- Stream mode DVMA

While programmed I/O requires direct CPU intervention, DVMA permits large amounts of data to be transferred between the SBus and memory without use of the processor. The SBI permits selection of transfer mode on a per-page basis. This permits a driver to use the transfer mode most appropriate to each task. For example, the driver for the differential SCSI host adapter uses programmed I/O for access to control registers but uses stream mode DVMA to transfer the large blocks of user data to and from the disk drives.

In Programmed I/O (PIO) mode, transfers are performed directly by the processor in physical address space and are not cacheable in either the processor's cache or in the I/O cache associated with the target SBus. This mode is provided for convenient access to memory-mapped I/O control registers and for transfer of small blocks of data.

Both DVMA modes use the I/O cache to achieve maximum performance. The two differ primarily in the way they present the memory model to the SBus. In consistent mode, all stores issued by an SBus board are guaranteed to be observed in issuing order by all processors. The practical impact is that the SBus permits only one pending transaction between each SBus board and system memory.

Stream mode DVMA uses buffers resident in the SBus interface chip. Each slot has its own buffers, used in a double-buffering arrangement. These buffers are not part of the system's shared memory image and therefore are not kept consistent by the XDBuses' cache coherency mechanism. As a result, consistency must be maintained by the device driver that must invalidate read buffers at the beginning of a DVMA read and flush write buffers at the end of a DVMA write. Stream mode is provided because full bandwidth can be achieved and sustained while the SBI buffers transactions into and out of the SBus. Unlike peripherals operating in consistent mode, each slot operating in stream DVMA mode may have more than one pending transaction. For example, one XDBus may be transferring into one of the stream buffers while the SBI is transferring the other buffer to the requesting device. In stream mode, each SBus can sustain 55 Mbytes/s when writing and 49 Mbytes/s when reading, using 64-byte bursts. Burst transfer speed is 80 Mbytes/s.

I/O Cache

SBus transactions can be many different sizes: 1, 2, 4, 8, 16, 32 or 64 bytes. Some other systems do not implement all transfer sizes on the SBus, and many SBus cards do not implement all transfer sizes. The SBus protocol negotiates the largest possible transfer size for each transaction and may break up large transfers into several smaller ones if necessary. The XDBus performs only 64-byte transfers, so an I/O cache is used to match up the transfers. A 64 byte block comes over the XDBus into the I/O cache and can be written on the SBus in several transactions. If an SBus card is performing DVMA, it may write small SBus transactions into the I/O cache; when the cache is full, a single 64-byte XDBus transfer occurs. One 64-byte buffer per SBus slot is provided in each I/O cache ASIC, so the SPARCcenter 2000 has a separate cache for each XDBus. The I/O cache is kept coherent with main memory in the same way as the CPU cache, by bus snooping logic.

I/O MMU

The SBus operates in virtual memory space, meaning that the SBus accepts virtual rather than physical addresses for main memory. Each SBus has a dedicated I/O memory management unit (MMU) for virtual address translation. The operating system is responsible for maintaining consistency between the processor's MMU(s) and the other SBus I/O MMUs.

The I/O MMU provides each SBus with a 64-Mbyte DVMA address space. The large DVMA address space provides the operating system great flexibility in choosing I/O buffers, thereby simplifying the processing of I/O. Additionally, because the SBuses are completely independent, their DVMA spaces may be configured separately, potentially using over 640 Mbytes of DVMA space in the SPARCcenter 2000 system and 256 Mbytes for the SPARCserver 1000.

SBus Interrupt Processing

Each SBus is provided with an interrupt target register that indicates which of a number of processors is to handle interrupts for the SBus. Each SBus may make arrangements for interrupt processing independently — any moment, any set of SBuses may be configured to send interrupts to arbitrary sets of processors. Groups of SBus target registers can also be updated in a single operation if this is desired. Normally, this is the approach taken by the operating system. The interrupt target registers could also be configured to shield one or more processors from SBus interrupts. This might be useful in a real-time environment.

Using /usr/kvm/prtdiag to Show the Configuration

The system configuration can be seen on SPARCserver1000 and SPARCcenter2000 machines with the /usr/kvm/prtdiag command. The following output shows the configuration of an 8-processor SPARCserver 1000 with 384 Mbytes of RAM and a 4-Mbyte bank of NVSIMM. The NVSIMM is incorrectly sensed as 8 Mbytes by the configuration software, but this does not cause any problems in operation. A substantial number of disk and network interfaces are configured on this system. The SCSI bus cards are a mixture of normal esp interfaces and wide SCSI isp interfaces. The network cards are a mixture of several buffered Ethernet les and an FDDI bf. To help identify each card, the vendor identity and part number is given for each one. Table 8-19 provides an example.

Table 8-19 Example Output from Prtdiag *for a SPARCserver 1000*

```
% prtdiag
System Configuration:  Sun Microsystems   sun4d SPARCserver 1000
System clock frequency: 40 MHz
Memory size: 392Mb
Number of XDBuses: 1
        CPU Units: Frequency Cache-Size      Memory Units: Group Size
             A: MHz MB    B: MHz MB      0: MB    1: MB    2: MB    3: MB
             ---------    ---------      -----    -----    -----    -----
Board0:       50 1.0       50 1.0         32       32       32       32
Board1:       50 1.0       50 1.0         32       32       32       32
Board2:       50 1.0       50 1.0         32       32       32       32
```

```
Board3:         50 1.0        50 1.0                  8        0        0        0
=====================SBus Cards=========================================
Board0:         0: dma/esp(scsi)          'SUNW,500-2015'
                   lebuffer/le(network)   'SUNW,500-2015'
                1: <empty>
                2: bf                     'SUNW,501-1732'
                3: QLGC,isp/sd(block)     'QLGC,ISP1000'
Board1:         0: dma/esp(scsi)          'SUNW,500-2015'
                   lebuffer/le(network)   'SUNW,500-2015'
                1: dma/esp(scsi)          'SUNW,500-2015'
                   lebuffer/le(network)   'SUNW,500-2015'
                2: <empty>
                3: <empty>
Board2:         0: dma/esp(scsi)          'SUNW,500-2015'
                   lebuffer/le(network)   'SUNW,500-2015'
                1: <empty>
                2: QLGC,isp/sd(block)     'QLGC,ISP1000'
                3: <empty>
Board3:         0: dma/esp(scsi)          'SUNW,500-2015'
                   lebuffer/le(network)   'SUNW,500-2015'
                1: <empty>
                2: <empty>
                3: <empty>

No failures found in System
===========================
```

Clustered System Architectures

Overview

In the convergence of the special purpose, massively parallel machines with networks of conventional machines, a hybrid approach has been developed. This approach uses special software to run parallelizable applications or server functions on a group of low-cost workstations. To improve performance, more network bandwidth than usual is configured between the machines in the cluster.

SPARCcluster 1

The SPARCcluster 1 consists of up to four SPARCstation 10 systems connected to a special Ethernet switch and using a dedicated connection for each system; many more Ethernets are used to connect users to the system. In its first incarnation, the SPARCcluster 1 is primarily intended as an NFS server and at introduction it was the highest-capacity NFS server available, rated on the SPEC SFS (LADDIS) benchmark at over 3000 NFS operations per second.

The special feature of the SPARCcluster 1 is that all the networks in the system are connected via a switch that filters Ethernet packets to ensure that they are seen only on networks that have the source or destination machine connected. This feature improves overall throughput substantially but, unlike a typical Ethernet router, all networks appear to be a single network with a single IP network address. This makes network configuration and installation much more flexible.

The SPARCcluster 1 uses the same rack-mounted server packaging as for a SPARCserver 690 or SPARCcenter 2000, with the same high-capacity disk options as for the SPARCcenter 2000. It also has special system administration tools that let you configure and manage all four machines as a single unit. Future directions for this product line include use as a database server and as a compute cluster.

The Solaris 2.4 version of the *SMCC NFS Server Performance and Tuning Guide* contains an overview of the architecture and capabilities of the SPARCcluster 1.

Clustering Software

Many software packages can be used to support application development on a cluster. Of particular note is the Parallel Virtual Machine (PVM) toolkit which is widely ported; source code is available on the Internet. Read the Internet Newsgroup `comp.parallel.pvm` to find out more about it. PVM can take advantage of a cluster of shared-memory multiprocessors for the best of both worlds.

8

Memory   9 ≡

Performance can vary even among machines that have the same CPU and clock rate if they have different memory systems. The interaction between caches and algorithms can cause performance problems, and an algorithm change may be called for to work around the problem. This chapter provides information on the CPU caches and memory management unit designs of various SPARC platforms so that application developers can understand the implications of differing memory systems[1]. This section may also be useful to compiler writers.

Cache Tutorial

Why Have a Cache?

Historically, the memory systems on Sun machines provided equal access times for all memory locations. This was true on the Sun-2™ machines and was true for data accesses on the Sun-3/50™ and Sun-3/60 machines.

Equal access was achieved by running the entire memory system as fast as the processor could access it. On Motorola 68010 and 68020 processors, four clock cycles were required for each memory access. On a 10 MHz Sun-2, the memory ran at a 400 ns cycle time; on a 20 MHz Sun-3/60, it ran at a 200 ns cycle time.

Unfortunately, although main memory chips (known as DRAM) have increased in size, its speed has increased only a little. SPARC processors rated at over ten times the speed of a Sun-3/60 run at a higher clock rate and access memory in a single cycle. The 40 MHz SPARCstation 2 requires 25 ns cycle times to keep running at full speed. The DRAM used is rated at 80 ns *access time*, which is less than a full single cycle of approximately 140 ns. The DRAM manufacturers have added special modes that allow fast access to a block of consecutive locations after an initial address has been loaded. These *page-mode* DRAM chips provide a block of data at the 50 ns rate required for an SBus block transfer into cache on the SPARCstation 2, after an initial delay to load up an address.

---

1. *High Performance Computing* by Keith Dowd, covers this subject very well.

The CPU cache is an area of fast memory made from *static* RAM or SRAM. SRAM is too expensive and would require too many chips for use for the entire memory system, so it is used in a small block of typically 64 Kbytes. It can operate at the full speed of the CPU (25 ns @ 40 MHz) in single-cycle reads and writes, and it transfers data from main DRAM memory using page mode in a block of typically 16 or 32 bytes at a time. Hardware keeps track of the data in the cache and copies data into the cache when required.

More advanced caches can have multiple levels and can be split so that instructions and data use separate caches. The SuperSPARC with SuperCache chip set used in the SPARCstation 10 model 51 has a 20-Kbyte instruction cache with 16-Kbyte data cache, which are loaded from a second-level 1-Mbyte combined cache that loads from the memory system. Simple caches are examined first before we look at the implications of more advanced configurations.

Cache Line and Size Effects

A SPARCstation 2 has its 64 Kbytes of cache organized as 2048 blocks of 32 bytes each. When the CPU accesses an address, the cache controller checks to see if the right data is in the cache; if it is, then the CPU loads it without stalling. If the data needs to be fetched from main memory, then the CPU clock is effectively stopped for 24 or 25 cycles while the cache block is loaded. The implications for performance tuning are obvious. If your application is accessing memory very widely and its accesses are *missing t*he cache rather than *hitting* the cache, then the CPU may spend a lot of its time stopped. By changing the application, you may be able to improve the *hit rate a*nd achieve a worthwhile performance gain. The 25-cycle delay is known as the *miss cost,* and the effective performance of an application is reduced by a large miss cost and a low hit rate. The effect of context switches is to further reduce the cache hit rate because after a context switch the contents of the cache will need to be replaced with instructions and data for the new process.

Applications access memory on almost every cycle. Most instructions take a single cycle to execute and the instructions must be read from memory; data accesses typically occur on 20–30 percent of the cycles. The effect of changes in hit rate for a 25-cycle miss cost are shown in Table 9-1 and Figure 9-1. in both tabular and graphical forms. A 25-cycle miss cost implies that a hit takes one cycle and a miss takes 26 cycles.

Table 9-1   Application Speed Changes as Hit Rate Varies with a 25-cycle Miss Cost

Hit Rate	Hit Time	Miss Time	Total Time	Performance
100%	100%	0%	100%	100%
99%	99%	26%	125%	80%
98%	98%	52%	150%	66%
96%	96%	104%	200%	50%

Figure 9-1   Application Speed Changes as Hit Rate Varies with a 25-cycle Miss Cost

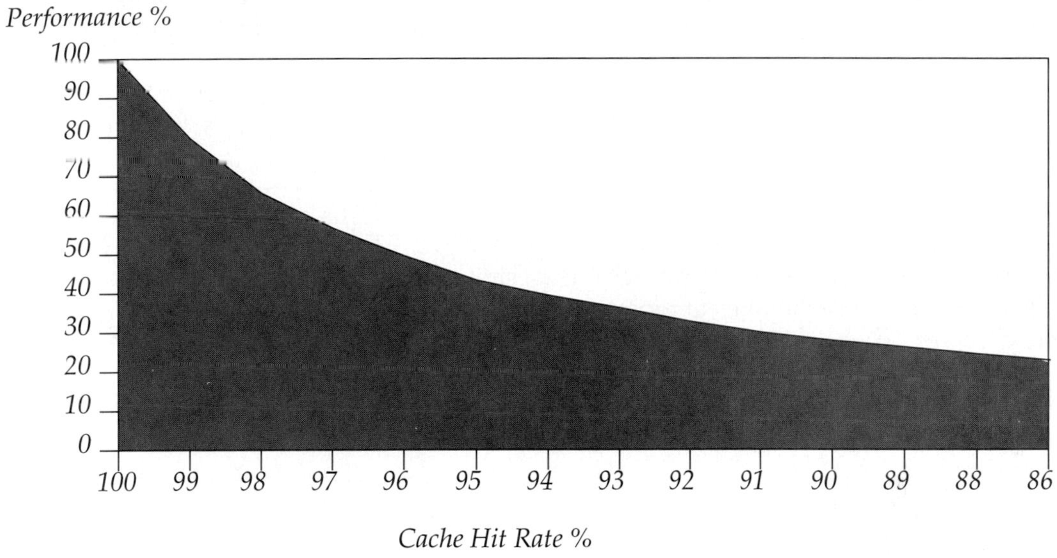

Performance %

Cache Hit Rate %

There is a dramatic increase in execution time as the hit rate drops. Although a 96 percent hit rate sounds quite high, you can see that the program will be running at half speed. Many small benchmarks like Dhrystone run at 100 percent hit rate. The SPEC92 benchmark suite runs at a 99 percent hit rate given a 1-Mbyte cache[2]. It isn't that difficult to do things that are bad for the cache, so it is a common cause of performance problems.

A Problem with Linked Lists

In "Algorithms" on page 35 I mentioned a CAD application that traversed a large linked list. Let's look at this in more detail and assume that the list has 5000 entries[3]. Each block on the list contains some data and a link to the next block. If we assume that the link is located at the start of the block and that the data is in the middle of a 100-byte block as shown in Figure 9-2, then the effect on the memory system of chaining down the list can be deduced.

---

2. See"The SuperSPARC Microprocessor Technical White Paper."

3. See also "The Cache-aligned Block Copy Problem" on page 162 for another example.

Figure 9-2   Linked List Example

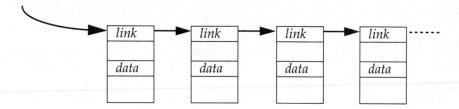

The code to perform the search is a tight loop, shown in Figure 9-3. This code fits in seven words, one or two cache lines at worst, so the cache is working well for code accesses. Data accesses occur when the link and data locations are read. If the code is simply looking for a particular data value, then these data accesses will occur every few cycles. They will never be in the same cache line, so every data access will cause a 25-cycle miss that reads in 32 bytes of data, when only 4 bytes were wanted. Also, only 2048 cache lines are available, so after 1024 blocks have been read in, the cache lines must be reused. This means that a second attempt to search the list will find that the start of the list is no longer in the cache.

The only solution to this problem is an algorithmic change. The problem will occur on any of the current generation of high performance computer systems. In fact, the problem gets worse as the processor gets faster since the miss cost tends to increase due to the difference in speed between the CPU and cache clock rate and the main memory speed.

Figure 9-3   Linked List Search Code in C

```
/* C code to search a linked list for a value and miss the cache a lot */

struct block {
        struct block *link;             /* link to next block */
        int pad1[11];
        int data;                       /* data item to check for */
        int pad2[12];
        } blocks[5000];

struct block *find(pb,value)
        struct block *pb;
        int value;
        {
        while(pb)                   /* check for end of linked list */
                {
                if (pb->data == value) /* check for value match */
                        return pb;      /* return matching block */
```

```
                    pb = pb->link;           /* follow link to next block */
                }
        return (struct block *)0; /* return null if no match */
        }
```

The while loop compiles with optimization to just seven instructions, including two loads, two tests, two branches, and a no-op as shown in Figure 9-4. Note that the instruction after a branch is always executed on a SPARC processor. This executes in 9 cycles on a SPARCstation 2 if it hits the cache, and in 59 cycles if both loads miss.

Figure 9-4   Linked List Search Loop in Assembler

```
LY1:                                  /* loop setup code omitted */
        cmp     %o2,%o1               /* see if data == value */
        be      L77016                /* and exit loop if matched */
        nop                           /* pad branch delay slot */
        ld      [%o0],%o0             /* follow link to next block */
        tst     %o0                   /* check for end of linked list */
        bne,a   LY1                   /* branch back to start of loop */
        ld      [%o0+48],%o2          /* load data in branch delay slot */
```

Cache Miss Cost and Hit Rates for Different Machines

Since the hardware details vary from one machine implementation to another and the details are sometimes hard to obtain, the cache architectures of some common machines are described below, divided into four main groups. Virtually and physically addressed caches with write-back algorithms, virtual write-through caches, and on-chip caches. For more details of the hardware implementation read the book *Multiprocessor System Architectures*, by Ben Catanzaro (SunSoft Press).

Virtual Write-through Caches

Example Machines

Most older desktop SPARCstations from Sun and the deskside SPARC system 300 series use virtual write-through caches.

How It Works

The virtual write-through cache works using virtual addresses to decide the location in the cache that has the required data in it. This avoids having to perform an MMU address translation except when there is a cache miss.

Data is read into the cache a block at a time, but writes go through the cache into main memory as individual words. This avoids the problem of data in the cache being different from data in main memory but may be slower since single word writes are less efficient than block writes would be. An optimization is for a buffer to be provided so that the word can be put into the buffer, then the CPU can continue immediately while the buffer is written to memory. The depth (one or two words) and width (32 or 64 bits) of the write buffer vary. If a number of words are written back-to-back then the write buffer may fill up and the processor will stall until the slow memory cycle has completed. A doubleword write on a SPARCstation 1 (and similar machines) will always cause a write-buffer overflow stall that takes 4 cycles.

On the machines listed in Table 9-2, the processor waits until the entire cache block has been loaded before continuing.

The SBus used for memory accesses on the SS2, IPX, and ELC machines runs at half the CPU clock rate. This may give rise to an extra cycle on the miss cost to synchronize the two buses and occurs half of the time on average.

Table 9-2   Virtual Write-through Cache Details

Machine	Clock	Size	Line	Read Miss	WB size	WB Full Cost
SS1, SLC	20 MHz	64 KB	16 B	12 cycles	1 word	2 cycles (4 dbl)
SS1+, IPC	25 MHz	64 KB	16 B	13 cycles	1 word	2 cycles (4 dbl)
SS330, 370, 390	25 MHz	128 KB	16 B	18 cycles	1 double	2 cycles
ELC	33 MHz	64 KB	32 B	24–25 cycles	2 doubles	4–5 cycles
SS2, IPX	40 MHz	64 KB	32 B	24–25 cycles	2 doubles	4–5 cycles

Virtual Write-back Caches

The larger desk-side SPARCservers from Sun use virtual write-back caches.

The cache uses virtual addresses as described above. The difference is that data written to the cache is not written through to main memory. This reduces memory traffic and allows efficient back-to-back writes to occur. The penalty is that a cache line must be written back to main memory before it can be reused, so there may be an increase in the miss cost. The line is written efficiently as a block transfer, then the new line is loaded as a block transfer. Most systems have a buffer that is used to store the outgoing cache line while the incoming cache line is loaded, then the outgoing line is passed to memory while the CPU continues. The SPARCsystem 400 backplane is 64 bits wide and runs at 33 MHz, synchronized with the CPU.The SPARCsystem 600 uses a 64-bit MBus and takes data from the MBus at full speed into a buffer; the cache itself is 32 bits wide, and takes extra cycles to pass data from the buffer in the cache controller to the cache itself. The cache coherency mechanisms required for a multiprocessor machine also introduce extra cycles. There is a difference between the number of MBus cycles taken for a cache miss (the bus occupancy) and the number of cycles that the CPU stalls for. A lower bus occupancy means that more CPUs can be used on the bus. Table 9-3 summarizes the details of the cache.

Table 9-3   Virtual Write-back Cache Details

Machine	Size	Line	Miss Cost	CPU Clock Rate
Sun-4/200 series	128 Kb	16 bytes	7 cycles	16 MHz
SPARCserver 400	128 Kb	32 bytes	12 cycles	33 MHz
SPARCserver 600 model 120	64 Kb	32 bytes	30 cycles	40 MHz

Physical Write-back Caches

The SPARCserver 600 and SPARCstation 10 with SuperCache, and the SPARCserver 1000 and SPARCcenter 2000 use physical write-back caches for their second-level cache. The first-level cache is described, in the section on on-chip caches.

The MMU translations occur on every CPU access before the address reaches the cache logic. The cache uses the physical address of the data in main memory to determine where in the cache it should be located. In other respects this type is the same as the virtual write-back cache described above.

The SuperCache controller implements subblocking in its 1 Mbyte cache. The cache line is actually 128 bytes but is loaded as four separate contiguous 32-byte lines. This cuts the number of cache tags required at the expense of needing an extra three valid bits in each tag. In XDBus mode for the SPARCserver 1000, the same chip set switches to two 64-byte blocks. The SPARCcenter 2000 takes advantage of this to use four 64-byte blocks per 256-byte line, for a total of 2 Mbytes of cache on a special module. This module cannot be used in any other systems since it requires the twin XDBus, as described in "CPU Building Blocks" on page 128.

In XDBus mode, the cache request and response are handled as separate transactions on the bus, and other bus traffic can interleave for better throughput but delayed response. The larger cache line takes longer to transfer, but the memory system is in multiple, independent banks, accessed over two interleaved buses on the SPARCcenter 2000. When many CPUs access memory at once, the single MBus memory system bottlenecks more quickly than with the XDBus. This two-level cache architecture is so complex that a single cache miss cost cannot be quoted. It can range from about 20 cycles in the ideal case, through about 40 cycles in a typical case, to even longer in the worst case. The worst case situation involves a read miss on a full but dirty cache line. Four blocks must be written back to main memory before the read data can be loaded. Table 9-4 summarizes details about the cache.

Table 9-4   Physical Write-back Cache Details

Machine	Size	Line (block)	Miss Cost	CPU Clock Rate
SPARCserver 600 model 41	1024 Kb	128 (32) bytes	Variable	40 MHz
SPARCstation 10 model 51	1024 Kb	128 (32) bytes	Variable	50 MHz
SPARCserver 1000	1024 Kb	128 (64) bytes	Variable	50 MHz
SPARCcenter 2000	2048 Kb	256 (64) bytes	Variable	50 MHz

On-chip Caches

Example Machines

Highly integrated SPARC chip sets like the Texas Instruments SuperSPARC (Viking) used in the SPARCstation 10, microSPARC (Tsunami) used in the SPARCstation LX and SPARCclassic, and the Fujitsu MB86930 (SPARClite) use on-chip caches. The Fujitsu/Ross HyperSPARC uses a hybrid on-chip instruction cache with off-chip unified cache. The latest SPARC design is the microSPARC II, which has four times the cache size of the original microSPARC and has other performance improvements. It is made by Fujitsu, who also recently bought Ross from Cypress. One other recent development is the Weitek PowerUP, which is a plug-in replacement for the SS2 and IPX CPU chip that adds on-chip caches and doubles the clock rate. At the time of writing, details of the UltraSPARC processor are not announced, and I have left it blank in Table 9-5 so that you can write in the details when it is introduced.

How It Works

Since the entire cache is on-chip, complete with its control logic, a different set of trade-offs apply to cache design. The size of the cache is limited, but the complexity of the cache control logic can be enhanced more easily. On-chip caches may be *associative* in that a line can exist in the cache in several possible locations. If there are four possible locations for a line, then the cache is known as a *four-way, set-associative cache.* It is hard to build off-chip caches that are associative, so they tend to be *direct mapped*, where each memory location maps directly to a single cache line.

On-chip caches also tend to be split into separate instruction and data caches, since this allows both caches to transfer during a single clock cycle, thus speeding up load and store instructions. This is not done with off-chip caches because the chip would need an extra set of pins and more chips would be needed on the circuit board.

More intelligent cache controllers can reduce the miss cost by passing the memory location that missed as the first word in the cache block, rather than starting with the first word of the cache line. The processor can then be allowed to continue as soon as this word arrives, before the rest of the cache line has been loaded. If the miss occurred in a data cache and the processor can continue to fetch instructions from a separate instruction cache, then this will reduce the miss cost. In contrast, with a combined instruction and data cache, the cache load operation keeps the cache busy until it has finished, so the processor cannot fetch another instruction anyway. SuperSPARC and microSPARC both implement this optimization.

microSPARC uses page-mode DRAM to reduce its miss cost. The first miss to a 1-Kbyte region takes 9 cycles for a data miss; consecutive accesses to the same region avoid some DRAM setup time and complete in 4 cycles.

The SuperSPARC processor implements subblocking in its instruction cache. The cache line is actually 64 bytes but is loaded as two separate contiguous 32-byte lines. If the on-chip cache is connected directly to main memory, it has a 10-cycle effective miss cost; if it is used with a SuperCache it can transfer data from the SuperCache to the on-chip cache with a 5 cycle cost. These details are summarized in Table 9-5.

Table 9-5   On-chip Cache Details

Processor	I-Size	I-line	I-Assoc	D-Size	D-line	D-Assoc	D-Miss
MB86930	2 KB	16	2	2 KB	16	2	N/A
microSPARC	4 KB	32	1	2 KB	16	1	4–9 cycles
microSPARC II	16 KB	32	1	8 KB	16	1	N/A
PowerUP	16 KB	32	1	8 KB	32	1	N/A
HyperSPARC	8 KB	32	1	256 KB[1]	32	1	10 cycles
SuperSPARC UltraSPARC	20 KB	64 (32)	5	16 KB	32	4	5–10 cycles

1. This is a combined external instruction and data cache.

The SuperSPARC with SuperCache Two-level Cache Architecture

As previously described, the SuperSPARC processor has two sophisticated and relatively large on-chip caches and an optional 1-Mbyte external cache, known as SuperCache or MXCC (for MBus XBus Cache Controller)[4]. It can be used without the external cache, and the on-chip caches work in write-back mode for transfers directly over the MBus. For multiprocessor snooping to work correctly and efficiently, the on-chip caches work in write-through mode when the external cache is used. This guarantees that the on-chip

---

4. See "The SuperSPARC Microprocessor Technical White Paper."

Memory Management Unit Designs

The Sun-4 MMU — sun4, sun4c, sun4e Kernel Architectures

Older Sun machines use a "Sun-4™" hardware memory management unit that acts as a large cache for memory translations. It is much larger than the MMU translation cache found on more recent systems, but the entries in the cache, known as PMEGs, are larger and take longer to load. A PMEG is a Page Map Entry Group, a contiguous chunk of virtual memory made up of 32 or 64 physical 8-Kbit or 4-Kbyte page translations. A SPARCstation 1 has a cache containing 128 PMEGs so a total of 32 Mbytes of virtual memory can be cached. Note that a program can still use 500 Mbytes or more of virtual memory on these machines, it is the size of the translation cache, which affects performance, that varies. The number of PMEGs on each type of Sun machine is shown in Table 9-6.

Table 9-6   Sun-4 MMU Characteristics

Processor Type	Page Size	Pages/PMEG	PMEGS	Total VM	Contexts
SS1(+), SLC, IPC	4 KB	64	128	32 MB	8
ELC	4 KB	64	128	32 MB	8
SPARCengine 1E	8 KB	32	256	64 MB	8
IPX	4 KB	64	256	64 MB	8
SS2	4 KB	64	256	64 MB	16
Sun 4/110, 150	8 KB	32	256	64 MB	16
Sun 4/260, 280	8 KB	32	512	128 MB	16
SPARCsystem 300	8 KB	32	256	64 MB	16
SPARCsystem 400	8 KB	32	1024	256 MB	64

In SunOS 4.0.3 and SunOS 4.1, there were two independent problems that only came to light when Sun started to ship 4-Mbit DRAM parts and the maximum memory on a SPARCstation 1 went up from 16 Mbytes to 64Mbytes. Memory prices also dropped and many more people loaded up their SPARCstation 1, 1+, SLC, or IPC with extra RAM. When the problem was discovered, a patch was made for SunOS 4.0.3 and SunOS 4.1. The patch is incorporated as standard into DBE 1.0 and later and SunOS 4.1.1 and later.

If you run within the limits of the MMUs 128 PMEG entries, the processor runs flat-out — faster than other MMU architectures, in fact. The problems occur when you run outside the limits of the MMU.

PMEG Reload-time Problem

When a new PMEG was needed, the kernel had to obtain information from a number of data structures, then process it to produce the values needed for the PMEG entry. This procedure took too long, and one of the symptoms of PMEG thrashing was that the system CPU time was very high, often over 50 percent for no apparent reason. The cure is to provide a secondary, software cache for the completed PMEG entries that can be resized if required. If a PMEG entry is already in the software cache, then it is block-copied into place. The effect is that the reload time is greatly reduced and the amount of system CPU used drops back to more reasonable levels.

PMEG Stealing

In order to load a new PMEG, the kernel had to decide which existing entry to overwrite. The original algorithm made the problem much worse, since it often stole a PMEG from an active process, which would then steal it back again, causing a thrashing effect. When a PMEG was stolen, its pages were put onto the free list. If every PMEG was stolen from a process, then every page would be on the free list and the system would decide to swap out the process. This gave rise to another symptom of PMEG thrashing — a large amount of free memory reported by vmstat and a lot of swapping reported by vmstat -S, even though no disk I/O was going on. The cure is to use a much better algorithm for deciding which PMEG to reuse and to stop putting pages on the free list when a PMEG is stolen.

Problem Solved

There are some performance graphs in the *SPARCstation 2 Performance Brief* that show the difference between SunOS 4.1 and SunOS 4.1.1 using a worst case test program. For a SPARCstation IPC, the knee in the curve that indicates the onset of PMEG thrashing is at 16 Mbytes for SunOS 4.1 and around 60 Mbytes for SunOS 4.1.1. Beyond that point SunOS 4.1 hits a brick wall at 24 Mbytes, while the IPC is degrading gracefully beyond 80 Mbytes with SunOS 4.1.1.

The SPARCstation 2, which has twice as many PMEGs, is flat beyond 80 Mbytes with no degradation.

If you are called on to tune a system that seems to have the symptoms described above, is running SunOS 4.0.3 or SunOS 4.1, and you cannot upgrade to SunOS 4.1.1, then you should contact Sun to get hold of the PMEGS patch.

Contexts in the Sun-4 MMU

Table 9-6 on page 164 shows the number of hardware contexts built into each machine. A hardware context can be thought of as a tag on each PMEG entry in the MMU that indicates which process that translation is valid for. This allows the MMU to keep track of the mappings for 8, 16, or 64 processes in the MMU, depending on the machine. When a context switch occurs, if the new process is already assigned to one of the hardware contexts, then some of its mappings may still be in the MMU and a very fast context switch can take place. For up to the number of hardware contexts available, this scheme is more efficient than a more conventional, TLB-based MMU. When the number of processes trying to run exceeds the number of hardware contexts, the kernel has to choose one of the hardware contexts to be reused, has to invalidate all the PMEGs for that context and load some PMEGs for the new context. The context-switch time starts to degrade gradually and probably becomes worse than a TLB-based system when there are more than twice as many active processes as contexts. This is one reason why a SPARCserver 490 can handle many more users in a time-sharing environment than the (apparently faster) SPARCstation 2, which would spend more time in the kernel shuffling the PMEGs in and out of its MMU. There is also a difference in the hardware interface used to control the MMU and cache; more work needs to be done in software to flush a context on a SPARCstation 1, and higher-level hardware support is provided for the SPARCstation 2 and SPARCserver 400. No new machines are being designed to use this type of MMU, but it represents a large part of the installed base.

Monitoring the Sun-4 MMU

The number of various MMU -related cache flushes can be monitored by means of vmstat -c.

```
% vmstat -c
flush statistics: (totals)
    usr     ctx     rgn     seg     pag     par
    821     960       0       0  123835      97
```

For Solaris 2 the required information can be obtained from the kernel statistics interface, by using the undocumented netstat -k option to dump out the virtual memory hardware address translation statistics (the vmhatstat section).

```
vmhatstat:
vh_ctxfree 650 vh_ctxstealclean 274 vh_ctxstealflush 209 vh_ctxmappings
4507
vh_pmgallocfree 4298 vh_pmgallocsteal 9 vh_pmgmap 0 vh_pmgldfree 3951
vh_pmgldnoctx 885 vh_pmgldcleanctx 182 vh_pmgldflush 0 vh_pmgldnomap 0
vh_faultmap 0 vh_faultload 711 vh_faultinhw 27667 vh_faultnopmg 3193
```

```
vmhatstat:
vh_faultctx 388 vh_smgfree 0 vh_smgnoctx 0 vh_smgcleanctx 0
vh_smgflush 0 vh_pmgallochas 123790 vh_pmsalloc 4 vh_pmsfree 0
vh_pmsallocfail 0
```

This output is very cryptic, and I haven't been able to work out any rules for which variables might indicate a problem. The Sun 4 MMU is rapidly becoming uninteresting, because the systems that use it are obsolete.

The SPARC Reference MMU — sun4m and sun4d Kernel Architectures

More recently Sun machines have started to use the SPARC Reference MMU, which has an architecture that is similar to many other MMUs in the rest of the industry. Table 9-7 lists the characteristics.

Table 9-7   SPARC Reference MMU Characteristics

Processor Types	Page Sizes	TLB	Contexts	Total VM
Cypress SPARC/MBus chip set, e.g.	4 KB	64	4096	256 KB
SPARCserver 600 -120 and -140 &	256 KB	64	4096	16 MB
Tadpole SPARCbook	16 MB	64	4096	1024 MB
Texas Instruments SuperSPARC e.g.	4 KB	64	65536	256 KB
SPARCserver 600 -41	256 KB	64	65536	16MB
SPARCstation 10 -30, -41, 51, and 61	16 MB	64	65536	1024 MB
SPARCserver 1000 and SC2000				
Fujitsu SPARClite embedded CPU	4 KB	32	256	128KB
	256 KB	32	256	8 MB
	16 MB	32	256	512 MB
Texas Instruments microSPARC e.g.	4 KB	32	64	128 KB
SPARCclassic and SPARCstation LX	256 KB	32	64	8 MB
	16 MB	32	64	512 MB

A detailed description of the hardware involved can be found in *Multiprocessor System Architectures*, by Ben Catanzaro.

There are four common implementations: the Cypress uniprocessor 604 and multiprocessor 605 MMU chips, the MMU that is integrated into the SuperSPARC chip, the Fujitsu SPARClite, and the highly integrated microSPARC.

Unlike the Sun-4 MMU there is a small, fully associative cache for address translations (a Translation Lookaside Buffer or TLB), which typically has 64 entries that map one contiguous area of virtual memory each. These areas are usually a single 4-Kbyte page but future releases of Solaris 2 may be optimized to use the 256 Kbytes or 16-Mbyte pages in certain cases, for mapping some frame buffers (the SX in Solaris 2.3) and parts of the kernel. This requires contiguous and aligned physical memory for each mapping, which is hard to allocate except for special cases. Each of the 64 entries has a tag that indicates what context the entry belongs to. This means that the MMU does not have to be flushed on a context switch. The tag is 12 bits on the Cypress/Ross MMU and 16 bits on the SuperSPARC MMU, giving rise to a much larger number of hardware contexts than the Sun-4 MMU, so that MMU performance is not a problem when very large numbers of users or processes are present.

The SPARC Reference MMU Table Walk Operation

The primary difference from the Sun-4 MMU is that TLB entries are loaded automatically by table-walking hardware in the MMU. The CPU stalls for a few cycles waiting for the MMU but unlike many other TLB-based MMUs or the Sun-4 MMU, the CPU does not take a trap to reload the entries itself using software. The kernel builds a table in memory that contains all the valid virtual memory mappings and loads the address of the table into the MMU once at boot time. The MMU then does a table walk by indexing and following linked lists to find the right page translation to load into the TLB, as shown in Figure 9-6.

The table walk is optimized by the MMU hardware, which keeps the last accessed context, region, and segment values in registers, so that the only operation needed is to index into the page table with the address supplied and load a page table entry. For the larger page sizes, the table walk stops with a special PTE at the region or segment level. The size of the page translation table is large enough for most purposes, but a system with a large amount of active virtual memory can cause a shortage of page table entries with effects similar to a PMEGS shortage. The solution is simply to increase the amount of kernel memory allocated to this purpose. The kernel variable *npts* controls how many PMEGS are allocated. Its calculation depends on the amount of physical memory in the system but can be set explicitly by patching *npts*. It was set too low in the GENERIC 4.1.2

kernel. DBE 1.2, SunOS 4.1.3, and Solaris 2 set *npts* much higher; it does not normally need to be tweaked. It should never be reduced below the calculated value and, if doubling it has no measurable effect on performance, then leave it alone.

Figure 9-6   SPARC Reference MMU Table Walk

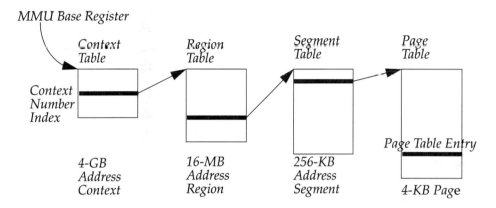

The Sun-4-MMU-based systems can cache sufficient virtual memory translations to run programs many Mbytes in size with no MMU reloads. When the MMU limits are exceeded there is a large overhead. The SPARC Reference MMU caches only 64 pages of 4 Kbytes at a time in normal use for a total of 256 Kbytes of simultaneously mapped virtual memory. The SRMMU is reloading continuously as the CPU uses more than this small set of pages, but it has an exceptionally fast reload, so there is a low overhead.

≡ 9

Sun Performance and Tuning

SPARC Implementations 10 ≡

This chapter looks at some SPARC implementations to see how the differences affect performance. A lot of hard-to-find details are documented. See also the recent book *"Multiprocessor System Architectures"* by Ben Catanzaro (SunSoft Press).

Architecture and Implementation

The SPARC architecture defines everything that is required to ensure application-level portability across varying SPARC implementations. It intentionally avoids defining some things, like how many cycles an instruction takes, to allow maximum freedom within the architecture to vary implementation details. This is the basis of SPARC's scalability from very low cost to very high performance systems. Implementation differences are handled by kernel code only, so that the instruction set and system call interface are the same on all SPARC systems. The SPARC Compliance Definition, controlled by the independent SPARC International organization, specifies this interface.   Within this standard there is no specification of the performance of a compliant system, only its correctness. The performance depends on the chip set used (i.e., the implementation) and the clock rate that the chip set runs at. To avoid confusion, some terms need to be defined.

Instruction Set Architecture (ISA)

The ISA is defined by the SPARC Architecture Manual. SPARC International has published Version 7, Version 8, and Version 9, and the IEEE has produced a standard based on Version 8, IEEE 1754. Version 9 defines major extensions including 64-bit addressing in an upward-compatible manner for user mode programs. Prentice Hall has published both the Version 8 and Version 9 SPARC Architecture manuals.

SPARC Implementation

A chip-level specification, the SPARC implementation defines how many cycles each instruction takes and other details. Some chip sets define only the integer unit (IU) and floating-point unit (FPU), others define the MMU and cache design and may include the whole lot on a single chip.

System Architecture

System architecture defines a board-level specification of everything the kernel has to deal with on a particular machine. It includes internal and I/O bus types, address space uses and built-in I/O functions. This level of information is documented in the SPARCengine™ User Guide[1] that is produced for the bare-board versions of Sun's workstation products. The information needed to port a real-time operating system to the board and physically mount the board for an embedded application is provided.

Kernel Architecture

A number of similar systems may be parameterized so that a single GENERIC kernel image can be run on them. This grouping is known as a kernel architecture. Sun has one for VME-based SPARC machines (Sun-4), one for SBus-based SPARC machines (Sun-4c), one for the VME and SBus combined 6U eurocard machines (Sun-4e), one for MBus-based machines and machines that use the SPARC reference MMU (Sun-4m), and one for XDBus based machines (Sun-4d). These are listed in Table 10-1 on page 174.

Register Windows and Different SPARC CPUs

SPARC defines an instruction set that uses 32 integer registers in a conventional way but has many sets of these registers arranged in overlapping *register windows*. A single instruction is used to switch in a new set of registers very quickly. The overlap means that 8 of the registers from the previous window are part of the new window, and these are used for fast parameter passing between subroutines. A further 8 global registers are always the same; of the 24 that make up a register window, 8 are passed in from the previous window, 8 are local, and 8 will be passed out to the next window. This usage is described further in the following references.

- *The SPARC Architecture Manual Version 8*

- "SPARC Strategy and Technology," March 1991

Some SPARC implementations have seven overlapping sets of register windows and some have eight. One window is always reserved for taking traps or interrupts, since these will need a new set of registers, the others can be thought of as a stack cache for six or seven levels of procedure calls with up to 6 parameters per call passed in registers. The other two registers are used to hold the return address and the old stack frame pointer. If

---

1. See the "SPARCengine IPX User Guide, "SPARCengine 2 User Guide," and "SPARCengine 10 User Guide."

there are more than six parameters to a call, then the extra ones are passed on the external stack as in a conventional architecture. It can be seen that the register windows architecture allows much faster subroutine calls and returns and faster interrupt handling than in conventional architectures that copy parameters out to a stack, make the call, then copy the parameters back into registers. Programs typically spend most of their time calling up and down a few levels of subroutines, however when the register windows have all been used, a special trap takes place, and one window (16 registers) is copied to the stack in main memory. On average, register windows seem to cut down the number of loads and stores required by 10–30 percent and provide a speedup of 5–15 percent. Care must be taken to avoid writing code that makes a large number of recursive or deeply nested calls and keeps returning to the top level. If very little work is done at each level and very few parameters are being passed then the program may generate a large number of save and restore traps. The SunPro SPARCcompiler optimizer performs tail recursion elimination and leaf routine optimization to reduce the depth of the calls.

If an application performs a certain number of procedure calls and causes a certain number of window traps, the benefit of reducing the number of loads and stores must be balanced against the cost of the traps. The overflow trap cost is very dependent on the time taken to store eight doublewords to memory. On systems with write through caches and small write buffers, like the SPARCstation 1, a large number of write stalls occur and the cost is relatively high. The SPARCstation 2 has a larger write buffer of two doublewords which is still not enough. The SuperSPARC chip in write through mode has an 8-doubleword write buffer, so will not stall; other systems with write-back caches will not stall (unless a cache line needs to be updated).

The SPARC V9 architecture supports a new, multiple level, trap architecture. This architecture greatly reduces the administrative overhead of register window traps, since the main trap handler no longer has to check for page faults. This feature is expected to increase the relative performance boost of register windows by reducing the trap time.

The Effect of Context Switches and Interrupts

When a program is running on a SPARC chip, the register windows act as a stack cache and provide a performance boost. Subroutine calls tend to occur every few microseconds on average in integer code but may be infrequent in vectorizable floating-point code. Whenever a context switch occurs, the register windows are flushed to memory and the stack cache starts again in the new context. Context switches tend to occur every few milliseconds on average, and a ratio of several hundred subroutine calls per context switch is a good one. There is time to take advantage of the register windows before they are flushed again. When the new context starts up, it loads in the register windows one at a time, so programs that do not make many subroutine calls do not load registers that they will not need. Note that a special trap is provided that can be called to flush the register windows; this trap is needed if you wish to switch to a different stack as part of a user written co-routine or threads library. When SunOS is running, a context switch rate of 1000 per second on each CPU is considered fast, so there are rarely any problems. There may be more concern about this ratio when running real-time operating systems on SPARC machines, but there are alternative ways of configuring the register windows that are more suitable for real-time systems[2]. These systems often run entirely in kernel mode and can perform special tricks to control the register windows.

The register window context switch time is a small fraction of the total SunOS context-switch time. On machines with virtual write-back caches, a cache flush is also required on some context switches. Systems have varying amounts of support for fast cache flush in hardware. The original SunOS 4.0 release mapped the kernel U-area at the same address for all processes, and the U-area flush gave the Sun-4/260 with SunOS 4.0 (the first SPARC machine) a bad reputation for poor context-switch performance that some people mistakenly blamed on the register windows.

Identifying Different SPARC CPUs

Table 10-1 can be used to find which SPARC CPU each machine has.

Table 10-1 Which SPARC IU and FPU Does Your System Have?

System (Kernel Architecture)	Clock	Integer Unit	Floating-point Unit
Sun-4/110 and Sun4/150 (sun4)	14 MHz	Fujitsu #1	FPC+Weitek 1164/5
Sun-4/260 and Sun4/280 (sun4)	16 MHz	Fujitsu #1	FPC+Weitek 1164/5
Sun-4/260 and Sun4/280 FPU2 (sun4)	16 MHz	Fujitsu #1	FPC2+TI 8847
SPARCserver 300 series (sun4)	25 MHz	Cypress 601	FPC2+TI 8847
SPARCserver 400 series (sun4)	33 MHz	Cypress 601	FPC2+TI 8847
SPARCstation 1 and SLC (sun4c)	20 MHz	LSI/Fujisu #2	Weitek 3170
SPARCstation 1+ and IPC (sun4c)	25 MHz	LSI/Fujitsu#2	Weitek 3170
Tadpole SPARCbook 1 (sun4m)	25 MHz	Cypress 601	Weitek 3171
SPARCstation ELC (sun4c)	33 MHz	Fujitsu #3	Weitek 3171 on chip
SPARCstation IPX (sun4c)	40 MHz	Fujitsu #3	Weitek 3171 on chip
SPARCstation 2 (sun4c)	40 MHz	Cypress 601	TI 602
SPARCserver 600 Model 120/140 (sun4m)	40 MHz	Cypress 601	Weitek 3171
SPARCstation 10 Model 20 (sun4m)	33 MHz	SuperSPARC	SuperSPARC

2. "SPARC Technology Conference Notes - 3 Intense Days of Sun" — Alternative Register Window Schemes. The Alewife Project at MIT has implemented one of these schemes for fast context switching.

Table 10-1 Which SPARC IU and FPU Does Your System Have?

System (Kernel Architecture)	Clock	Integer Unit	Floating-point Unit
SPARCstation 10 Model 30 (sun4m)	36 MHz	SuperSPARC	SuperSPARC
SPARCstation 10 Model 40, 402 (sun4m)	40 MHz	SuperSPARC	SuperSPARC
SPARCstation 10 Model 41, 412 (sun4m)	40 MHz	SuperSPARC	SuperSPARC
SPARCstation 10 model 51, 512, 514 (sun4m)	50MHz	SuperSPARC	SuperSPARC
SPARCstation 20 Model 50, 502 (sun4m)	50MHz	SuperSPARC	SuperSPARC
SPARCstation 20 Model 61, 612 (sun4m)	60MHz	SuperSPARC	SuperSPARC
Cray SuperServer CS6400 (sun4d)	60MHz	SuperSPARC	SuperSPARC
SPARCclassic & SPARCstation LX (sun4m)	50MHz	microSPARC	microSPARC
SPARCcenter 1000 & 2000 (sun4d)	50MHz	SuperSPARC	SuperSPARC
Cray S-MP & FPS 500EA (sun4)	66MHz	BIT B5000	BIT B5010
SPARCstation Voyager (sun4m)	60MHz	microSPARC II	microSPARC II
SPARCstation 5 Model 70 (sun4m)	70MHz	microSPARC II	microSPARC II
SPARCstation 5 Model 70 (sun4m)	85MHz	microSPARC II	microSPARC II
SPARC PowerUP (sun4c)	80MHz	Weitek	Weitek on-chip
UltraSPARC details not announced ( )			

Sun engineering teams designed many of the integer units, listed in Table 10-1 by the vendor that manufactured and sold the parts. Sun has often dual-sourced designs and several designs have been cross-licensed by several vendors. The basic designs listed in Table 10-1 are:

- The original gate array IU design sold by Fujitsu (#1) as the MB86901, used an FPU based on the Weitek 1164 and 1165. Initially the design used a floating-point controller (FPC) ASIC but later moved to the Texas Instruments 8847 with a new FPC design.

- A tidied-up, semi custom gate array version for higher clock rates is sold by Fujitsu and LSI Logic (#2) as the L64911. It takes two cycles to issue operations to the companion, single-chip Weitek 3170 FPU.

- A full-custom CMOS version with minor improvements and higher clock rates is sold by Cypress as the CY7C601, which was licensed by Fujitsu (#3) and combined with a Weitek 3171 FPU into a single chip sold by both Fujitsu and Weitek as the MB86903. FPU operations are issued in one cycle to either a Texas Instruments 602 or a Weitek 3171 FPU.

- A high clock-rate ECL implementation with an improved pipeline is sold by BIT as the B5000. It has its own matching FPU design based on a custom ECL FPC and a standard BIT multiplier and accumulator.

- A second generation, superscalar BICMOS implementation, known as SuperSPARC with its own on-chip FPU, is sold by Texas Instruments as the TMS390Z50. The companion SuperCache controller chip is the TMS390Z55.

- A highly integrated, very low cost custom CMOS implementation, known as microSPARC with an on-chip FPU derived from a design by Meiko Ltd. is sold by Texas Instruments as the TMS390S10.

- The microSPARC II design with higher performance and even higher integration than microSPARC is made by Fujitsu.

Several SPARC chips are designed independently of Sun, including the Fujitsu MB86930 SPARClite embedded controller, the Matsushita MN10501 used by Solbourne, and the Fujitsu HyperSPARC™. The Ross division of Cypress was bought by Fujitsu in 1993.

The Weitek SPARC PowerUP Upgrade

Weitek has modified the basic design used in the MB86903 to double the internal clock rate and provide 24 Kbytes of on-chip caches. This design is sold as a chip-level upgrade for SPARCstation 2 and IPX machines, and its 80 MHz operation runs some programs between one and a half and two times faster than on the basic 40 MHz SPARCstation 2 or IPX.

Superscalar Operations

The main superscalar SPARC chips are the Texas Instruments SuperSPARC and the Cypress/Ross HyperSPARC. These chips can both issue multiple instructions in a single cycle.

SuperSPARC

The SuperSPARC can issue three instructions in one clock cycle; just about the only instructions that cannot be issued continuously are integer multiply and divide, floating point divide, and square root, as shown in Table 10-2. A set of rules controls how many instructions are grouped for issue in each cycle. The main ones are that instructions are executed strictly in order and subject to the following conditions[3]:

- Three instructions in a group

- One load or store anywhere in a group

- A control transfer (branch or call) ends a group at that point

---

3. See "The SuperSPARC Microprocessor Technical White Paper."

- One floating point operation anywhere in a group

- Two integer word results or one double word result (including loads) per group

- One shift can cascade into another operation, but not vice-versa

Dependent compare and branch is allowed, and simple ALU cascades are allowed (a + b + c). Floating point load and a dependent operation is allowed, but dependent integer operations have to wait for the next cycle after a load.

SuperSPARC is shipping at 40, 50, and 60 MHz. A derived SuperSPARC II design is part of the SPARC futures road map for higher performance.

Cypress/Fujitsu Ross HyperSPARC

The HyperSPARC design can issue two instructions in one clock cycle. The combinations allowed are more restrictive than with SuperSPARC, but the simpler design allows a higher clock rate to compensate. HyperSPARC is shipping at 55 MHz and 66 MHz and is targeting 80 MHz and 100 MHz. The performance of a 66 MHz HyperSPARC is comparable to that of a 50 MHz SuperSPARC.

UltraSPARC

In 1993 Sun announced a SPARC road map for the following five years. Apart from higher clock rates, the next major development is the superscalar UltraSPARC. This design implements the 64-bit SPARC V9 architecture and will run at well over 100 MHz. Performance levels in the 200 to 300 region for SPECint92 and SPECfp92 are expected, depending upon cache size and a range of clock rates.

Low-cost Implementations

The main low-cost SPARC chips are the Fujitsu SPARClite, a development aimed at the embedded control marketplace; and the Texas Instruments microSPARC, a highly integrated "workstation on a chip." The microSPARC integer unit is based on the old BIT B5000 pipeline design, although it has a new low-cost FPU based upon a design by Meiko. The chip integrates IU, FPU, caches, MMU, SBus interface, and a direct DRAM memory interface controller.

Floating-point Performance Comparisons

Table 10-2 indicates why some programs that use divide or square root intensively may run better on a SPARCstation 2 than on a SPARCstation IPX, for example. The old Weitek 1164/5 did not implement square root in hardware, and there were bugs in some early versions. The SunPro code generator avoids the bugs and the square root instruction in

-cg87 mode, but goes faster in -cg89 (optimized for the SPARCstation 2) or in -cg92 (optimized for the SuperSPARC) mode if you know you do not have to run on the oldest type of machine. Solaris 2 disables the Weitek 1164/5 CPU so that -cg89 can be used as the default; however, this means that some old machines will revert to software FPU emulation. SunPro provides a command called fpversion that reports what you have in your machine microSPARC has an iterative FPU that is data dependent; minimum, typical and maximum times are given. I don't have microSPARC II details.

Most SPARC Instructions execute in a single cycle. The main exceptions are floating point operations, loads, stores and a few specialized instructions. The time taken to complete each floating point operation in cycles is shown in Table 10-2.

Table 10-2 Floating-point Cycles per Instruction

Instruction	FPC & TI 8847	Weitek 3170 & 3171	Texas 602	BIT B5000	microSPARC min	microSPARC typ	microSPARC max	Super SPARC
fitos	8	10	4	2	5	6	13	1
fitod	8	5	4	2	4	6	13	1
fstoir, fstoi	8	5	4	2	6	6	13	1
fdtoir, fdtoi	8	5	4	2	7	7	14	1
fstod	8	5	4	2	2	2	14	1
fdtos	8	5	4	2	3	3	16	1
fmovs	8	3	4	2	2	2	2	1
fnegs	8	3	4	2	2	2	2	1
fabss	8	3	4	2	2	2	2	1
fsqrts	15	60	22	24	6	37	51	6
fsqrtd	22	118	32	45	6	65	80	10
fadds, fsubs	8	5	4	2	4	4	17	1
faddd, fsubd	8	5	4	2	4	4	17	1
fmuls	8	5	4	3	5	5	25	1
fmuld	9	8	6	4	7	9	32	1
fdivs	13	38	16	14	6	20	38	4
fdivd	18	66	26	24	6	35	56	7
fcmps, fcmpes	8	3	4	2	4	4	15	1
fcmpd, fcmped	8	3	4	2	4	4	15	1

Integer Performance Comparisons

Table 10-3 lists the register windows and integer cycles per instruction. The main points to note are (1) microSPARC is similar to the B5000 in that they share the same basic pipeline design, but floating-point loads and stores are faster on the B5000, and (2) SuperSPARC can issue up to three instructions in a clock cycle according to grouping rules mentioned previously. SPARClite does not include an FPU.

Table 10-3 Number of Register Windows and Integer Cycles per Instruction

Instruction	Fujitsu/LSI #1, #2	Cypress/ Fujitsu #3	microSPARC (&B5000)	Fujitsu SPARClite	Super SPARC
(register windows)	7	8	7	8	8
ld (32 bit integer)	2	2	1	1	1
ldd (64 bit integer)	3	3	2	2	1
ld (32 bit float)	2	2	1	1	1
ldd (64 bit double)	3	3	2 (1)	2	1
st (32 bit integer)	3	3	2	1	1
std (64 bit integer)	4	4	3	2	1
st (32 bit float)	3	3	2 (1)	1	1
std (64 bit double)	4	4	3 (2)	2	1
taken branches	1	1	1	1	1
untaken branches	2	1	1	1	1
jmpl and rett	2	2	2	2	1
integer multiply	N/A	N/A	19	?	4
integer divide	N/A	N/A	39	?	18
issue FP operation	2	1	1	N/A	1

Kernel Algorithms and Tuning 11

This chapter explains the inner workings of the kernel so that you can understand the output of commands like `vmstat` and `sar`. The two parts of the kernel that are of most interest are the file attribute caches, and the paging algorithm. This chapter also describes buffer sizes and variables that can be changed by a system administrator when building or tuning a kernel. Appendix A, "Rules and Tunables Quick Reference Tables," contains a quick summary of when to tune and what can safely be changed.

The kernel algorithms have changed in many places between SunOS 4.x and Solaris 2. The differences are noted as SVR4 changes if they are generic and as Solaris 2 if Solaris 2 is different from generic SVR4. Later releases of SunOS 4.x have Solaris 1.x names, which I have avoided for clarity (although this is not considered the correct use of the terms). The kernel part of Solaris 2.x is known as SunOS 5.x, but this name is not often used.

SunOS and Solaris Release Overview

The number of fixed-size tables in the kernel has been reduced in each release of SunOS. Most are now dynamically sized or are linked to the *maxusers* calculation, which is now also sized automatically. My own personal tuning recommendations for each release vary as shown in Table 11-1. In most cases, tuning is only needed on large servers.

Table 11-1 Tuning SunOS Releases

Release	Tuning Recommendations for Large Servers
SunOS 4.1/Solaris 1.0	Add PMEGS patch tape or DBE-1.0, set *maxusers*.
SunOS 4.1.1/Solaris 1.0.1	Add DBE-1.1, increase buffer cache, set *maxusers*.
SunOS 4.1.2/Solaris 1.0.2	Add DBE-1.2, add I/O patch 100575-02, tune pager, set *maxusers*.
SunOS 4.1.3/Solaris 1.1	Add DBE-1.3, increase *maxslp*, tune pager, set *maxusers*.
SunOS 4.1.3U1/Solaris 1.1.1	Add DBE-1.3.1, increase *maxslp*, tune pager, set *maxusers*.
SunOS 5.0/Solaris 2.0	Tune pager, check `/etc/TIMEZONE`, set *maxusers*, upgrade!
SunOS 5.1/Solaris 2.1	Tune pager, double `ufs_ninode`, set *maxusers*.
SunOS 5.2/Solaris 2.2	Tune pager, double *ufs_ninode*.
SunOS 5.3/Solaris 2.3	Tune pager, double *ufs_ninode*, set *pt_cnt* for time-share.
SunOS 5.4/Solaris 2.4	Set *pt_cnt* for time-share.

Solaris 2 Performance Tuning Manuals

There is a manual section called *Administering Security, Performance, and Accounting in Solaris 2*. Read it, but beware that early releases contain a few typos and errors. The manual was written for Solaris 2.0, and some changes in the Solaris 2.2 and 2.3 kernel have made parts of the manual obsolete. The manual has been revised and corrected for Solaris 2.4, along with a completely rewritten *SMCC NFS Server Performance and Tuning Guide*. The first of these manuals is part of the *SunSoft™ System Software AnswerBook*, the second is part of the *Sun Microsystems Computer Corporation Hardware AnswerBook*.

Using /etc/system to Modify Kernel Variables in Solaris 2

In SunOS 4.x the kernel must be recompiled after values in param.c or conf.c are tweaked to increase table sizes. In Solaris 2 there is no need to recompile the kernel; it is modified by changing /etc/system and rebooting. /etc/system is read by the kernel at startup. It configures the search path for loadable kernel modules and allows kernel variables to be set. See the manual page for system (4) for the full syntax[1].

Be very careful with set commands in /etc/system; they basically cause arbitrary, unchecked and automatic changes to variables in the kernel, so there is plenty of opportunity to break your system. If your machine will not boot and you suspect a problem with /etc/system use the boot -a option. With this option, the system prompts (with defaults) for its boot parameters. One of these is the configuration file /etc/system. Either enter the name of a backup copy of the original /etc/system file or enter /dev/null. Fix the file and reboot the machine immediately to check that it is now working properly.

Watch for messages at boot time. If an error is detected or a variable doesn't exist, then a message is displayed on the console during boot.

General Solaris 2 Performance Improvements

The initial developers' release of Solaris 2.0 is slower than SunOS 4.1.3. Solaris 2.1 performance improved substantially, particularly for interactive desktop use. Solaris 2.2 had further improvements, with an emphasis on database performance, I/O throughput and multiprocessor scalability. Solaris 2.3 benefited from another six months of performance tuning and bug fixes, with an emphasis on network throughput, multiuser performance, and high-end multiprocessor scalability. Very high SPEC LADDIS NFS performance numbers obtained using Solaris 2.3 have been released. The latest set of

---

1. The command to use is man -s 4 system, since there are other things called "system" in the manual.

changes in Solaris 2.4 focus on improving interactive performance in small memory configurations, improving overall efficiency, and providing better support for large numbers of connected time-sharing users with high-end multiprocessor machines.

The Solaris 2 kernel is on a diet! It will get slimmer and quicker in subsequent releases for better performance on everything from the smallest SPARCclassic to the 20-CPU SPARCcenter 2000.

Some of the changes that improve performance on the latest processor types and improve high-end multiprocessor scalability could cause a slight reduction in performance on earlier processor types and on uniprocessors. Trade-offs like this are carefully assessed; in most cases, when changes to part of the system are made, an improvement must be demonstrated on all configurations.

In general, Solaris 2 still requires more memory than SunOS 4.1.3 requires. On small memory systems (16 Mbytes) SunOS 4.1.3 will be faster because it will be paging less[2]. On larger memory systems Solaris 2 is faster than SunOS 4.1.3 for some things and slower for others. In some areas, internationalization and stricter conformance to standards from the SVID, POSIX, and X/Open cause higher overheads compared to SunOS 4.1.3.

The base Solaris 2 operating system contains support for international locales that require 16 bit characters, whereas the base SunOS 4 is always 8-bit. The internationalized and localized versions of SunOS 4 were recoded and released much later than the base version. Solaris 2 releases have a much simpler localization process. One side effect of this is that the Solaris 2 `sort` command deals with 16-bit characters and localized collation ordering. If you only deal with the simple 8-bit locales and use `sort` a lot, then it can be faster to use the SunOS 4.1.3 version of `sort` running in binary compatibility mode on a Solaris 2 system.

Using Solaris 2 with Large Numbers of Active Users

Problems supporting a large number of active users tend to start at about the level of 200 active users. This level was rarely encountered in SunOS 4 and early Solaris 2 releases, since the CPU was usually maxed out in any case well before this point. The SPARCserver 1000 and SPARCcenter 2000 changed this by providing abundant CPU power and RAM. The problem is a well-known generic issue with UNIX and TCP/IP networking protocols.

To connect large numbers of users into a system, Ethernet terminal servers using the Telnet protocol are normally used. Characters typed by several users at one terminal server cannot be multiplexed into a single Ethernet packet; a separate packet must be sent

---

2. See "Solaris 2 Tweaks" on page 214 for a way to free up some memory and help performance.

for any activity on each Telnet session. The data is processed by a pair of Telnet daemons, one for each direction for each user, so the action of echoing a single character typed at a terminal involves the following steps, which are illustrated in Figure 11-1. (The `rlogin` process is very similar.)

1. **Send an Ethernet packet from a terminal server to Solaris.**
   The terminal server gets a character from a serial port and puts it in a Telnet packet on the Ethernet.

2. **Send the packet to the user's incoming `telnetd`.**
   On the server the Ethernet device driver passes the packet up through TCP/IP protocol processing to a Telnet daemon process.

3. **Send the characters to an application.**
   The Telnet protocol processing is performed, and the character is written down the pseudo-terminal to the application. The application decides what to send back to the user, and a bunch of characters may be written.

4. **Send the echo characters to the user's outgoing Telnet.**
   The characters written to the pseudo-terminal are picked up and processed by the outgoing telnet daemon, which handles the Telnet protocol and writes it back down through TCP/IP to the Ethernet driver.

5. **Send back the Ethernet packet from Solaris to a terminal server.**
   An individual Ethernet packet is sent back to the terminal server, which writes the characters to a serial port.

Figure 11-1   Terminal Server Telnet Processing

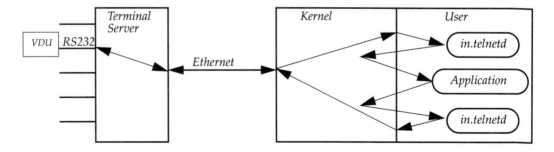

This process involves context switches between three UNIX processes, a lot of protocol processing, and several system calls for each interaction with each user. This is the situation that exists in all SunOS 4.X releases, generic BSD and SVR4 UNIX, and Solaris 2. There are several ways that it can be made more efficient.

The system calls involved include `poll`, which is implemented with single-threaded code in releases before Solaris 2.4. This prevents raw CPU power from being used to solve this problem, as the effect in Solaris 2.3 and earlier releases is that a large amount of CPU time is wasted in the kernel contending on `poll`, and adding another CPU has no useful effect. This limits the number of active Telnet-connected users per machine to about 200 in practice. In Solaris 2.4, `poll` is fully multithreaded, so, with sufficient CPU power, Telnet no longer limits the number of users and kernel CPU time stays low to 500 users and beyond. Now that the Telnet and `poll` limit has gone, any subsequent limit is much more application-dependent. Tests on a 16-processor SPARCcenter 2000 failed to find any significant kernel-related limits before the machine ran out of CPU power.

Another approach is to take the Telnet and Rlogin daemons out of the normal path; a single daemon remains to handle the protocol itself, but the regular character data that is sent backward and forward is processed entirely within the kernel, using new streams modules that take the characters directly from the TCP/IP stack and put them directly into the pseudo-terminal. This makes the whole process much more efficient and, since the poll system call is no longer called, also bypasses the contention problems. This Rlogin and Telnet solution is being developed for release as a patch for Solaris 2.4.

The underlying efficiency of the network protocol is part of the problem, and one solution is to abandon the Telnet protocol completely. There are two good options, but both have the disadvantage of using a proprietary protocol. The terminal server that Sun supplies is made by Xylogics, Inc. Xylogics has developed a multiplexed protocol that takes all the characters from all the ports on their terminal server and sends them as a single large packet to Solaris. A new protocol streams driver that Xlogics supplies for Solaris de-multiplexes the packet and writes the correct characters to the correct pseudo-terminal. This product is expected to become available from Xylogics in mid-1994. Another possible alternative is to use the DECnet LAT protocol, which addresses the same issues. Many terminal servers support LAT because of its widespread use in DEC sites. There are several implementations of LAT for Solaris; for example, Meridian does one which is implemented as a stream module, so should be quite efficient.

The Performance Implications of Patches

Every release has a set of patches for the various subsystems, the patches generally fall into three categories; security-related patches, reliability-related patches and performance related patches. In some cases, the patches are derived from the ongoing development work on the next release, where changes have been back-ported to previous releases for immediate availability. Some patches are also labeled as recommended patches, particularly for server systems. You should resist the temptation to apply every patch you find since as some of the reliability-related patches are for fairly obscure problems and may reduce the performance of your system. If you are benchmarking, try to get benchmark results with and without patches so that you can see the difference.

The Amdahl Solaris A+ Edition Product

Amdahl Corp. resells the SPARCserver 1000 and SPARCcenter 2000. Amdahl has made changes to the Solaris 2 code based on experience with their mainframe UNIX SVR4 based UTS4.2 release. There are several components to this product, but the most interesting one is a modified version of the kernel. The SunSoft kernel patch releases are tracked as they occur and incorporated into new versions of A+.

A+ makes changes in areas that are not used much by the main industry-standard benchmarks. The changes primarily help the system manage virtual memory more efficiently. This speeds up process creation and related tasks. The benchmarks that show the most benefit are the little-used SPEC multiuser benchmarks SDET and Kenbus1.

The initial A+ release does not address the Telnet issues mentioned in "Using Solaris 2 with Large Numbers of Active Users" on page 183. However, Amdahl has developed a 2.3-based patch for `poll` that does help many Telnets to run efficiently. A+ also makes little difference to NFS and database throughput, as measured by LADDIS and TPC benchmarks; the base Solaris 2 release has already been well-tuned for these workloads. Solaris 2.4 solves some of the performance problems that are fixed by A+ and some others besides, but it does not include the main A+ improvements. Amdahl is expected to incorporate the best of both in a 2.4A+ release.

The A+ patch is available only for the *sun4d* kernel architecture, so it will only run on SPARCserver 1000 and SPARCcenter 2000 systems. It is priced on a per CPU basis; and in many cases fewer CPUs will be needed for the same performance level.

Basic Sizing with Maxusers

When BSD UNIX was originally developed, its designers addressed the problem of scaling the size of several kernel tables and buffers by creating a single sizing variable. The scaling needed was related to the number of time-sharing terminal users the system could support, so the variable was named *maxusers*. Nowadays, so much has changed that there is little direct relationship between the number of users a system supports and the value of *maxusers*. Increases in memory size and more complex applications require much larger kernel tables and buffers for the same number of users.

Parameters Derived from maxusers

The calculation of parameters derived from maxusers is basically the same in both SunOS 4 and Solaris 2. The inode and name cache variables are described in more detail later in this chapter. The other variables are not performance-related.

Table 11-2 Default Settings for Kernel Parameters

Kernel Resource	Variable	Default Setting
Processes	max_nprocs	10 + 16 * maxusers
Callout Queue	ncallout	16 + max_nprocs[1]
Inode Cache	ufs_ninode	max_nprocs + 16 + maxusers + 64
Name Cache	ncsize	max_nprocs + 16 + maxusers + 64
Quota Table	ndquot	(maxusers * NMOUNT)/4 + max_nprocs
User Process Limit	maxuprc	max_nprocs - 5

1. *ncallout* no longer exists in Solaris 2.2 and later releases. The callout queue is now dynamically sized as required.

Changing maxusers in SunOS 4

The *maxusers* parameter is set in the kernel configuration file, and a replacement kernel is compiled and linked using the new value. *maxusers* defaults to 16 for the sun4m architecture, but in other architectures it defaults to 8 for a GENERIC kernel and 4 for a GENERIC_SMALL kernel. These values are suitable for single-user workstations that are short of RAM, but in most cases a substantial increase in *maxusers* is called for. A safe upper limit is documented in the SunOS 4.1.2 (about 100) and 4.1.3 (about 200) manuals in the Read This First section. A rough guideline would be to set to the number of megabytes of RAM in the system for a workstation and twice that for an NFS server (subject to the limits mentioned above). Because of a shortage of kernel memory in SunOS 4.1.2, the safe upper limit is *reduced* to about 100 for systems that have large amounts of RAM, since kernel memory is used to keep track of RAM as well as to allocate tables. The kernel base address was changed in 4.1.3 to allow a safe limit of about 200 for sun4m kernel architecture systems. The limit for other kernel architectures may be less, and if a system will not boot, reduce *maxusers* to 100 or less and try again.

Changing maxusers and Pseudo-ttys in Solaris 2

The effect of *maxusers* has not changed, but it now defaults to 8 in Solaris 2.0 and 2.1 and is dynamically sized in Solaris 2.2, Solaris 2.3, and Solaris 2.4 depending on the amount of RAM configured in the system. It is modified by placing a command in /etc/system to override the default value.

The variable that really limits the number of user logins on the system is *pt_cnt*. It may be necessary to set the number of pseudo-ttys higher than the default of 48, especially in a time-sharing system that uses Telnet-from-Ethernet terminal servers to connect users to the system. Solaris 2.2 has a limit of 1000 pseudo-ttys, since the /dev/pts entries can only go from /dev/pts/0 to /dev/pts/999. This restriction was lifted for Solaris 2.3,

The only upper limit is the amount of kernel memory used by the inodes. The tested upper limit in Solaris 2.3 corresponds to *maxusers = 2048,* which is the same as *ncsize* at 34906. Use `sar -k` to report the size of the kernel memory allocation; each inode uses 512 bytes of kernel memory from the lg_mem pool. In Solaris 2.4, the inodes are packed together and use around 300 bytes each. Since it is just a limit, *ufs_ninode* can be tweaked with `adb` on a running system with immediate effect.

Inode cache statistics can be seen on later Solaris 2 releases using `netstat -k` to dump out the raw kernel statistics information as shown in Figure 11-6.

If the *maxsize_reached* value is higher than the *maxsize* (this variable is equal to *ufs_ninode*), then the number of *active* inodes has exceeded the cache size at some point in the past, so you should increase *ufs_ninode*. Set it on a busy NFS server by editing `param.c` and rebuilding the kernel in SunOS 4 and by adding the following line to `/etc/system` for Solaris 2.

```
set ufs_ninode=10000          For Solaris 2.2 and 2.3 only
set ufs_ninode=5000           For Solaris 2.4 only
```

Figure 11-6   Example `netstat` *Output to Show Inode Statistics*

```
% netstat -k
inode_cache:
size 1200 maxsize 1200 hits 722 misses 2605 mallocs 1200 frees 0
maxsize_reached 1200
puts_at_frontlist 924 puts_at_backlist 1289 dnlc_looks 0 dnlc_purges 0
```

Warning – `netstat -k` is an undocumented and unsupported option. The output is an almost raw dump of the undocumented kernel statistics interface, which is subject to change in each release of Solaris 2. Do not depend upon it.

Rnode Cache

A similar cache, the rnode cache, is maintained on NFS clients to hold information about files in the NFS filesystem. The data is read by NFS `getattr` calls to the NFS server, which keeps the information in a vnode of its own. The default rnode cache size is twice the DNLC size and should not need to be changed.

Suggested Tuning Changes for DNLC and Inode Caches

The inode cache size should end up twice the DNLC size for older releases. This change is not needed in Solaris 2.4. If your Solaris 2 NFS server has over 256 Mbytes of RAM or has maxusers set over 256, the cache size will already be over 5000. Do not reduce it with this fix, but do double the inode cache size.

Table 11-4 Suggested Changes for `ufs_ninode` *for SunOS 4.X and Solaris 2.0 to Solaris 2.3*

Machine Type	Default Setup	Suggested Changes
Default	ufs_ninode = ncsize = maxusers*17+90	ufs_ninode = 2 * ncsize
NFS Server	ufs_ninode = ncsize = maxusers*17+90	ufs_ninode = 5000 ncsize = 10000

Buffer Cache

The buffer cache is used to cache all UFS disk I/O in SunOS 3 and BSD UNIX. In SunOS 4, generic SVR4, and Solaris 2 it is used to cache inode-, indirect block-, and cylinder group- related disk I/O only.

In Solaris 2 *nbuf* is used to keep track of how many page sized buffers have been allocated, and a new variable called *p_nbuf* (default value 100) defines how many new buffers are allocated in one go. A variable called *bufhwm* controls the maximum amount of memory allocated to the buffer and is specified in Kbytes. The default value of *bufhwm*, allows up to two percent of system memory to be used. On systems that have a large amount of memory, two percent of the memory is too much and the buffer cache can cause kernel memory starvation as described in "Kernel Memory Allocation" on page 216. The *bufhwm* tunable can be used to fix this by limiting the buffer cache to a few Mbytes as shown below.

```
set bufhwm = 8000
```

In Solaris 2 the buffer cache can be monitored by using `sar -b`, which reports a read and a write hit rate for the buffer cache, as shown in Figure 11-7. "Administering Security, Performance, and Accounting in Solaris 2" contains unreliable information about tuning the buffer cache.

Figure 11-7   Example `Sar` *Output to Show Buffer Cache Statistics*

```
# sar -b 5 10
SunOS hostname 5.2 Generic sun4c    08/06/93
23:43:39 bread/s lread/s %rcache bwrit/s lwrit/s %wcache pread/s pwrit/s
...
Average         0      25     100       3      22      88       0       0
```

An alternative look at the buffer cache hit rate can be calculated from part of the output of `netstat -k`, as shown in Figure 11-8.

Figure 11-8 Example `netstat` *Output to Show Buffer Cache Statistics*

```
% netstat -k
biostats:
buffer cache lookups 9705 buffer cache hits 9285 new buffer requests 0
waits for buffer allocs 0 buffers locked by someone 3 duplicate buffers
found 0
```

Comparing buffer cache hits with lookups (9285/9705) shows a 96 percent hit rate since reboot, which seems to be high enough.

The Paging Algorithm and Memory Usage

The paging algorithm manages and allocates physical memory pages to hold the active parts of the virtual address space of processes running on the system. First the monitoring statistics are explained; then the algorithm is explained; then recommended changes in the tuning parameters for different circumstances are made. The most important reason to understand paging is that you can then tell when adding more RAM will make a difference to performance.

MMU Algorithms and PMEGS

A fundamental part of the kernel functionality is concerned with managing virtual and physical memory. It is useful to understand the differences between various machines in the way that virtual to physical memory translations are performed. The two types of MMU hardware have already been described in "Memory Management Unit Designs" on page 164.

Understanding vmstat and sar Output

The paging activity on a Sun can be monitored by means of `vmstat` or `sar`. `sar` is better for logging the information, but `vmstat` is more concise and crams more information into each line of text for interactive use. There is a simple correspondence between most of the values reported by `sar` and `vmstat`.

Unfortunately, the `vmstat` manual page does not explain how to interpret the information, so clarification of some fields is in order. At this stage, don't worry if the explanations make little sense — this chapter looks deeper and deeper into the paging algorithms as it goes on. The kernel variables that control the algorithm are described later. The Solaris 2 version of the `vmstat` command is explained; the SunOS 4 version doesn't show free swap space but labels that column `avm` and always reports zero as the value. This is a hangover from the redesign of the virtual memory system between the BSD 4.2-based SunOS 3 and SunOS 4.

Runnable Queue: `vmstat procs r` **and** `sar -q runq-sz, runocc`

The runnable queue is the primary measure that can be used to decide whether a system needs more CPU power. If a process is ready to run but there is no free CPU to run on, then the process waits in this queue. This is a bit like going to the bank at lunchtime and waiting in line to be served. If the line is long, so is the wait. If more bank clerks service the line, it moves faster so a longer line is OK. On a multiprocessor machine, the queue empties more quickly than on a uniprocessor; a crude estimate of the service time is the length of the queue divided by the number of CPUs. A CPU time slice is about 50 to 100 ms, and a service time of up to four time-slices is usually perceived to be acceptable performance. `runocc` is the proportion of the time that there is something in the run queue.

Blocked Queue: `vmstat procs b`

This is the number of processes that are ready to run but are blocked for resources, paging, I/O, and so forth.

Swapped Queue: `vmstat procs w` **and** `sar -q swpq-sz, swpocc`

This is the number of processes swapped out due to lack of RAM. You are unlikely to see this nonzero unless you are running Solaris 2.4. `swpocc` is the proportion of the time that there is something in the swap queue.

Swap Space: `vmstat swap`, `sar -r freeswap` **and** `swap -s`

`vmstat swap` shows the available swap in Kbytes, `sar -r freeswap` shows the free swap in 512-byte blocks, and `swap -s` shows several measures including available swap. They do not measure the same thing! In the example shown in Figure 11-9, available swap is about 34 Mbytes whereas free swap is about 42 Mbytes, the 8 Mbytes of reserved swap shown by `swap -s` is the difference. `swap -s available + swap -s reserved = sar -r freeswap`.

Figure 11-9   Three Ways to Look at Swap Space

```
hostname% sar -r 1
SunOS hostname 5.3 Generic sun4c     06/26/94
16:46:36 freemem freeswap
16:46:37     307     85104
hostname% swap -s
```

```
total: 35856k bytes allocated + 8532k reserved = 44388k used, 34172k
available
hostname% vmstat 1
 procs      memory            page            disk          faults      cpu
 r b w    swap  free   re  mf pi po fr de sr f0 s3 s5 --   in   sy   cs us sy id
 0 0 0    8808  4200    0   3  1  0  0  0  0  0  0  0    78  284  192  6  3 92
 0 0 0   34144  1320    0  14  0  0  0  0  0  0  0  0    30  169  144  1  2 97
```

Please refer to "Virtual Swap Space in SunOS" by Howard Chartock and Peter Snyder for an explanation. When available swap is exhausted, the system will not be able to use more memory.

Free Memory: vmstat free **and** sar -r freemem

> vmstat reports the free memory in Kbytes, that is the pages of RAM that are immediately ready to be used whenever a process starts up or needs more memory. sar reports freemem in pages. The kernel variable *freemem* that they report is discussed later. The absolute value of this variable has no useful meaning. Its value relative to some other kernel thresholds is what is important.

Reclaims: vmstat re

> This is the number of pages reclaimed from the free list. The page had been stolen but had not yet been reused so it can be reclaimed avoiding a full page fault that would need I/O. This is described in "The Life Cycle of a Typical Physical Memory Page" on page 200.

Minor Faults: vmstat mf **and** sar -p vflt

> A minor fault is caused by an address space or hardware address translation fault.

Other Fault Types: sar -p pflt, slock, vmstat -s copy-on-write, zero fill

> There are many other types of page faults. Protection faults are caused by illegal accesses of the kind that produce "segmentation violation - core dumped" messages. Copy-on-write and zero-fill faults are described in "The Life Cycle of a Typical Physical Memory Page" on page 200. Protection and copy-on-write together make up sar -p pflt. Faults caused by software locks held on pages are reported by sar -p slock. The total counts of several of these fault types are reported by vmstat -s.

Attaches To Existing Pages: vmstat at **and** sar -p atch

This is the number of attaches to shared pages already in use by other processes (reference count is incremented).

Pages Swapped In: vmstat -S si **and** sar -w swpin, bswin

vmstat -S si reports the number of Kbytes/s swapped in, sar -w swpin reports the number of swap-in operations, and sar -w bswin reports the number of 512- byte blocks swapped in.

Pages Swapped Out: vmstat so **and** sar -w swpot, bswot

vmstat -S so reports the number of Kbytes/s swapped out, sar -w swpot reports the number of swap-out operations and sar -w bswot reports the number of 512- byte blocks swapped out.

Pages Paged In: vmstat pi **and** sar -p pgin, ppgin

vmstat pi reports the number of Kbytes/s and sar reports the number of page faults and the number of pages paged in by swap space or file system reads. Since the filesystem block size is 8 Kbytes, there are often two pages or 8 Kbytes, paged in per page fault.

Pages Paged Out: vmstat po **and** sar -p pgout, ppgout

vmstat po reports the number of Kbytes/s and sar reports the number of page-outs and the number of pages paged out to the swap space or file system. Because of the clustering that occurs on swap space writes, there may be very many pages written per page-out. "Virtual Swap Space in SunOS" by Howard Chartock and Peter Snyder describes how this works.

Pages Freed: vmstat fr **and** sar -g pgfree

Pages freed is the rate at which memory is being put onto the free list by the page scanner daemon. vmstat fr is in Kbytes freed per second, and sar -g pgfree is in pages freed per second. Pages are usually freed by the page scanner daemon, but there are other mechanisms as well.

The Short Term Memory Deficit: vmstat de

In SunOS 4 and Solaris 2 as far as 2.3, an artificial memory deficit is set at swap-out to prevent processes from immediately swapping back in. It decays over time after the swap-out. In practice, swapping does not normally occur, so it can be ignored. In

Solaris 2.4 the swapping and paging algorithms have been redesigned. The deficit is now a paging parameter that provides some hysteresis for the page scanner when there is a period of high memory demand. If it is nonzero, then memory is being consumed quickly.

The Page Daemon Scanning Rate: vmstat sr **and** sar -g pgscan

These commands report the number of pages scanned by the page daemon as it looks for pages to steal from processes that aren't using them often. This is the key memory shortage indicator if it stays above 200 pages per second for long periods.

Example vmstat **Output**

To illustrate the dynamics of vmstat output, Figure 11-10 presents an annotated vmstat log taken at 5-second intervals. It was taken during an Empower RTE-driven 200 user test on a SPARCserver 1000 configured with Solaris 2.2, 128 Mbytes of RAM and four CPUs. Emulated users logged in at 5-second intervals and ran an intense, student-style, software development workload, that is, edit, compile, run, core dump, debug, look at man pages, and so forth. I have highlighted in bold type the numbers in the vmstat output that I take note of as the test progresses. Long sequences of output have been replaced by comments to reduce the log to a manageable length. As is often the case with Empower-driven workloads, the emulation of 200 dedicated users who never stop to think for more than a few seconds at a time provides a much higher load than 200 real life-students.

Figure 11-10 Example Vmstat 5 *Output for a SPARCserver 1000 with 200 Users*

procs			memory				page						disk					faults			cpu		
r	b	w	swap	free	re	mf	pi	po	fr	de	**sr**	s0	s1	s2	s3	in	sy	cs	us	sy	id
0	0	0	330252	**80708**	0	2	0	0	0	0	**0**	0	0	0	1	18	107	113	0	1	**99**
0	0	0	330252	**80708**	0	0	0	0	0	0	**0**	0	0	0	0	14	87	78	0	0	**99**
...users begin to login to the system																					
4	0	0	320436	**71448**	0	**349**	7	0	0	0	**0**	2	1	0	12	144	4732	316	65	35	0
6	0	0	318820	**69860**	0	**279**	25	0	0	0	**0**	0	0	0	2	54	5055	253	66	34	0
7	0	0	317832	**68972**	0	**275**	3	0	0	0	**0**	1	0	0	1	48	4920	278	64	36	0
...lots of minor faults are caused by processes starting up																					
50	0	0	259592	**14880**	0	**283**	8	0	0	0	**0**	1	0	0	2	457	5098	289	57	43	0
50	0	0	258716	**14040**	0	**311**	2	0	0	0	**0**	1	0	0	1	447	4822	306	59	41	0
51	0	0	256864	**12620**	0	**266**	2	0	0	0	**0**	3	1	0	12	543	3686	341	66	34	0
...at this point the free list drops below 8MB and the pager starts to scan																					
56	0	0	251620	**8352**	0	321	4	1	1	0	**0**	1	1	0	1	461	4837	342	57	43	0
60	0	0	238280	**5340**	5	596	1	371	1200	0	**4804**	0	0	0	6	472	3883	313	48	52	0
59	0	0	234624	**10756**	**97**	172	0	1527	1744	0	**390**	0	0	0	14	507	4582	233	59	41	0
60	0	0	233668	**10660**	9	297	2	0	0	0	**0**	4	2	0	12	539	5223	272	57	43	0
61	0	0	232232	**8564**	2	225	0	75	86	0	**87**	0	0	0	2	441	3697	217	71	29	0
62	0	0	231216	**8248**	2	334	11	500	547	0	**258**	1	0	0	7	484	5482	292	52	48	0

procs			memory		page							disk				faults			cpu		
r	b	w	swap	free	re	mf	pi	po	fr	de	**sr**	s0	s1	s2	s3	in	sy	cs	us	sy	id
...some large processes exit, freeing up RAM and swap space																					
91	0	0	**196868**	**7836**	0	227	8	511	852	0	**278**	1	7	0	5	504	5278	298	50	50	0
91	1	0	**196368**	**8184**	1	158	3	1634	2095	**0**	652	0	37	0	5	674	3930	325	50	50	0
92	0	0	**200932**	**14024**	0	293	85	496	579	0	**42**	0	17	0	21	654	4416	435	47	53	0
93	0	0	**208584**	**21768**	1	329	9	0	0	0	**0**	0	0	0	3	459	3971	315	62	38	0
92	1	0	**208388**	**20964**	0	328	12	0	0	0	**0**	3	3	0	14	564	5079	376	53	47	0
...it was steady like this for a long time. RAM is OK, need more CPUs																					
189	0	0	41136	**8816**	3	99	32	243	276	0	**160**	1	1	0	9	500	3804	235	67	33	0
190	0	0	40328	**8380**	6	**65**	76	0	0	0	**0**	3	2	0	19	541	3666	178	71	29	0
190	0	0	**40052**	**7976**	1	**56**	102	58	65	0	**32**	0	1	0	15	457	3415	158	72	28	0
...users exit causing an I/O block as closing files flushes changes to disk																					
57	**14**	0	**224600**	**55896**	5	114	284	0	0	0	**0**	0	1	0	69	843	368	436	84	16	0
39	**10**	0	**251456**	**61136**	37	117	246	0	0	0	**0**	1	4	0	70	875	212	435	81	19	0
19	**15**	0	**278080**	**65920**	46	129	299	0	0	0	**0**	0	1	0	74	890	223	454	82	18	0
3	**5**	0	**303768**	**70288**	23	88	248	0	0	0	**0**	0	1	0	59	783	324	392	60	11	29
0	**1**	0	**314012**	**71104**	0	47	327	0	0	0	**0**	0	3	0	47	696	542	279	12	5	83
0	**0**	0	**314012**	**69528**	1	39	304	0	0	0	**0**	0	3	0	38	636	109	205	14	3	83

Virtual Memory Basics

All the RAM in a system is managed in terms of pages (usually 4 Kbytes in size, but some older machines used 8 Kbytes), these are used to hold the *physical address space* of a process. The kernel manages the *virtual address space* of a process by maintaining a complex set of data structures. Each process has a single-address space structure, with any number of segment data structures to map each contiguous segment of memory to a backing device, which holds the pages when they are not in RAM. The segment keeps track of the pages that are currently in memory, and from this information, the system can produce the PMEG or PTE data structures that each kind of MMU reads directly to do the virtual-to-physical translations. The machine-independent routines that do this are called the *hat* (hardware address translation) layer. This architecture is generic to SunOS 4.X, SVR4 and Solaris 2. Figure 11-11 illustrates the concept. This diagram has been greatly simplified. In practice there are many more segments than are shown here!

The code segment contains executable instructions, the data segment contains pre-initialized data, such as constants and strings. BSS stands for Block Starting with Symbol and holds uninitialized data that will be zero to begin with.

10. Attach — A Popular Page

Another process using the same shared library page faults in the same place. It discovers that the page is already in memory and attaches to the page, increasing its vnode reference count by one.

11. COW — Making a Private Copy

If one of the processes sharing the page tries to write to it, copy-on-write (COW) page fault occurs. Another page is grabbed from the free list, and a copy of the original is made. This new page becomes part of a privately mapped segment backed by anonymous storage (swap space) so it can be changed, but the original page is unchanged and can still be shared. Shared libraries contain jump tables in the code that are patched, using COW as part of the dynamic linking process.

12. File Cache — Not Free

The entire window system exits, and both processes go away. This time the page stays in use, attached to the vnode of the shared library file. The vnode is now inactive but will stay in its cache[4] until it is reused, and the pages act as a file cache in case the user is about to restart the window system again.

13. Fsflush — Flushed by the Sync

Every 30 seconds all the pages in the system are examined in physical page order to see which ones contain modified data and are attached to a vnode. The details differ between SunOS 4 and Solaris 2, but essentially any modified pages will be written back to the filesystem, and the pages will be marked as clean.

This example sequence can continue from Step 4 or Step 9 with minor variations. The fsflush process occurs every 30 seconds by default for all pages, and whenever the free list size drops below a certain value, the `pagedaemon` scanner wakes up and reclaims some pages.

The detailed implementation of the paging algorithm and its parameters is now described for SunOS 4, followed by a description of the changes made for Solaris 2.

The Paging Algorithm in SunOS 4

When new pages are allocated from the free list, there comes a point when the system decides that there is no longer enough free memory (less than *lotsfree*) and it goes to look for some pages that haven't been used recently to add to the free list. At this point the `pagedaemon` is awakened. The system also checks the size of the free list four times per second and may wake up the `pagedaemon`. After a wakeup, the `pagedaemon` is

---

4. This subject was covered in "Vnodes, Inodes and Rnodes" on page 189. The filesystem could be UFS or NFS.

scheduled to run as a process inside the kernel and assumes that it runs four times per second, so it calculates a scan rate, then divides by four to get the number of pages to scan before it goes back to sleep.

The `pagedaemon`'s scanning algorithm works by regarding all the pagable RAM in order of its physical address as if it were arranged in a circle. Two pointers are used like the hands of a clock; the distance between the two hands is controlled by *handspread*. When there is a shortage of free pages (less than *lotsfree*) the hands start to move round the clock at a slow rate *(slowscan)*, which increases linearly to a faster rate *(fastscan)* as free memory tends to zero. If the pages for each hand are not locked into memory, on the free list, or otherwise busy then a flag (which is set every time the pages are referenced) is examined. If the pages have not been referenced, they can be freed. The first hand then clears the referenced flag for its page so that when the second hand gets round to the page, it will be freed unless it has been referenced since the first hand got there. If the freed page contained modified data it is paged out to disk. If there is a lot of memory in the system, then the chances of an individual page being referenced by a CPU in a given time span are reduced.

If the shortage of memory gets worse (less than *desfree*), there are two or more processes in the run queue, and it stays at that level for more than 30 seconds, then swapping will begin. If it gets to a minimum level (*minfree*), swapping starts immediately. If after going twice through the whole of memory there is still a shortage, the swapper is invoked to swap out entire processes. The algorithm limits the number of pages scheduled to be paged out to 40 per second (*maxpgio*) since this is approximately how many random I/Os per second a single disk can support at the 66 percent busy level. If you have swap spread across several disks, then increasing *maxpgio* may improve paging performance and delay the onset of swapping. Note that `vmstat po` reports the number of kilobytes per second paged out, which can be compared to *maxpgio* * *pagesize*.

Figure 11-12 illustrates parameters to control page scanning in SunOS 4.

Figure 11-12 Parameters to Control Page Scanning Rate and Onset of Swapping in SunOS 4

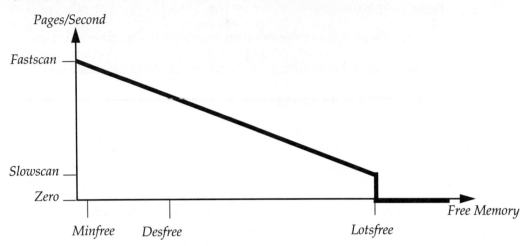

Kernel Variables to Control Paging in SunOS 4

The default values change in each OS release and vary for each kernel architecture for the same release of SunOS 4.

physmem

Physmem is set to the number of pages of usable physical memory. Some other variables are based on *physmem*. Pages are 4 Kbytes on most SPARC machines[5]. `adb` prints out *physmem* in hexadecimal when it is used to patch a live system.

minfree

Minfree is the absolute minimum memory level that can be tolerated by the system. If (freemem − deficit) is less than *minfree*, the system immediately swaps processes out rather than paging. It is usually set to 8 pages and clamped at *desfree*/2. The SunOS 4 sun4m kernel sets it to 128 pages.

---

5. See Table 9-6 on page 164 for a full list.

desfree

Desfree represents a *desperation* level, if free memory stays below this level for more than 30 seconds then paging is abandoned and swapping begins. *desfree* is usually set to 25 pages and is clamped to (*physmem*/16). The SunOS 4 sun4m kernel sets the value to 256 pages

lotsfree

Lotsfree is the memory limit that triggers the `pagedaemon` to start working if free memory drops below its value. *lotsfree* is usually set to 64 pages and is clamped at (*physmem*/8). The SunOS 4 sun4m kernel sets it to 512 pages.

fastscan

Fastscan is the number of pages scanned per second by the algorithm when there is no memory available and it is usually set to 1000. There is a linear ramp up from `slowscan` to `fastscan` as free memory goes from `lotsfree` to zero. The SunOS 4 sun4m kernel sets it to (physmem/2).

slowscan

Slowscan is the number of pages scanned per second by the algorithm when there is just under *lotsfree* available; it is usually set to (*fastscan*/10). There is a linear ramp up from *slowscan* to *fastscan* as free memory goes from *lotsfree* to zero

maxpgio

Maxpgio is the maximum number of page-out I/O operations per second that the system will schedule. The default is 40 pages per second, which is set to avoid saturating random access to a single 3600 rpm (60 rps) disk at two-thirds of the peak rate. It can be increased if more or faster disks are being used for the swap space. Many systems now have 5400 rpm (90 rps) disks; see Table 5-1 on page 64 for disk specifications.

handspread

Handspread is set to (*physmem*pagesize*/4), but is increased during initialization to be at least as large as fastscan, which makes it (*physmem*pagesize*/2) on sun4m machines.

Swapping Out and How to Get Back in (SunOS 4)

Swap-outs Based on Sleep Time

If a process has been sleeping for more than 20 seconds, then it is very likely to be swapped out even if a lot of free memory is available. This means that the update process, which synchronizes the disks every 30 seconds, is continually being swapped in and out, since it tends to sleep for 30 seconds. It also means that window system tools that wake up regularly (like the clock) swap in every minute to update the time. This concept seems to generate more overhead than it saves; it can be disabled by setting *maxslp* to 128. The kernel only keeps track of process sleep time in a single byte and it stops counting at 127 seconds. Large time-sharing MP servers running SunOS 4.1.2 or 4.1.3 can be helped significantly due to a reduction in unnecessary system time overhead.

The current values for all processes can be seen by means of `pstat -p` (in the SLP column), and information on a single process can be seen by means of `pstat -u` *pid* (where *pid* is the process ID). The `pstat` manual page is helpful, but intimate knowledge of kernel internals is assumed in too many cases.

These operations are also known as *soft swaps* and are not included in the swap-outs reported by `vmstat -S`. In practice, only the private pages for the process are swapped out, and these pages are put on the free list. When the swap-in occurs, the pages may still be on the free list so can be reclaimed without any disk reads.

Swap-outs Based on Memory Shortage

The SunOS 4 kernel keeps track of the ten biggest processes according to their resident set size (RSS). When there is a memory shortage (see the description of *minfree* and *desfree* in the previous section) it selects the four largest and swaps out the oldest or one that has been sleeping longer than *maxslp*. The deficit (`vmstat de`) is increased to prevent the process from swapping back in immediately. This is also known as a *hard swap* and is reported by `vmstat -S` `so` in Kbytes swapped out per second. It is very rare for memory to become scarce enough for this type of swap-out to occur.

Swap-ins

The first processes to be swapped back in are the smallest ones that have been asleep for longest and are not running at low priority. A process will be swapped back in when half of the number of pages it freed on swap-out are available, although only the basic few pages are swapped in at one time; the rest are paged in as needed.

The Paging Algorithm in Solaris 2

The basic paging algorithm is similar to that in SunOS 4, but the details have changed sufficiently for the tuning parameters to have different meanings in some cases (although they have the same names). This part of Solaris 2 has some tuning variables derived from System V and some from BSD4.3 via SunOS 4, but the algorithm now uses Solaris 2 kernel threads and works alongside the scheduler. Swapping is now a scheduler function, and Solaris 2.1 and 2.2 machines do not perform any swapping in normal operation. Solaris 2.3 swaps in some extreme circumstances; Solaris 2.4 implements a new swapping algorithm, designed to help performance on small-memory desktop machines. Page-outs are now queued and clustered so that the random page-outs are reorganized into large sequential writes. This makes page-out very efficient, but page-in is still random.

Swap Space

One other swapping change is that swap space on disk is no longer required to backup physical RAM. The total allocatable memory in SunOS 4.X is equal to the swap space, and large memory machines require an even larger swap space to back up the RAM. In Solaris 2, if you have enough RAM, you do not need to configure any swap space at all, so page-outs cannot occur! If you ran on SunOS 4.X with 30–40 Mbytes of swap space, then you could configure Solaris 2 with 48 Mbytes of RAM and no swap disk. The page scanning algorithm still needs to find unused pages to put on the free list, but it cannot cause page-outs. This is described further in "Virtual Swap SunOS" by Howard Chartock and Peter Snyder. Figure 11-13 illustrates parameters to control page scanning in Solaris 2.4.

Figure 11-13 Parameters to Control Page Scanning Rate and Onset of Swapping in Solaris 2.4

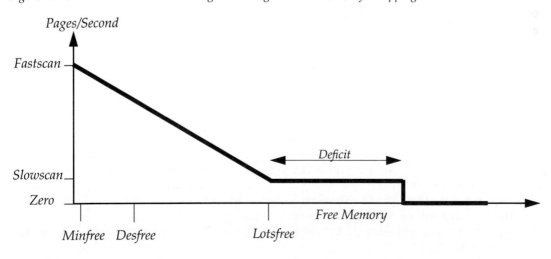

Tuning Parameters

The tuning parameters are described in the following.

 Caution – The kernel algorithms are subject to change, and the algorithms described are only valid for Solaris 2.1 through 2.4. 2.1 through 2.3 are identical, but Solaris 2.4 has changes to both the algorithms and the default values.

physmem

Physmem is set to the number of pages of usable physical memory. As previously mentioned, the *maxusers* calculation is based upon *physmem* in Solaris 2.2, 2.3, and 2.4. If you are investigating system performance and want to run tests with reduced memory on a system, you can set *physmem* in /etc/system and reboot to prevent a machine from using all its RAM. The unused memory still uses some kernel resources, and the page scanner still scans it, so if the reduced memory system does a lot of paging, the effect will not be the same as physically removing the RAM.

minfree

Minfree is set to (*physmem*/64) in Solaris 2.1 through 2.3 and is fixed at 50 pages for sun4d kernels and 25 pages for all others in 2.4. The kernel uses *minfree* for the following purposes:

- In Solaris 2.4, if the short-term (5-second) average free memory is less than *minfree*, then processes will be swapped out.
- When running exec on a small program (under 280K, which is set by *pgthresh*), the entire program is loaded in at one time rather than being paged in piecemeal, as long as doing so would not reduce *freemem* below *minfree*.

desfree

Desfree is set to (*physmem*/32) in Solaris 2.1 through 2.3 and is fixed at 100 pages for sun4d kernels and at 50 for all others in Solaris 2.4. The kernel uses *desfree* for the following purposes:

- In Solaris 2.4, if a 30 second average of free memory is less than *desfree*, then processes will be swapped out.
- At the point where pages are taken from the free list, if *freemem* is less than *desfree*, then an immediate wakeup call is sent to the pageout daemon, rather than waiting for pagedaemon to be awakened by the clock interrupt. This is similar to SunOS 4.

lotsfree and deficit

Lotsfree is set to (*physmem*/16) in Solaris 2.1 through 2.3; it is fixed at 256 pages for sun4d kernels and at 128 pages for all others in 2.4.

The kernel uses *lotsfree* for the following purposes:
- During the 100 Hz clock routine, a test is made four times a second to see if *freemem* is less than *lotsfree*. If so a wakeup, is sent to the `pageout` daemon.
- *Lotsfree* is the baseline for the scan rate interpolation. When *freemem* is the same as *lotsfree*, then the scan rate is set to *slowscan*.
- The *deficit* value is dynamically calculated and is displayed as `vmstat de`. It varies between zero and *lotsfree* and is added to *lotsfree* so that the system will continue to scan at the slow rate in anticipation of future, large, memory demands. It decays over time when memory demand drops.

fastscan

Fastscan is set to (*physmem*/2) in Solaris 2.1 through 2.3 and (*physmem*/4) with a limit of 64 Mbytes (16384) in Solaris 2.4. It is used in the scan rate interpolation as the notional scan rate when *freemem* is zero.

slowscan

Slowscan is the number of pages scanned per second by the algorithm when there is `exactly` *lotsfree* available. It is set to (*fastscan*/10) in Solaris 2.1 through 2.3 and is fixed at 100 in Solaris 2.4. There is a linear ramp-up from *slowscan* to *fastscan* as free memory goes from *lotsfree* to zero.

maxpgio

Maxpgio is the maximum number of page out I/O operations per second that the system will schedule. The default is 40 in Solaris 2.1 through 2.3, which is set to avoid saturating random access to a single 3600 rpm (60 rps) disk at two-thirds of the rotation rate. *Maxpgio* can be increased if more or faster disks are being used for the swap space. Since many systems now have 5400 rpm (90 rps) disks, *maxpgio* is set to 60 for sun4d kernels only in Solaris 2.4. See Table 5-1 on page 64 for disk specifications. The value is divided by four during system initialization, since the `pageout` daemon runs four times per second and the resulting value is the limit on the number of page-outs that the `pageout` daemon will add to the page-out queue in each invocation. Note that in addition to the clock-based invocations, an additional invocation will occur whenever more memory is allocated and *freemem* is less than *desfree*, so more than *maxpgio* pages can be queued per second when a lot of memory is allocated in a short time period.

Note – Changes to *maxpgio* only take effect after a reboot, so it cannot be tweaked on a running system.

---

handspreadpages

Handspreadpages is set to (*physmem*/4), but is increased during initialization to be at least as big as *fastscan,* which makes it (*physmem*/2) for Solaris 2.1 through 2.3. It is usually set to the same value as *fastscan*. In Solaris 2.4 it is limited to 64 Mbytes like *fastscan*. Note that the definition of this variable changed from *handspread*, measured in bytes in SunOS 4, to *handspreadpages* measured in pages in Solaris 2.

tune_t_ gpgslo

Tune_t_gpgslo is a feature derived from UNIX System V.3. In Solaris 2.1 to 2.3, it defaults to 25 pages and is the threshold used by the scheduler to decide whether to begin swapping-out processes. In Solaris 2.4 it is no longer used.

autoup and tune_t_fsflushr

Unlike SunOS 4 where the update process does a full sync of memory to disk every 30 seconds, Solaris 2 uses the fsflush daemon to spread out the sync workload. *Autoup* is set to 30 seconds by default, and this is the maximum age of any memory resident filesystem pages that have been modified. Unlike update, fsflush wakes up every 5 seconds (set by *tune_t_fsflushr*) and checks a portion of memory on each invocation (5/30= one-sixth of total RAM by default). The pages are queued on the same list that the pageout daemon uses and are formed into clustered sequential writes.

On machines with more than a few hundred Mbytes of RAM, fsflush can take over almost an entire CPU in the worst case, where very many pages are being modified. This problem can be avoided by reducing the rate at which fsflush checks memory. It should still always wake up every few seconds, but *autoup* can be increased from 30 seconds to a few hundred seconds if required. In most cases, files that are being written are closed before fsflush gets around to them. For NFS servers all writes are synchronous so fsflush is hardly needed at all. Note the time and the CPU usage of fsflush, then watch it later and see if its CPU usage is more than five percent. If it is, increase *autoup* as shown in Figure 11-15.

Figure 11-14 shows commands for evaluating fsflush.

Figure 11-14 Measuring Fsflush CPU Usage

```
% ps 3
    PID TT       S   TIME COMMAND
      3 ?        S 169:19 fsflush
% uptime
  10:09pm  up 2 day(s),  7:09,  4 users,  load average: 0.25, 0.23, 0.23
```

Since boot fsflush has used 169:19 = 10159 seconds of CPU time in a total of 112140 seconds elapsed time which is about 9% of a CPU. This system has 896 Mbytes of RAM and has an idle database running on it. When the database is active fsflush uses more CPU.

Figure 11-15 Reducing Fsflush CPU Usage By Increasing autoup in `/etc/system`

```
set autoup=240
```

max_page_get

Max_page_get is set to half the number of pages in the system and limits the maximum number of pages that can be allocated in a single operation. In some circumstances a machine may be sized to run a single very large program that has a data area or single `malloc` space of more than half the total RAM. It will be necessary to increase *max_page_get* in that circumstance.

Warning – If *max_page_get* is increased too far and reaches *total_pages* (a little less than *physmem*), then deadlock can occur and the system will hang trying to allocate more pages than exist.

Swapping Out and How to Get Back in (Solaris 2)

Under extreme, artificially induced conditions, a Solaris 2.2 system was made so short of memory that it was observed to swap out a process, but for all practical purposes, swapping can be ignored in Solaris 2.1 or 2.2. The time based soft swapouts that occur in SunOS 4.X are no longer implemented. `vmstat -s` will report total numbers of swap-ins and swap-outs, which are always zero. In Solaris 2.3, the code was changed so that prolonged memory shortages can trigger swap-outs of inactive processes. This has been refined in Solaris 2.4 to make it more likely that completely inactive processes will be swapped out during a memory shortage; this helps performance of 16 Mbyte machines, in particular.

11

Sensible Tweaking

The default settings for SunOS 4.X were derived from the BSD4.3 values designed to handle machines with at most 8 Mbytes of RAM and around one MIP performance. These settings were tinkered with for the SPARCserver 600MP (the initial sun4m machine) and were overhauled for Solaris 2.1, where they were optimized for good overall window system performance with 16 Mbytes. No changes were made to the defaults for Solaris 2.2 or 2.3. More changes were made for Solaris 2.4.

Note – The suggestions below are a mixture of theory, informed guesswork, and trial and error testing. There are no right answers, as the ideal parameters depend upon the application workload. The default parameters do not scale ideally for use on very large memory systems in Solaris 2.1 through 2.3, this was fixed in 2.4, and a Solaris 2.4 system is unlikely to need tuning.

Varying Lotsfree

An interactive time-sharing system will often be continuously starting new processes; interactive window system users will keep opening new windows. This type of system can benefit from a large free list to cope with frequent and large memory allocation demands. A pure database server, compute server, or single-application document-publishing, or CAD workstation may startup, then stay very stable, with a long time between process startups. This type of system can use a small free list, as the pages are better utilized by the application rather than sitting idly in the free list.

Take a window system example: When a new process starts, it consumes free memory very rapidly before reaching a steady state so that the user can begin to use the new window. If the process requires more than the current free memory pool, then it will get partway through its startup then the paging algorithm will take over the CPU and look for more memory at up to *fastscan* rates. When the memory has been found the process continues, and the situation can repeat several times. These interruptions in process startup time can be apparent to the user as poor interactive response. To improve the interactive response `lotsfree` can be increased so that there is a large enough pool of free memory for most processes to start-up without running out. Of course, if this means that pages are stolen from other processes, then performance will go down.

In the past, the SunOS 4 default free pool of 64 8-Kbit pages provided 512 Kbytes, when the page size went to 4 Kbytes for the desktop sun4c kernel architecture, the free pool went to 256 Kbytes. On the sun4m kernel architecture, it is set to 512 pages or 2048 Kbytes. The problems occur on the sun4c machines since the move from SunView to OpenWindows/X11 seemed to coincide with an increase in startup memory requirements to more than 256 Kbytes for most applications. Solaris 2.1 through 2.3 set *lotsfree* to (*physmem*/16), which results in an improvement in startup times but contributes to a large increase in paging rates when 16-Mbyte machine is upgraded from SunOS 4. I recommend setting the *lotsfree* parameter to 512 Kbytes per CPU on all machines as a compromise. The idea is that the more CPU power there is, the bigger the short-term demand for memory can be. *Desfree* should be set to half of *lotsfree*. You can try out tweaks by timing a process startup in one window[6], monitoring vmstat in another window, and *lotsfree* can be changed with immediate effect using adb in a third window to try different settings. Take care if you try this! See the tweaking sections for examples of using adb.

If you are running a large stable workload and are short of memory, it is a bad idea to increase *lotsfree,* because more pages will be stolen from your applications and put on the free list. You want to have a small free list so that all the pages can be used by your applications. A small free list with an enhanced paging and swapping algorithm is now the default in Solaris 2.4.

Changing Fastscan and Slowscan

The *fastscan* parameter is set to 1000 pages per second in SunOS 4 machines, except for the sun4m architecture, where it is set to (*physmem*/2) pages (e.g. about 4000 on a 32-Mbyte machine and about 125,000 on a 1-Gbyte machine). *Slowscan* is set to 100 or on sun4m, set to (*fastscan*/10) (e.g., about 400 on a 32-Mbyte machine and about 12,500 on a 1-Gbyte machine). Solaris 2.0 used fixed scan rates, but Solaris 2.1, 2.2 and 2.3 use the same scaled rates described above for all machines. These very high-scaled scan rates do not allow enough memory references to occur, so all but the most active pages will be put on the free list, and unnecessary page-outs may occur. The pageout daemon may also consume excessive system CPU time. *Slowscan* should be set quite low at a fixed, unscaled level of perhaps 100 pages/s, so that the number of pages scanned at the slowest rate doesn't immediately cause a paging I/O overload. *Fastscan* should be halved to (*physmem*/4), which automatically removes the override that currently forces the *handspread* value up from 90° to 180°. The ramp-up from *slowscan* to *fastscan* as free memory drops is steep, so there is no need to increase *slowscan* as memory is added.

 Warning – These values should be scaled according to the configuration of the machine being tuned. Save an unpatched copy of the kernel and be very careful when using adb. Errors can crash the system or render it unbootable.

---

6. For OpenWindows applications, "time toolwait application" will show the elapsed startup time.

SunOS 4 Tweaks For Large Memory Sun4m

In the large memory sun4m systems, the scan rate variables need to be modified to reduce *slowscan* to about 100 and to lower *fastscan*. Twin 5400 rpm, 90 rps swap disks are assumed, so *maxpgio* can be set to 2*(90*2/3) = 120.

```
# cp /vmunix /vmunix.notpatched
# adb -k -w /vmunix /dev/mem
physmem 3ffd              physmem is the total number of physical memory
                          pages in hex
maxslp?W0t128            disable maxslp in /vmunix
maxslp/W0t128            disable current operating maxslp
maxpgio?W0t120           set maxpgio to 120 pages/sec in /vmunix
fastscan?W0t8192         set fastscan to 8192 pages/sec in /vmunix
fastscan/W0t8192         set current fastscan to 8192 pages/sec
slowscan?W0t100          set slowscan to 100 pages/sec in /vmunix
slowscan/W0t100          set current slowscan to 100 pages/sec
```

Solaris 2 Tweaks

 Warning – The following tweaks will change the current operating copy only; this is useful for experimenting but be careful that you keep *lotsfree* > *desfree* > *minfree* at all times!

The following numbers are for a 16-Mbyte machine running Solaris 2.1 to 2.3 with a relatively constant workload. Changes are not needed on Solaris 2.4.

```
# adb -k -w /dev/ksyms /dev/mem
physmem ffd              physmem is the total number of physical memory
                         pages in hex
slowscan/W0t100          set slow scan rate to 100 pages/second
fastscan/W0t1024         set fast scan rate to 1024 pages/second
minfree/W0t25            set minfree to 100KB - not needed on 2.4
desfree/W0t50            set desfree to 200KB - not needed on 2.4
lotsfree/W0t128          set current lotsfree to 512 KB - not needed on 2.4
```

The following commands should be placed at the end of /etc/system and they will be automatically applied at the next reboot.

```
# Settings for 16MB of RAM - not needed on 2.4
set slowscan = 100       # set slow scan rate to 100 pages/second
set fastscan = 1024      # set fast scan rate to 1024 pages/second
set lotsfree = 128       # set lotsfree to 128 pages, 512KB
set maxpgio  = 60        # set maxpgio to 60 pages/sec
```

At the other end of the scale, on an 8-CPU, 1 GB machine with four swap disks and a very active workload (compiles or batch streams of small jobs), *slowscan* should be set to 100, *fastscan* should be limited (these changes are not needed on Solaris 2.4), *lotsfree* should be set to 8 x 512 Kbytes, and *desfree* and *minfree* should be scaled as well. *Maxpgio* should be set to 4 x 60.

```
set fastscan = 16000    # set fastscan rate to 16000 pages/sec
set slowscan = 100      # fix initial scan rate at 100
set maxpgio  = 240      # set maxpgio to 60 pages/sec for each
                          of four 90 rps disks
set lotsfree = 1024     # 128 pages for each of 8 CPUs
set desfree = 512       # scaled appropriately, half lotsfree
set minfree = 128       # scaled appropriately, half desfree
```

To decide whether the system is active, creates a lot of process, and needs a large free list, use `sar -c` to monitor the number of `fork` and `exec` system calls. If there are a lot fewer than 1 per second averaged over a 20-minute period, then the free list can be reduced in size.

Tools for Measuring the Kernel

This section explains how you can use the tools provided to monitor the algorithms described earlier in this chapter.

Using Pstat In SunOS 4 To Examine Table Sizes

The occupancy and size of some of the tables can be seen by means of the `pstat -T` command. The example shown in Figure 11-16 is for a SPARCstation 1 running SunOS 4.1.1 with *maxusers* set to 8.

Figure 11-16 Example Pstat Output To See Table Sizes In SunOS 4

```
% pstat -T
217/582 files        The system wide open file table
166/320 inodes       The inode cache
 48/138 processes    The system wide process table
13948/31756 swap     Kilobytes of swap used out of the
                     total
```

The `pstat` command only shows a few of the tables. Before SunOS 4.1, it showed another entry, confusingly also labeled files, which was in fact the number of streams. From SunOS 4.1 on, the number of streams is increased dynamically on demand, so this entry was removed.

Using `sar` Effectively in Solaris 2

The `sar` utility has a huge number of options and some very powerful capabilities. One of its best features is that you can log its full output in date-stamped binary form to a file. You can even look at a few selected measures interactively, then go back to look at all the other measures if you need to. `sar` generates average values automatically and can be used to produce averages between specified start and end times from a binary file. Many of the `sar` options have already been described in "Vnodes, Inodes and Rnodes" on page 189 and "Understanding vmstat and sar Output" on page 194.

One particularly useful facility is that the system is already set up to capture binary `sar` records at 20-minute intervals and to maintain one-month's worth of past records in `/var/adm/sa`. This feature can easily be enabled by uncommenting three lines in the file `/var/spool/cron/crontabs/sys` and making sure that `/etc/rc2.d/S21perf` is enabled (the default). You will then be collecting a complete, historical system-load profile, so when the system is behaving "badly," the records can be compared with some previous time when the system was behaving "well." This is discussed further in "Collecting Long-term System Utilization Data" on page 26.

Using `sar` in Solaris 2 to Examine Table Sizes

`sar` likes to average sizes over time, so `sar -v 1` tells `sar` to make one measure over a one second period. The proc-sz, inod-sz, and file-sz fields are reporting the same thing as `pstat -T`. The file table is no longer a fixed-size data structure in Solaris 2, so its size is given as zero. The examples in Figure 11-17 were taken on a 32-Mbyte desktop machine with *maxusers* set at the default value of 30.

Figure 11-17 Example `sar` *Output to See Table Sizes in Solaris 2*

```
% sar -v 1
SunOS hostname 5.3 Generic sun4c     03/01/94
22:34:02  proc-sz    ov  inod-sz    ov  file-sz    ov  lock-sz
22:34:03   41/490     0  600/600     0   255/0      0   2/0
```

Kernel Memory Allocation

There is no easy way to find out how much kernel memory SunOS 4 is using, but it is measured and reported in Solaris 2. The kernel is probably using more memory than you expect. Kernel memory usage increases as you add RAM, CPUs, and processes to a system. You need to monitor usage on very large active systems because it is possible for the kernel to reach its *kernelmap* limit. When this happens, processes and streams fail and a reboot is often needed.

Solaris 2.0, 2.1, 2.2, and 2.3 Kernel Memory Allocation

The kernel dynamically allocates memory from the global free list as it needs it. All allocations are rounded up to a power of two. Allocations of 256 bytes or less are made from a small block pool, and allocations of 512 bytes to 2 Kbytes are made from a large block pool. The total pool sizes never decrease, although the amount allocated will fluctuate. Allocations of over 2 Kbytes are rounded up to 4 Kbytes and oversize allocations of 4 Kbytes or more are made by allocating pages directly. These are freed for general use when no longer required. On desktop workstations between 5 and 10 Mbytes can be used up in this way. On high-end MP machines with a lot of processes, hardware, and RAM to keep track of it is not unusual for the kernel to use several tens of Mbytes. Solaris 2.3 seems to use less than Solaris 2.2, but this memory usage is one of the main reasons why Solaris 2.3 requires more memory than SunOS 4.X to run the same workload. Figure 11-18 is an example.

Figure 11-18 Example sar *Output to Show Kernel Memory Allocation*

```
% sar -k 1
SunOS hostname 5.3 Generic sun4c     03/01/94
22:19:28 sml_mem    alloc   fail  lg_mem    alloc   fail  ovsz_alloc   fail
22:19:29   422400   413952     0 2138112  1924608      0     2711552      0
```

Solaris 2.4 Kernel Memory Allocation

A completely new kernel memory allocation system is implemented in Solaris 2.4. It has less CPU overhead and allocates packed data structures in a way that saves space and improves CPU cache hit rates. On desktop workstations this allocation frees up a Mbyte or more and helps bring the memory requirements down much closer to SunOS 4.X levels. The allocation statistics are summarized as before for reporting via sar, but the details of the allocations at each block size can be seen via part of the netstat -k output, as shown in Figure 11-19.

> **Warning –** netstat -k is an undocumented[7] and unsupported option. The output is an almost raw dump of the undocumented kernel statistics interface, which is subject to change in each release of Solaris 2. Do not depend upon it.

Figure 11-19 Example Kernel Memory Statistics Reported by Netstat *-k in Solaris 2.4*

```
kmem_misc:
arena_size 14848000 huge_alloc 107 huge_alloc_fail 0 perm_size 126976
perm_alloc 956 perm_alloc_fail 0

kmem_slab_cache:
buf_size 32 align 16 chunk_size 32 slab_size 4096 color 0 max_color 0
alloc 1142 alloc_fail 0 buf_avail 7 buf_reapable 0 buf_total 1143
buf_max 1143 slab_create 9 slab_destroy 0 slab_reapable 0 hash_size 0
hash_lookup_depth 0 hash_rescale 0

kmem_bufctl_cache:
buf_size 12 align 16 chunk_size 16 slab_size 4096 color 0 max_color 0
alloc 1634 alloc_fail 0 buf_avail 167 buf_reapable 0 buf_total 1778
buf_max 1778 slab_create 7 slab_destroy 0 slab_reapable 0 hash_size 0
hash_lookup_depth 0 hash_rescale 0

kmem_alloc_8:
buf_size 8 align 8 chunk_size 8 slab_size 4096 color 0 max_color 0
alloc 8159 alloc_fail 0 buf_avail 4 buf_reapable 0 buf_total 3556
buf_max 3556 slab_create 7 slab_destroy 0 slab_reapable 0 hash_size 0
hash_lookup_depth 0 hash_rescale 0

kmem_alloc_16:
buf_size 16 align 8 chunk_size 16 slab_size 4096 color 0 max_color 0
alloc 3651 alloc_fail 0 buf_avail 114 buf_reapable 0 buf_total 1524
buf_max 1778 slab_create 7 slab_destroy 1 slab_reapable 0 hash_size 0
hash_lookup_depth 0 hash_rescale 0
[... many more buffer sizes omitted ...]
inode_cache:
buf_size 304 align 8 chunk_size 304 slab_size 4096 color 88 max_color 112
alloc 20217 alloc_fail 0 buf_avail 95 buf_reapable 0 buf_total 4537
buf_max 4537 slab_create 349 slab_destroy 0 slab_reapable 0 hash_size 0
hash_lookup_depth 0 hash_rescale 0
```

---

7. The documentation for the kstat library is in the header file /usr/include/sys/kstat.h. In Solaris 2.4 manual pages
   for kstat have been added.

A lot of information is presented; the most useful is the arena_size value at the start which is the total amount of RAM allocated by the kernel in subpage sized chunks, in this case about 15 Mbytes on a large SPARCcenter 2000 configuration that had recently been rebooted. `sar` totals the chunks smaller than 512 bytes for its sml_mem statistic and chunks between 512 bytes and a whole page for its lg_mem statistic. The oversized allocations are mostly done by using whole pages.

It is useful to be able to see how much space the inode cache actually uses per entry (chunk_size = 304 bytes) and how much space it is currently using (chunk_size * buf_total = 1.3MB, in this case). The inode cache is described in "The Inode Cache and File Data Caching" on page 191.

Kernel Profiling with `kgmon` in Solaris 2

The kernel can be profiled in the same way that user programs can be profiled by using special compiler options and the `gprof` command. The standard kernel has clock sample profiling enabled; for SunSoft's own in-house performance tuning work, the kernel can be recompiled to include call graph profiling as well.

 Warning – Kernel profiling is an unsupported and undocumented capability. The interface and capabilities may change in each release of Solaris 2. If the system misbehaves or crashes while profiling is enabled, you are on your own.

The profile is collected with the `/usr/bin/kgmon` utility, which allocates some profiling buffers, collects the profile, and dumps the results to be processed by `gprof`. The utility must be run as root. An example sequence of commands is shown in the following.

There is no manual page, to show the options, use the command shown in the follow.

```
# kgmon --
Usage: kgmon [ -i -b -h -r -p -s -d ]
    -i = initialize profiling buffers
    -b = begin profiling
    -h = halt profiling
    -r = reset the profiling buffers
    -p = dump the profiling buffers
    -s = snap shot the profiling data
    -d = deallocate profiling buffers
# kgmon -i
one moment
NOTICE: Profiling kernel, textsize = 626692 [f0004000..f009d004]
NOTICE: Profiling modules, size = 5267000 [ff011000..ff516e38] (954282
used)
```

```
NOTICE: need 139600 bytes per cpu for clock sampling
profiling has been initialized
WARNING: call graph profiling is not compiled into this kernel
WARNING: only clock sample profiling is available
# kgmon -b
kernel profiling is running
```

Run the workload at this point.

```
# kgmon -h
kernel profiling is off
# kgmon -p
dumping cpu 0 - one moment
a.out symbols for the kernel and modules have been dumped to gmon.syms
profiling data has been dumped to gmon[n].out
# kgmon -d
profiling buffers have been deallocated
# /usr/ccs/bin/gprof gmon.syms gmon.out >kgmon.gprof
```

Since call graph profiling is not enabled, the first part of the output file is not very
interesting. The "flat" profile at the end is the most useful part and it is shown in the
following. In this case, the profile was collected for about 30 seconds on a SPARCstation 1
that was mostly idle and user CPU-bound, with some I/O activity. On multiprocessor
machines, the idle loop also calls disp_getwork, which means that the idle CPU is
checking the cache affinity algorithm to see if a process should be migrated off the
dispatch queue of a busy CPU.

```
granularity: each sample hit covers 4 byte(s) for 0.03% of 32.83 seconds
   %   cumulative    self              self    total
 time    seconds    seconds  calls  ms/call  ms/call  name
66.3      21.77      21.77                             idle [1]
 1.8      22.37       0.60                             vac_usrflush [2]
 1.6      22.90       0.53                             bcopy [3]
 1.6      23.43       0.53                             sunm_pmgswapptes [4]
 1.3      23.86       0.43                             _level10 [5]
 1.2      24.25       0.39                             mutex_enter [6]
 0.9      24.54       0.29                             mutex_exit [7]
 0.8      24.79       0.25                             syscall [8]
 0.6      24.99       0.20                             sunm_pmgload [9]
 0.5      25.17       0.18                             .syscall [10]
 0.5      25.34       0.17                             sunm_ptesync [11]
 0.5      25.50       0.16                             blkclr [12]
 0.5      25.65       0.15                             clock [13]
 0.5      25.80       0.15                             hmetopmg [14]
 0.4      25.94       0.14                             pgcopy [15]
 0.4      26.07       0.13                             poll [16]
```

```
0.4        26.19       0.12                              _interrupt [18]
0.4        26.31       0.12                              fsflush [17]
0.3        26.42       0.11                              .div [19]
0.3        26.53       0.11                              resume [20]
0.3        26.64       0.11                              rw [21]
0.3        26.75       0.11                              strpoll [22]
.... and so on
```

The kernel routine names are fairly descriptive, but access to kernel source code or a Solaris System Internals course is needed to make good use of this information.

Monitoring the System with Proctool

Proctool is a freely available tool developed by Walter Nielsen and Morgan Herrington of Sun. It can be obtained via anonymous ftp on the Internet from the machine opcom.sun.ca in the directory /pub/binaries/proctool. Proctool uses features found only in Solaris 2 and is release specific. Proctool 2.2 works only with Solaris 2.2, Proctool 2.3 is for Solaris 2.3 only.

Proctool monitors and controls processes on a system, providing a GUI interface to ps(1) and providing more flexibility than the public domain top utility. It extracts a huge amount of information from the data structures maintained in /proc for each process and can plot a variety of data graphically on a per-system or a per-process basis.

Setting Default Limits

There is sometimes a need to change the default hard and soft limit values. Maybe the maximums need to be reduced to keep processes from hogging the system, or perhaps the default number of files needs to be increased. Rather than setting limits in every user login script, the global default limits in the kernel can be changed. In generic UNIX System V Release 4, this is performed by setting some symbolic variables and rebuilding the kernel. In Solaris 2 the /etc/system method cannot be used, since there are no variables corresponding to the individual limits, just a single rlimits data structure. The kernel must be patched by means of adb. The elements are laid out by the sysdef -i command, which lists the values in hexadecimal as shown in Figure 11-20.

Figure 11-20 Example System-wide Resource Limits Shown by `Sysdef`

```
% sysdef -i
...
     Soft:Hard          Resource            byte offset in hex in a decimal
 Infinity:Infinity      cpu time                  0: 4
 Infinity:Infinity      file size                 8: c
 1fefe000:1fcfc000      heap size                10:14
   800000: ff00000      stack size               18:1c
 Infinity:Infinity      core file size           20:24
       40:     400      file descriptors         28:2c
 Infinity:Infinity      mapped memory            30:34
 ...
```

The hard limits for data size and stack size vary. Some older machines with the Sun-4 MMU can only map 1 Gbyte of virtual address space, so stack size is restricted to 256 Mbytes and data size is restricted to 512 Mbytes. For recent machines with the SPARC Reference MMU, the maximums are 2 Gbytes each[8].

To increase the default number of file descriptors per process, rlimits+0x28 must be patched with `adb`.

Note that the industry-standard definition for the `stdio` library can only handle 256 files at most, but raw read/write will work up to 1024. The commands shown in Figure 11-21 permanently patch the default number of file descriptors to 128 (0x80) in the `/kernel/unix` file by using "?" and also patch the current copy in memory by using "/."

Figure 11-21 How to Permanently Increase the Default Number of File Descriptors

```
# cp /kernel/unix /kernel/unix.orig
# adb -k -w /kernel/unix /dev/mem
rlimits,e?X
rlimits:
rlimits:    7fffffff         7fffffff         7fffffff         7fffffff
            1fefe000         1fefe000         800000           ff00000
            7fffffff         7fffffff         40               400
            7fffffff         7fffffff
rlimits+28?W80
rlimits+28/W80
rlimits,e?X
rlimits:
rlimits:    7fffffff         7fffffff         7fffffff         7fffffff
```

---

8. See "Memory Management Unit Designs" on page 164.

1fefe000	1fefe000	800000	ff00000
7ffffff	7ffffff	80	400
7ffffff	7ffffff		

Caution – Using `adb` to patch the kernel directly is a potentially dangerous operation. Mistyping a command could crash the system or render it unbootable. Save an unpatched kernel copy. Do not increase the hard limits.

Configuring Devices

Kernel Configuration in SunOS 4.X

Kernel configuration is one of the most obvious tuning operations for systems that are running short of memory. It is particularly important to configure 8-Mbyte diskless SPARCstation ELCs to have as much free RAM as possible, since it will be used to cache the NFS accesses. A diskless machine can have many filesystem types and devices removed (including the nonexistent floppy on the ELC), which can free up over 500 Kbytes. The DL60 configuration file with all framebuffer types except mono removed and with TMPFS added and enabled in `/etc/rc.local` makes a good DL25 kernel for the ELC.

Kernel Configuration in Solaris 2

There is no need to configure the kernel in Solaris 2, since it is dynamically linked at runtime. All the pieces of the kernel are stored in a `/kernel` directory and the first time a device or filesystem type is used, it is loaded into memory. The kernel can unload some of the devices if they are not being used.

Mapping Device Nicknames to Full Names in Solaris 2

The boot sequence builds a tree in memory of the hardware devices present in the system, which is passed to the kernel and can be viewed with the `prtconf` command. This tree is mirrored in the `/devices` and `/dev` directories; after hardware changes are made to the system, these directories must be reconfigured with `boot -r`. See also the `drvconfig` `tapes` and `disks` commands that allow you to configure a system manually. The file `/etc/path_to_inst` maps hardware addresses to symbolic device names. An extract from a simple configuration with the symbolic names added is shown in Figure 11-22.

When a large number of disks are configured, it is important to know this mapping so that `iostat` and related commands can be related to the output from `df`. The sbus@1 part tells you which SBus is used (an SC2000 can have up to 10 separate SBuses) the

11

esp@0 part tells you which SBus slot the esp (SCSI) controller is in. The sd@0 part tells you that this is SCSI target address 0. The /dev/dsk/c0t0d0s2 device name indicates SCSI target 0 on SCSI controller 0 and is a symbolic link to a hardware specification similar to that found in /etc/path_to_inst. The extra :c at the end of the name in /devices corresponds to the s2 at the end of the name in /dev. Slice s0 is partition :a, s1 is :b, s2 is :c, and so forth.

Figure 11-22 Mapping Solaris 2 Device Nicknames into Full Names

```
% more /etc/path_to_inst
...
"/fd@1,f7200000" 0                                fd0
"/sbus@1,f8000000/esp@0,800000/sd@3,0" 3     sd3
"/sbus@1,f8000000/esp@0,800000/sd@0,0" 0     sd0
"/sbus@1,f8000000/esp@0,800000/sd@1,0" 1     sd1
```

```
% iostat -x
                            extended disk statistics
disk    r/s  w/s  Kr/s  Kw/s wait actv  svc_t  %w  %b
fd0     0.0  0.0  0.0   0.0  0.0  0.0    0.0    0   0
sd0     0.1  0.1  0.4   0.8  0.0  0.0   49.3    0   1
sd1     0.1  0.0  0.8   0.1  0.0  0.0   49.0    0   0
sd3     0.1  0.1  0.6   0.8  0.0  0.0   75.7    0   1
```

```
% df -k
Filesystem          kbytes    used    avail capacity  Mounted on
/dev/dsk/c0t3d0s0    19107   13753    3444    80%     /              sd3
/dev/dsk/c0t3d0s6    56431   46491    4300    92%     /usr           sd3
/proc                    0       0       0     0%     /proc
fd                       0       0       0     0%     /dev/fd¹
swap                  2140      32    2108     1%     /tmp
/dev/dsk/c0t3d0s5    19737   17643     124    99%     /opt           sd3
/dev/dsk/c0t1d0s6    95421   71221   14660    83%     /usr/openwin   sd1
/dev/dsk/c0t0d0s2   308619  276235    1524    99%     /export        sd0
```

1. /dev/fd is a file descriptor filesystem type, nothing to do with floppy disks!

```
% ls -l /dev/dsk/c0t0d0s2
lrwxrwxrwx  1 root          51 Jun  6 15:59 /dev/dsk/c0t0d0s2 ->
../../devices/sbus@1,f8000000/esp@0,800000/sd@0,0:c
```

A Command Script To Do It For You

The `csh/nawk` script presented in Figure 11-23 can be used to print out the device-to-nickname mappings. Enter it with three long command lines starting with `set`, `if`, and `nawk`, — it doesn't work if you try to use multiple lines or backslash continuation.

Figure 11-23 `Whatdev` - *Device to Nickname Mapping Script*

```
#!/bin/csh
# print out the drive name - st0 or sd0 - given the /dev entry
# first get something like "/iommu/.../.../sd@0,0"
set dev = `/bin/ls -l $1 | nawk '{ n = split($11, a, "/");
split(a[n],b,":"); for(i = 4; i < n; i++) printf("/%s",a[i]);
printf("/%s\n", b[1]) }'`
if ( $dev == "" ) exit
# then get the instance number and concatenate with the "sd"
nawk -v dev=$dev '$1 ~ dev { n = split(dev, a, "/"); split(a[n], \
b, "@"); printf("%s%s\n", b[1], $2) }' /etc/path_to_inst
```

An example of its use:

```
% foreach device (/dev/dsk/c?t?d?s2)
> echo -n $device " ---- "
> whatdev $device
> end
/dev/dsk/c0t3d0s2   ---- sd3
/dev/dsk/c0t5d0s2   ---- sd5
```

References

- *Administering Security, Performance, and Accounting in Solaris 2*

- *"Building and Debugging SunOS Kernels"* by Hal Stern

- *The Design and Implementation of the 4.3BSD UNIX Operating System,* by Leffler, McKusick, Karels, and Quarterman

- *SunOS System Internals Course Notes*

- *System Performance Tuning,* by Mike Loukides

≡ *11*

Rules and Tunables Quick Reference Tables

A

This appendix summarizes some of the advice given in the rest of this book into rules and lists the kernel variables that are tunable. The data is tabulated with references to the rest of the book for more information and explanation. I'm assuming that you have read the rest of the book, so there is no need to repeat explanations here.

If you have one of the many performance management tools that lets you set thresholds or rules, then you can use these tables to set up your tool.

Notation Used in Tables

Rules

To refer to a measured result, I use the name of the command with any options, then a "." followed by the variable name identification. Spaces are removed whenever the resulting name is unambiguous. For example, to indicate disk service time using `iostat -x` with a 30-second interval, I would specify `iostat-x30.svc_t`.

Variables are combined using the usual C language operators with "&&" for logical AND, "||" for logical OR, and "==" to test for equality. Temporary variables and multistage rules may be used. A range test expression, for example, $0 <= X < 100$ is used for brevity.

Levels

The level entry in the table indicates how serious the situation is. The color coding used is white for low usage, blue for underutilization or imbalance of an expensive resource, green for target utilization levels or no problem, amber for a warning level, red for a critical level that needs to be fixed for good performance, and black for problems that can prevent your application or system from running at all.

Actions

The action to be taken when the rule is true is explained below the tables in a numbered paragraph. The action field contains a terse reminder of the problem and the number of the relevant statement where necessary.

A

Disk I/O Rules

Table A-1   Disk I/O Performance Rules for SunOS 4

Rule for Each Disk Drive	Level	Action
(iostat-D30.util < 5%) && (other disks white or green)	White	No Problem
(iostat-D30.util < 5%) && (other disks amber or red)	Blue	1. Idle Disk
5% <= iostat-D30.util < 35%	Green	No Problem
35% <= iostat-D30.util < 65%	Amber	2. Busy Disk
65% <= iostat-D30.util	Red	2. Busy Disk

Table A-2   Disk I/O Performance Rules for Solaris 2

Rule for Each Disk Drive	Level	Action
(iostat-x30.b < 5%) && (other disks white or green)	White	No Problem
(iostat-x30.b < 5%) && (other disks amber or red)	Blue	1. Idle Disk
(5% <= iostat-x30.b) && (iostat-x30.svc_t < 30 ms)	Green	No Problem
(20% <= iostat-x30.b) && (30 ms <= iostat-x30.svc_t < 50 ms)	Amber	2. Busy Disk
(20% <= iostat-x30.b) && (50 ms <= iostat-x30.svc_t)	Red	2. Busy Disk
(20% <= iostat-x30.b) && (50 ms <= iostat-x30.svc_t) && (iostat-x30.disk == "fd0" || iostat-x30.disk == "sd6")	Amber	3. Floppy/CD
0% == iostat-x30.w	Green	No Problem
0% < iostat-x30.w < 5%	Amber	4. SCSI Busy
5% <= iostat-x30.w	Red	4. SCSI Busy

1. **Idle Disk**
   An idle disk is a waste of I/O throughput when other disks are overloaded. Rebalance the load or stripe this disk together with a busy one.

2. **Busy Disk**
   A busy or slow disk reduces system throughput and increases user response times. Rebalance the load or stripe this disk together with an idle one. If there are no idle disks then reduce the I/O load somehow or configure more disks. See "Load Monitoring and Balancing" on page 75.

3. **Floppy/CD**
   To prevent the rules from being applied to much slower devices, check for the disk type of fd0, indicating a floppy. A CD appears as a normal but very slow disk that has never been written to, and there is no simple way to exclude it without accidentally excluding a very overloaded, read-only hard disk. The CD is often configured as target number 6 on the first SCSI bus, so specifying sd6 is a crude

workaround for this problem. If the floppy or CD are active for long periods, then something somewhere is running slowly, and the data should be moved to a faster disk.

4. **SCSI Busy**
   If disk commands have to wait before they can be sent to the disk, then the waiting may be due to an overloaded SCSI bus. There are no direct measures of SCSI bus utilization levels.

Network Rules

Table A-3 Network Performance Rules Based on Ethernet Collisions

Rule or Each Network Interface	Level	Action
(0 < `netstat-i30.output.packets` < 10) && (100 * `netstat-i30.output.colls` / `netstat-i30.output.packets` < 0.5%) && (`other nets white or green`)	White	No Problem
(0 < `netstat-i30.output.packets` < 10) && (100 * `netstat-i30.output.colls` / `netstat-i30.output.packets` < 0.5%) && (`other nets amber or red`)	Blue	1. Inactive Net
(10 <= `netstat-i30.output.packets`) && (0.5% <= 100 * `netstat-i30.output.colls` / `netstat-i30.output.packets` < 2.0%)	Green	No Problem
(10 <= `netstat-i30.output.packets`) && (2.0% <= 100 * `netstat-i30.output.colls` / `netstat-i30.output.packets` < 5.0%)	Amber	2. Busy Net
(10 <= `netstat-i30.output.packets`) && (5.0% <= 100 * `netstat-i30.output.colls` / `netstat-i30.output.packets`)	Red	2. Busy Net
network type is not `ie`, `le`, `ne`, or `qe`; it is `bf` or `nf`.	Green	3. Not Ether

1. **Inactive net**
   An inactive network is a waste of throughput when other networks are overloaded. Rebalance the load so that all networks are used more evenly.

2. **Busy Net**
   A network with too many collisions reduces throughput and increases response time for users. Move some of the load to inactive networks if there are any. Add more Ethernets or upgrade to a faster interface type like FDDI, 100-Mbit Ethernet, or ATM.

3. **Not Ether**
   If the last letter of the interface name is not `e` then this is not an Ethernet, so the collision-based network performance rule should not be used.

A

NFS Client Rules

Table A-4 NFS Client Performance Rules

Rule for Each NFS Client	Level	Action
`0 == nfsstat-rc.calls`	White	No Client NFS
`nfsstat-rc.timeout` < 0.05 * `nfsstat-rc.calls`	Green	No Problem
0.05 * `nfsstat-rc.calls` <= `nfsstat-rc.timeout` && `nfsstat-rc.badxid` == 0	Red	1. Bad Net
0.05 * `nfsstat-rc.calls` <= (`nfsstat-rc.timeout` == `nfsstat-rc.badxid`)	Red	2. Slow NFS

1. **Bad Net**
    Packets are not making it to or from the NFS server. Fix the network hardware or reduce NFS packet sizes.

2. **Slow NFS**
    The NFS server is so slow that it is processing duplicate requests from the clients that were sent after time-outs. Increase client time-out.

Memory Rules

Table A-5   Virtual Memory Rules for SunOS 4

Virtual Memory Rule	Level	Action
100000k <= pstat-s.available	White	1. Swap Waste
10000k <= pstat-s.available < 100000k	Green	No Problem
4000k <= pstat-s.available < 10000k	Amber	2. Swap Low
1000k <= pstat-s.available < 4000k	Red	2. Swap Low
pstat-s.available < 1000k	Black	3. No Swap

Table A-6   Virtual Memory Rules For Solaris 2

Virtual Memory Rule	Level	Action
100000k <= vmstat30.swap	White	1. Swap Waste
10000k <= vmstat30.swap < 100000k	Green	No Problem
4000k <= vmstat30.swap < 10000k	Amber	2. Swap Low
1000k <= vmstat30.swap < 4000k	Red	2. Swap Low
vmstat30.swap < 1000k	Black	3. No Swap

1. **Swap Waste**
   You have a lot of unused swap space.

2. **Swap Low**
   There is not much swap space left, so the system may soon run out of virtual memory. Reduce the number and size of the programs running on the system or add more swap space before it runs out completely. See "Swap Space" on page 4.

3. **No Swap**
   The system has effectively run out of swap space. Programs will fail or hang. Add more swap space or shut down applications immediately.

A

Table A-7 *Physical Memory Rules for SunOS 4 and Solaris 2*

Physical Memory Rule	Level	Action
`vmstat30.sr == 0`	White	1. RAM Waste
`0 < vmstat30.sr < 200`	Green	No Problem
`200 <= vmstat30.sr < 300`	Amber	2. RAM Low
`300 <= vmstat30.sr`	Red	2. RAM Low

1. **RAM Waste**
   You have more RAM than you need. The system does not even need to reclaim inactive pages.

2. **RAM Low**
   The system is scanning through memory looking for pages to free at a high rate. This indicates that, as well as inactive pages, active pages may be stolen from processes.

Table A-8 *Kernel Memory Rules for Solaris 2*

Kernel Memory Rule	Level	Action
`((0 < sar-k1.sml_mem.fail) || (0 < sar-k1.lg_mem_fail) ||` `(0 < sar-k1.ovsz.alloc.fail)) && (64 < sar-r1.freemem)`	Black	1. No Kmap
`((0 < sar-k1.sml_mem.fail) || (0 < sar-k1.lg_mem_fail) ||` `(0 < sar-k1.ovsz.alloc.fail)) && (sar-r1.freemem <= 64)`	Black	2. No Kmem

1. **No Kmap**
   There are available memory pages, but the kernel cannot allocate more memory. The *kernelmap* or kernel address space has been used up; see "Kernel Memory Allocation" on page 216. Several parts of the system may fail; a reboot is advised to restore the system to a known stable state. Reducing *maxusers* and limiting the buffer cache size may help. See "Basic Sizing with Maxusers" on page 186 and "Buffer Cache" on page 193.

2. **No Kmem**
   The system is short of memory; when the kernel tried to allocate pages for its own use there was no free RAM. This is likely to occur only with Solaris 2.4, which has a smaller free list than earlier releases do. On a high-end MP server that has a lot of minor faults and page-ins this problem can be avoided by setting *lotsfree* higher to increase the free list size. See the description of "lotsfree and deficit" on page 209.

CPU Rules

The number of CPUs in use on this system must be known. It is referred to as *ncpus* in the rules. For SunOS 4, the /usr/kvm/mpstat command shows you how many CPUs are on SPARCserver 600MP systems. For Solaris 2, the psrinfo command or the sysinfo library routine can be used. The run queue length is divided by the number of CPUs because every CPU takes a job off the run queue in each time slice.

Table A-9 CPU Rule for SunOS 4 And Solaris 2

CPU Rule	Level	Action
$0 == $ vmstat30.r	White	1. CPU Idle
$0 < ($vmstat30.r$ / $ ncpus$) < 3.0$	Green	No Problem
$3.0 <= ($vmstat30.r$ / $ ncpus$) <= 5$	Amber	2. CPU Busy
$5.0 <= ($vmstat30.r$ / $ ncpus$)$	Red	2. CPU Busy
mpstat30.smtx < 200	Green	No Problem
$200 <= $ mpstat30.smtx < 400	Amber	3. Mutex Stall
$400 <= $ mpstat30.smtx	Red	3. Mutex Stall

1. **CPU Idle**
   The CPU power of this system is underutilized. Fewer or less powerful CPUs could be used to do this job.

2. **CPU Busy**
   There is insufficient CPU power, and jobs are spending an increasing amount of time in the queue before being assigned to a CPU. This reduces throughput and increases interactive response times.

3. **Mutex Stall**
   If the number of stalls per CPU per second exceeds the limit, mutex contention is happening in the kernel, which wastes CPU time and degrades multiprocessor scaling.

A

Kernel Tables Rules

Table A-10 Kernel Table Rules for SunOS 4

Kernel Table Rule	Level	Action
`vmstat-s.name.hits < 90%`	Red	1. DNLC Miss
`90% <= vmstat-s.name.hits < 95%`	Amber	1. DNLC Miss
`95% <= vmstat-s.name.hit <= 100%`	Green	No Problem

Table A-11 Kernel Table Rules for Solaris 2

Kernel Table Rule	Level	Action
`dnlc.hitrate = 100 * (sar-a30.namei - sar-a30.iget) / sar-a30.namei`	All	Define
`(dnlc.hitrate < 90%) && (50 < sar-a30.namei)`	Amber[1]	1. DNLC Miss
`90% <= dnlc.hitrate <= 100% || (sar-a30.namei <= 50)`	Green	No Problem
`0.00% == sar-g1.ufs_ipf`	Green	No Problem
`0.00% < sar-g1.ufs_ipf <= 100.00%`	Amber	2. Inode Flush

1. This condition is given an Amber level because it needs more research to verify that it is the right threshold and rule.

1. **DNLC Miss**

   The directory name lookup cache is too small and a lot of inodes are being read. See "Directory Name Lookup Cache" on page 189.

2. **Inode Flush**

   The inode cache limit is set too low, and file data is being flushed as inodes are being reused. Try doubling *ufs_ninode*. See "The Inode Cache and File Data Caching" on page 191.

Tunable Kernel Parameters

The kernel chapter of this book explains how the main kernel algorithms work. The kernel tunable values listed in this section include *the main tunables that are worth worrying about*. There are a huge number of global values defined in the kernel; if you hear of a tweak that is not listed in this book, think twice before using it. The algorithms, default values, and existence of many of these variables vary from one release to the next. Do not assume that an undocumented tweak that works well for one kernel will apply to other releases, other kernel architectures of the same release, or even a different patch level.

Table A-12 Primary Configuration Variables in Solaris 2.3 and Solaris 2.4

Name	Default	Min	Max	Reference
maxusers	MB available RAM (*physmem*)	8	2048	"Autoconfiguration of maxusers in Solaris 2.3 and Solaris 2.4" on page 188
pt_cnt	48	48	3000	"Changing maxusers and Pseudo-ttys in Solaris 2" on page 187

Table A-13 File Name and Attribute Cache Sizes for SunOS 4 and Solaris 2

Name	Default	Min	Max	Reference
ncsize	(*maxusers* * 17) + 90	226	34906	"Directory Name Lookup Cache" on page 189
ufs_ninode	(*maxusers* * 17) + 90	226	34906	"The Inode Cache and File Data Caching" on page 191

Table A-14 Hardware-specific Configuration Tunables

Name	Default	Min	Max	Reference
use_mxcc_prefetch	0 (sun4d) 1 (sun4m)	0	1	"The SuperSPARC with SuperCache Two-level Cache Architecture" on page 159.
npts	dynamic, based on memory	default, do not set lower	2 * default	"The SPARC Reference MMU Table Walk Operation" on page 168

Shared memory parameters are usually set based on the needs of specific application programs.

Table A-15 Shared Memory and Semaphore Tunables in Solaris 2

Name	Default	Min	Max	Reference
shmsys:shminfo_shmmax	1048576	1048576	Available RAM	Maximum shm segment size in bytes
shmsys:shminfo_shmmin	1	1		Minimum shm segment size in bytes
shmsys:shminfo_shmni	100	100		Number of shm identifiers to pre-allocate
shmsys:shminfo_shmseg	6	6		Maximum number of shm segments per process
semsys:seminfo_semmap	10	10		Number of entries in semaphore map
semsys:seminfo_semmni	10	10	65535	Number of semaphore identifiers
semsys:seminfo_semmns	60			Number of semaphores in system
semsys:seminfo_semmnu	30			Number of undo structures in system
semsys:seminfo_semmsl	25			Maximum number of semaphores per ID
semsys:seminfo_semopm	10			Maximum number of operations per semop call
semsys:seminfo_semume	10			Maximum number of undo entries per process
semsys:seminfo_semusz	96	-	-	Size in bytes of undo structure, derived from semume
semsys:seminfo_semvmx	32767			Semaphore maximum value
semsys:seminfo_semaem	16384			Adjust on exit maximum value

References B

References throughout this book are collected here in alphabetical order (by title) with a few words to indicate what is of interest in the reference and, when appropriate, where the reference can be obtained.

Internet Resources

Many of the white papers can be obtained over the Internet as compressed PostScript documents. Good places to try:

- `http://www.sun.com/` is Sun's main service for the World Wide Web, or Mosaic users.

- The ftp server opcom.sun.ca mainly provides information specific to the Solaris 2 upgrade transition support.

- SunSite at the University of Northern Carolina, sunsite.unc.edu, is the USA-based Sun-sponsored Internet resource, with ftp and mosaic support.

- SunSite at Imperial College, London, UK, doc.ic.ac.uk, is the European-based, Sun-sponsored Internet resource. Check out ftp to the `/sun/papers` directory.

- The Uunet organization server at ftp.uu.net also has `/systems/sun/papers`, mirroring Imperial College.

Document Descriptions

2.1Gb 5.25-inch Fast Differential SCSI-2 Disk Products

Describes Sun's 2.1-Gbyte disk drive, which introduces several new technologies. Fast SCSI at 10 Mbits/s, differential drive to provide 25 meter cable lengths, and tagged command queueing to optimize multiple commands inside the drive are discussed in detail.

Administering Security, Performance, and Accounting in Solaris 2

This document is the basic reference on Solaris 2 and is part of the manual set on AnswerBook CD. It describes the tweakable parameters that can be set in `/etc/system` and provides a tutorial on how to use performance analysis tools such as `sar` and `vmstat`.

An Analysis of TCP Processing Overhead

by David Clark, Van Jacobson, John Romkey, Howard Salwen

Describes the things that can be tuned to improve TCP/IP and Ethernet throughput. IEEE Communications, June 1989.

The Art of Computer Systems Performance Analysis

by Raj Jain

This recent book is a comprehensive and very readable reference work covering techniques for experimental design, measurement, simulation and modelling. Published by Wiley, ISBN 0-471-50336-3.

Building and Debugging SunOS Kernels

by Hal Stern

This Sun white paper provides an in-depth explanation of how kernel configuration works in SunOS 4.X, with some performance tips.

A Cached System Architecture Dedicated for the System IO Activity on a CPU Board

by Hseih, Wei, and Loo.

Describes the patented Sun I/O cache architecture used in the SPARCserver 490 and subsequent server designs. Proceedings of the International Conference on Computer Design, October 2 1989.

Computer Architecture - A Quantitative Approach

by John Hennessy and David Patterson

The definitive reference book on modern computer architecture. ISBN 1-55860-069-8.

Configuration and Capacity Planning for Solaris,

by Brian Wong

This book tells you how to think about the job of configuring a server to perform a task. It contains detailed guidelines and case studies for the configuration of NFS, database, and time-shared servers. It also contains the performance characteristics of most Sun peripheral options and an extensive section on the theory and practice of the SCSI interface. At the time of writing it is scheduled for publication in early 1995 by SunSoft Press/PTR Prentice Hall. ISBN 0-13-349952-9.

The Design and Implementation of the 4.3BSD UNIX Operating System
by Leffler, McKusick, Karels and Quarterman

This book describes the internal design and algorithms used in the kernel of a very closely related operating system. SunOS 3.X was almost a pure BSD4.3, SunOS 4 redesigned the virtual memory system, and UNIX System V Release 4 is about 80 percent based on SunOS 4 with about 20 percent UNIX System V.3. Solaris 2 has been further rewritten to support multiple processors. Despite the modifications over time this is a definitive work, and there are few other sources for insight into the kernel algorithms. ISBN 0-201-06196-1.

Extent-like Performance from a UNIX File System
by L. McVoy and S. Kleiman

This paper was presented at Usenix in Winter 1991. It describes the filesystem clustering optimization that was introduced in SunOS 4.1.1.

Graphics Performance Technical White Paper

This provides extensive performance figures for PHIGS and GKS running a wide variety of benchmarks on various hardware platforms. It is becoming a little out of date, as new versions of PHIGS, GKS and hardware have superseded those tested but is still very useful. January 1990.

High Performance Computing
by Keith Dowd

This is a very recent book that covers the architecture of current high-performance workstations, compute servers, and parallel machines. It is full of examples of the coding techniques required to get the best performance from the new architectures, and contrasts vector machines with the latest, microprocessor-based technologies. The importance of coding with caches in mind is emphasized. The book is essential reading for FORTRAN programmers trying to make numerical codes run faster, and is recommended for all programmers. Published by O'Reilly, ISBN 1-56592-032-5.

Managing NFS and NIS
by Hal Stern

Network administration and tuning is covered in depth. An essential reference published by O'Reilly, ISBN 0-937175-75-7.

Multiprocessor System Architectures
by Ben Catanzaro
> This book is a great reference to all the details of SPARC based system hardware. It describes all the chip sets and system board designs, including the latest multiprocessor systems. Published by SunSoft Press/PTR Prentice Hall. ISBN 0-13-089137-1.

Networks and File Servers: A Performance Tuning Guide
> This is the best of the network tuning white papers. It is starting to get a little out of date.

New Technology for Flexibility, Performance and Growth, The SPARCserver 600 Series
> This white paper, despite its overblown title, provides a very good technical overview of the architecture of the hardware and how SunOS 4.1.2 works on a multiprocessor system. It also describes the SPARC Reference MMU in some detail in an appendix. A new version called "SPARCserver 10 and SPARCserver 600 Performance Brief" is also available.

Optimization in the SPARCompilers
by Steven Muchnick
> This document provides a description of the SPARC compilers and how they work. A Sun white paper and several Sun User Group conference proceedings on this subject are also available.

Performance Tuning an Application
> This book is part of the SPARCworks on-line AnswerBook with the compiler products and the Teamware manuals. Defined are new tools that may be unfamiliar to many users doing software development.

Realtime Scheduling In SunOS 5.0
by Sandeep Khanna, Michael Sebrée, John Zolnowsky
> This paper was presented at Usenix Winter '92 and describes the implementation of the kernel in Solaris 2.0. It covers how kernel threads work, how real-time scheduling is performed, and the novel priority-inheritance system.

SBus /SCSI Developers Kit, Release III
> A comprehensive, 4-manual set for developers creating SBus cards and SCSI device drivers. The kit includes Openboot Command Reference, The SBus Handbook, SunOS 5.3 Writing Device Drivers, and Writing FCode Programs. ISBN 0-13-107202-1, SunSoft Press/Prentice Hall.

A Scalable Server Architecture for Department to Enterprise — The SPARCserver 1000 and the SPARCcenter 2000

by Adrian Cockcroft

This is the architecture white paper for the SS1000 and SC2000. The paper progresses logically into more and more detail, so start at the beginning and read until you've had enough. May 1993.

SCSI-2 Terms, Concepts, and Implications Technical Brief

There is much confusion and misuse of terms in the area of SCSI buses and standards. This paper clears up the confusion.

SCSI and IPI Disk Interface Directions

After many years of IPI being the highest-performance disk technology, the time has come when SCSI disks are not only less expensive, but are also higher performance. SCSI disks with on-disk buffers and controllers are beginning to include the optimizations previously found only in IPI controllers.

SMCC NFS Server Performance and Tuning Guide

This guide was first issued as part of the Solaris 2.3, SMCC, hardware-specific manual set and AnswerBook CD. It contains a good overview of how to size an NFS server configuration, but its tuning recommendations should be considered a first draft, as there are many errors and inconsistencies. It actually covers SunOS 4.1.3/Solaris 1.1 NFS server tuning as well as Solaris 2.

The Solaris 2.4 version of this guide has been completely rewritten and is highly recommended.

Solaris 2.0 Multithread Architecture White Paper

The overall, multiprocessor architecture of Solaris 2.0 is described. In particular the user level thread model is explained in detail. This paper has also appeared as "SunOS Multithread Architecture" at Usenix Winter '91 and has been superseded by the SunOS 5 Guide to Multithread Programming, which is part of the Solaris 2.2 and later manual set.

Solaris XIL 1.0 Imaging Library White Paper

This paper describes the XIL Imaging Library functions and how specific applications may require XIL functions. It includes a glossary of imaging and video terminology. February 1993.

The SPARC Architecture Manual Version 8

This manual is available as a book from Prentice Hall. It is also available from the IEEE as the IEEE 1754 standard is based on SPARC version 8. ISBN 0-13-825001-4.

The SPARC Architecture Manual Version 9

This has also been publsihed by Prentice Hall as a book. It includes upwards compatible extensions to version 8. A new kernel interface and 64-bit addressing modes are the main changes. ISBN: 0-13-099227-5.

The SPARCcenter 2000 Architecture and Implementation White Paper

This paper contains an immense amount of detail on this elegant but sophisticated large- scale multiprocessor server. A good understanding of computer architecture is assumed.

SPARCcompiler Optimization Technology Technical White Paper

This paper describes the optimizations performed by Sun compilers. Knowing what the compiler is looking for, it can help guide your coding style.

SPARCengine IPX User Guide

This can be ordered from Sun using the product code SEIPX-HW-DOC. It provides the full programmers model of the SPARCstation IPX CPU board including internal registers and address spaces and a full hardware description of the board functions.

SPARCengine 2 User Guide

This guide can be ordered from Sun by the product code SE2-HW-DOC. It provides the full programmer's model of the SPARCstation 2 CPU board, including internal registers and address spaces and a full hardware description of the board functions.

SPARCengine 10 User Guide

This guide can be ordered from Sun's SPARC Technology Business Unit. It provides the full programmer's model of the SPARCstation 10 CPU board, including internal registers and address spaces and a full hardware description of the board functions.

SPARC Strategy and Technology

This paper contains an excellent introduction to the SPARC architecture, as well as the features of SunOS 4.1.1, the migration to SVR4, and the SPARC cloning strategy. It is probably out of stock and no longer available. March 1991.

SPARC Technology Conference Notes - 3 Intense Days of Sun

The SPARC Technology Conference toured the world during 1991 and 1992. It was particularly aimed at SPARC hardware and real-time system developers. You need to have attended to get the notes!

SPARCclassic X Performance Brief

Xmarks, X11perf v1.2, and Xbench numbers for the SPARCclassic X Terminal. Descriptions of the benchmarks and product highlights are included. July 1993.

SPARCserver 10 and SPARCserver 600 Performance Brief

The standard benchmark performance numbers for SuperSPARC-based SPARCserver 10 and SPARCserver 600 systems running SunOS 4.1.3 are published in this document.

SPARCserver 1000 and SPARCcenter 2000 Performance Brief

All the standard benchmark results are listed in this white paper. March 1994.

SPARCserver 1000 Compute White Paper

This paper covers the requirements of a compute server, a hardware overview, Solaris features, and development of applications for multithreading and multiprocessing. May 1993.

SPARCserver 1000 Performance Brief

SPECint92, SPECfp92, SPECrate_int92, SPECrate_fp92, Linpack1000, AIM3, 097.LADDIS (SFS), and TPC-A information for the SS1000, Solaris 2.2. May 1993.

SPARCserver Sizing Guide for X terminals

This guide answers the question "How many SPARCclassic X-based Frame or Wabi users should be configured on a SPARCserver 10 or 1000 with two or four CPUs and from 64 to 256 Mbytes of RAM?" August 1993.

SPARCstation 2 Performance Brief

This old white paper contains some useful information, not repeated in later performance briefs on the performance characteristics of the Sun-4 MMU, and some Ethernet-routing performance benchmarks.

SPARCstation 10 Performance Brief

This document contains SPECint92, SPECfp92, Dhrystone V1.1, Linpack DP 1000, SPECrate_int92, SPECrate_fp92 benchmark information for the SS10 30LC,40, 41, 51, 402, 512, and 54. Solaris 2.2, April 1993.

SPARCstation 10 Product Line Technical White Paper

This paper explains the differences between various uniprocessor and multiprocessor SPARCstation 10 models and provides results of many application and benchmark tests on each model. It also contains a simplified architectural overview of the machine. June 1993.

SPARCstation 10 System Architecture - White Paper

A comprehensive overview of the SPARCstation 10.

SPARCstation 10SX Graphics Technology, A White Paper

This is a very hot product and the white paper does it justice. It does a nice job of discussing why the SX is a good fit for various markets, with the right number of buzzwords and right amount of detail. It then goes into the architecture and software implications. July 1993.

SPARCstation 10ZX and SPARCstation ZX Graphics Technology, A White Paper

The paper is broken down into features, architecture, and software. The paper is chock full of clearly presented information. You do need to be a graphics person to fully appreciate it. July 1993.

SPARCstation LX and SPARCclassic Performance Brief

This is the complete SPARCstation LX and SPARCclassic Performance Brief; it is based on Solaris 2.1 and is dated November 1992. There have been significant performance improvements in some areas since then.

SPARCstation ZX, SPARCstation 10ZX and SPARCstation 10 TurboGXplus Graphics Performance Brief

GPC, X11perf, and primitive test benchmarks for the products listed in the title are discussed. Descriptions of the benchmarks and product highlights are included. July 1993.

SPARCstation Products Performance Brief

Desktop machines, including the SPARCclassic, SPARCstation 5, SPARCstation 10 and SPARCstation 20, are compared using a standard set of CPU and graphics benchmarks. June 1994.

Statistical Models in S
by John M. Chambers and Trevor J. Hastie

This book is specific to the S Language and the S-Plus statistical package, but because the raw statistical techniques are wrapped up in library functions, it is easier to get into than a pure statistics textbook. The book contains many examples of methods that can be used to extract patterns and relationships from large amounts of raw, incomplete, and error-prone data. Published by Wadsworth and Brooks/Cole 1992. ISBN 0-534-16764-0.

Sun Systems and their Caches
by Sales Tactical Engineering

This explains Sun caches in great detail, including the I/O cache used in high-end servers. It does not include miss cost timings, however. June 1990.

SunOS 4.1 Performance Tuning
by Hal Stern

This white paper introduces many of the new features that were introduced in SunOS 4.1. It complements this overview document, as I have tried to avoid duplicating detailed information. It is essential reading, although it is getting out of date now.

SunOS System Internals Course Notes

These notes cover the main kernel algorithms, using pseudo-code and flowcharts to avoid source code licensing issues. The notes are from a 5-day course that is run occasionally by Sun.

SunPHIGS / SunGKS Technical White Paper

There is little explicit performance information in this paper, but it is a very useful overview of the architecture of these two graphics standards and should help developers choose an appropriate library to fit their problems.

The SuperSPARC Microprocessor Technical White Paper

This paper provides an overview to the architecture, internal operation, and capabilities of the SuperSPARC microprocessor used in the SPARCstation 10, SPARCserver 600, and SPARCcenter 2000 machines.

System Performance Tuning
by Mike Loukides

This reference book covers tuning issues for SunOS 4, BSD, System V.3 and System V.4 versions of UNIX. It concentrates on tuning the operating system as a whole, particularly for multiuser loads, and contains a lot of information on how to manage a system, how to tell which part of the system may be overloaded, and what to tweak to fix it. ISBN 0-937175-60-9. Published by O'Reilly.

tmpfs: A Virtual Memory File System
by Peter Snyder
> This Sun white paper discusses the design goals and implementation details of tmpfs.

Tuning the SPARCserver 490 for Optimal NFS Performance
> This paper describes the results of some NFS performance testing and provides details of scripts to modify and monitor the buffer cache. February 1991.

TurboGXplus Graphics Technology, A White Paper
> Lots of good information, including features, architecture, and software. Clearly written, a good description of the TGX. July 1993.

Virtual Swap Space in SunOS
by Howard Chartock and Peter Snyder
> The concept of swap space in SunOS 5 has been extended by the abstraction of a virtual swap filesystem, which allows the system to treat main memory as if it were a backing store. Further, this abstraction allows for more intelligent choices to be made about swap space allocation.This paper contrasts the existing mechanisms and their limitations with the modifications made to implement virtual swap space. May 1992.

XGL Graphics Library Technical White Paper
> A standard Sun white paper describing the highest-performance graphics library available on Sun systems.

You and Your Compiler
by Keith Bierman
> This is the definitive guide to using the compilers effectively for benchmarking or performance tuning. It has been modified as a performance tuning chapter in the manual set for FORTRAN 1.4 and later.

Index

≡ *Index*

≣ *Index*

Sun Performance and Tuning